GCSE AQA
English Literature

If you're taking AQA GCSE English Literature, you'll know the examiners have pretty *Great Expectations*. Not to worry — this brilliant CGP book has everything you need to make your exams feel like *Much Ado About Nothing*.

It's packed with clear study notes for poetry, drama and prose — plus plenty of realistic exam-style questions for all the set texts on the AQA course.

We've also included worked answers, brilliant advice on how to approach the exam, and a full set of practice papers to make sure you're prepared for the real thing.

How to access your free Online Edition

This book includes a free Online Edition to read on your PC, Mac or tablet.
You'll just need to go to **cgpbooks.co.uk/extras** and enter this code:

1009 9959 6486 8970

By the way, this code only works for one person. If somebody else has used this book before you, they might have already claimed the Online Edition.

Complete
Revision & Practice
Everything you need to pass the exams!

Contents

Section Five — Poetry

Section Six — Poetry Anthology

Section Seven — Unseen Poetry

Practice Papers

Published by CGP

Editors:
Izzy Bowen
Emma Crighton
Sean Walsh

With thanks to Louise McEvoy for the proofreading
and Jan Greenway for the copyright research.

Acknowledgements:
Page 80: 'Ghosts' by Robert W. Service used by courtesy of Mrs Anne Longepe.

Page 83: 'At Sea' by Jennifer Copley.

Page 107: Fleur Adcock, Poems 1960-2000 (Bloodaxe Books, 2000). www.bloodaxebooks.com

Page 108: 'The Beautiful Lie' is from 'The Beautiful Lie' by Sheenagh Pugh (Seren, 2002)

Every effort has been made to locate copyright holders and obtain permission to reproduce sources.
For those sources where it has been difficult to trace the copyright holder of the work, we would be grateful
for information. If any copyright holder would like us to make an amendment to the acknowledgements,
please notify us and we will gladly update the book at the next reprint. Thank you.

ISBN: 978 1 78294 413 3

Clipart from Corel®
Printed by Elanders Ltd, Newcastle upon Tyne.

Based on the classic CGP style created by Richard Parsons.

Exam Structure

It's time to get to grips with English Literature — here's what to expect...

There are **Two Exams** for AQA English Literature

1) For your English Literature GCSE, you'll have to sit <u>two exams</u> — <u>Paper 1</u> and <u>Paper 2</u>.

2) <u>Paper 1</u> lasts <u>1 hour 45 minutes</u>. It's worth <u>64</u> marks (<u>40%</u> of the GCSE).

3) Paper 1 is split into <u>two</u> sections:

> - <u>Section A</u>: an essay question about a <u>Shakespeare play</u> (see p.30-34)
>   — e.g. 'Macbeth', 'The Merchant of Venice'.
> - <u>Section B</u>: an essay question about a <u>novel</u> from the <u>19th century</u> (see p.44-46)
>   — e.g. 'A Christmas Carol', 'Jane Eyre'.

4) <u>Paper 2</u> lasts <u>2 hours 15 minutes</u>. It's worth <u>96</u> marks (<u>60%</u> of the GCSE).

5) Paper 2 is split into <u>three</u> sections:

> - <u>Section A</u>: an essay question asking you about a modern text, written after 1914 — e.g. 'Blood Brothers', 'Animal Farm'. This could be a <u>play</u> (see p.28-29) or a <u>novel</u> (see p.41-43).
> - <u>Section B</u>: a question about a cluster of <u>poems</u> from the AQA poetry anthology — you'll study either the '<u>Love and Relationships</u>' cluster or the '<u>Power and Conflict</u>' cluster (see p.63-74).
> - In <u>Section C</u>, there'll be two <u>unseen poems</u> — you'll have to <u>analyse</u> and <u>compare</u> them (see p.75-84).

Assessment Objectives are the **Skills** you need for the **Exam**

The <u>assessment objectives</u> cover all the things you need to do to get a <u>good grade</u> in the exams. They are:

AO1
- Give your own <u>thoughts</u> and <u>opinions</u> on the text.
- <u>Back up</u> your interpretations using <u>evidence</u> from the text (e.g. quotes).

AO2
- <u>Explain</u> how writers use <u>language</u>, <u>structure</u> and <u>form</u>, and what <u>effect</u> this has on the reader.
- Use <u>technical terms</u> to support your analysis.

AO3
- Show that you understand how the text relates to the <u>context</u> in which it was written or set.

AO3 is tested everywhere <u>except</u> the unseen poetry section of Paper 2.

AO4
- Use a range of <u>sentence structures</u> and <u>vocabulary</u>, so that your writing is <u>clear</u> and <u>effective</u>.
- Write <u>accurately</u>, paying particular attention to spelling, punctuation and grammar.

AO4 is only tested in Section A of each paper. It counts for 5% of your overall mark.

You don't need to remember the assessment objectives word for word...

There's no need to memorise these assessment objectives — they're just here to give you an idea of the things you need to think about when you're revising, and when you're writing your answers in the exam.

Planning Answers

We've all been there — you turn over your exam paper, read the question, notice that time's slipping away and start scribbling your answer. But I promise, if you take a few minutes to plan, you won't regret it.

Read the question **Carefully** and **Calmly**

1) Before you start writing an answer, give yourself time to read through the <u>question</u> properly. If you're given an <u>extract</u> from a text you've studied or any <u>poems</u> to go with the question, read those too.

2) Always <u>read the question</u> before any extracts or poems that go with the question — that way, you'll know what to look out for.

3) Make sure you're clear about what the question is <u>asking</u> you to do by <u>underlining</u> the <u>key words</u>.

> How does Brontë <u>present</u> the <u>changing relationship</u> between <u>Jane</u> and <u>Mr Rochester</u>?

PAPER 1

4) Once you've read the question, carefully <u>read</u> through any <u>extracts</u> or <u>poems</u> that are part of the question. It's a good idea to <u>highlight</u> key <u>words</u> or <u>phrases</u> that will help you to answer the questions — but don't spend ages doing this.

Remember, it's your exam paper and you can write on it if it helps you.

Jot down your **Main Ideas** before you start writing

1) You'll need to spend a <u>few minutes planning</u> most of your answers.

2) Don't go into too much <u>detail</u> — just get your <u>main ideas</u> down and <u>outline</u> the <u>structure</u> of your answer.

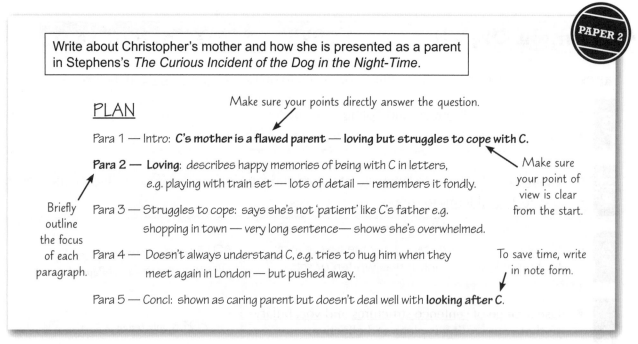

Write about Christopher's mother and how she is presented as a parent in Stephens's *The Curious Incident of the Dog in the Night-Time*.

PAPER 2

PLAN

Make sure your points directly answer the question.

Para 1 — Intro: **C's mother is a flawed parent — loving but struggles to cope with C.**

Para 2 — **Loving:** describes happy memories of being with C in letters, e.g. playing with train set — lots of detail — remembers it fondly.

Briefly outline the focus of each paragraph.

Para 3 — Struggles to cope: says she's not 'patient' like C's father e.g. shopping in town — very long sentence— shows she's overwhelmed.

Para 4 — Doesn't always understand C, e.g. tries to hug him when they meet again in London — but pushed away.

Para 5 — Concl: shown as caring parent but doesn't deal well with **looking after C.**

Make sure your point of view is clear from the start.

To save time, write in note form.

3) If the question is only worth a <u>few marks</u> (e.g. in the unseen poetry section), you might not need to do a full plan — just <u>jot down a few ideas</u> before you start.

Planning will keep your writing focused...

You need to stick to the question you've been asked in the exam, or you won't get the marks. Planning will help keep you on track when you're writing your answer. Don't forget to check your work at the end, too.

P.E.E.D.

To get good marks, you need to explain and develop your ideas properly. That's why P.E.E.D. is useful.

P.E.E.D. stands for **Point, Example, Explain, Develop**

To write good English essays about texts you've read, you must do <u>four</u> things:

1) Make a <u>point</u> to answer the question you've been given.

2) Then give an <u>example</u> from the text (see page 4 for more on this).

3) After that, <u>explain</u> how your example backs up your point.

4) Finally, <u>develop</u> your point — this might involve saying what the <u>effect on the reader</u> is, saying what the <u>writer's intention</u> is, <u>linking</u> your point to another part of the text or giving your <u>own opinion</u>.

The <u>explanation</u> and <u>development</u> parts are very important. They're your chance to show that you <u>really understand</u> and have <u>thought about</u> the text. Here are a couple of <u>examples</u>:

PAPER 1

Read Act 1, Scene 7, from "Was the hope drunk..." to "... as you have done to this." Using this extract as a starting point, explore how Shakespeare presents Lady Macbeth's attitude to power.

This introduces the main <u>point</u> of the paragraph. → **Shakespeare presents Lady Macbeth as even more obsessed with power than Macbeth himself**. She calls Macbeth a **"coward"** and says that he **"dare not"** murder Duncan in order to become king. Manipulating him to commit a terrible crime **shows how desperate she is for Macbeth to attain power so that she can rule alongside him**. In Shakespeare's day, **women were seen as gentler and less ambitious than men, so Lady Macbeth's quest for power would have shocked an audience of the time.**

Quotes are used as the <u>example</u> here.

This <u>explains</u> the effect of the example.

This <u>develops</u> the point further by relating it to context.

PAPER 2

Compare how getting older is presented in C. Day Lewis's 'Walking Away' and one other poem you have studied.

Start with a <u>point</u> that mentions both poems. → Both 'Walking Away' and 'Mother, Any Distance' show how **children become more independent over time**. Day Lewis uses the simile **"like a satellite / Wrenched from its orbit"** to describe his young son travelling away from him; **the verb "Wrenched" shows that the child has moved away suddenly**. Similarly, Armitage describes moving away from his mother as a **"space-walk", suggesting that it is a new experience for him**. In both poems, **space imagery shows how the process of growing up and becoming independent is an exciting adventure, but also one that is scary for both parents and their children.**

Give <u>examples</u> from both poems.

<u>Explain</u> how the examples relate to your opening point.

Sometimes you can <u>develop</u> your point for both poems at the same time.

P.E.E.D. should help you to explain and develop your points...

Other versions of P.E.E.D. also focus on explaining and developing — P.E.E.R. (Point, Example, Explain, Relate), P.E.E.C.E. (Point, Example, Explain, Compare, Explore) and so on. Use the one you've been taught.

Using Examples

However fabulous the point you make in your answer is, it won't get you top marks unless you can back it up with examples from the text. Cue a page that shows you how it's done...

Use **Details** from the text to **Back Up** your points

Whenever you make a <u>point</u> about a text, you need to use short pieces of <u>evidence</u> to <u>back it up</u>.

The woman was cruel to her dog.

This answer doesn't give any evidence.

The woman was cruel to her dog: she kept him chained up in the sun all day with very little food and no water.

This is much better — it gives <u>examples</u> to back up the point.

Your evidence can be **Quotes** or **Examples**

1) Your evidence could be a <u>quote</u> from the text. If you use a quote, keep it <u>short</u>. It'll really impress the examiner if you <u>embed</u> it in a sentence, like this:

The writer refers to the situation as "indefensible", suggesting that he is extremely critical of the way it has been handled.

Using short embedded quotes like this lets you combine the 'example' and 'explain' parts of P.E.E.D. (see p.3) in one sentence.

2) <u>Paraphrased details</u> from the text also work well as examples. You just need to describe one of the <u>writer's techniques</u>, or one of the <u>text's features</u>, in your own words, like this:

Tennyson uses a rhetorical question in the final stanza, which emphasises the heroism of the Light Brigade.

3) Here's an <u>example</u> to show you how to work your evidence into your answer:

Read Act 2, Scene 1, from "If this were true..." to "And not my husband's secrets?". Using this extract as a starting point, write about how Shakespeare presents femininity in *Julius Caesar*.

In 'Julius Caesar', femininity appears to be defined by its weakness. For example, in Act 2, Scene 1, Portia believes that she is a strong person despite her gender rather than because of it. She states: **"I grant I am a woman, but withal / A woman that Lord Brutus took to wife"**. The verb "grant" shows that she sees being a woman as a failing, which is only overcome by her position as Brutus's "wife" and also as "Cato's daughter". It is clear she believes these men in her life are the primary source of her strength: it is because of how she is **"fathered"** and **"husbanded"** that she is able to be **"stronger than"** other women. This shows that she considers femininity to be inherently weaker than masculinity.

If you use a longer quote, make sure you copy it correctly and use the correct punctuation.

Embedding short quotes will help your answer to flow smoothly.

Use examples to support your ideas...

Whether you paraphrase or use a quote, backing up your points with evidence from the text is really crucial in your English Literature exams. Just make sure that you then explain how the evidence supports your point.

Writing Well

In these exams, it's not just what you write that's important — it's how you write as well.

Keep your writing **Formal** but **Interesting**

1) For these exams, it's important that you write in Standard English.

2) Standard English is the version of English that most people think is 'correct'. There are a few simple rules that you can follow to make sure you're writing in Standard English:

- Avoid using informal words and phrases (e.g. putting 'like' after sentences).
- Avoid using slang or local dialect words that some people might not understand.
- Use correct spelling, punctuation and grammar (have a look at pages 7-8).

Use clear **Explaining Words** and **Phrases**

1) You should use explaining words and phrases to make your answers easy to follow.

- This signifies that...
- This is reminiscent of...
- This highlights the fact that...
- Furthermore...
- This imagery reflects...
- This continues the idea of...

2) Using words and phrases like these makes your writing sound more professional.

3) They're also really useful when it comes to P.E.E.D. (see page 3). They help you to link the explanation and development parts of your answer to your main point.

Use **Paragraphs** to structure your answer

1) Your points need to be clearly organised and linked together. To do that you need to write in paragraphs.

2) You can use different paragraph structures to organise your points in different ways. For example:

- You could write a paragraph for every point you want to make, and each paragraph could have a P.E.E.D. structure (see page 3).
- You could make two points that contrast or agree with each other within a paragraph — this can be useful when comparing two texts.
- You could make one point and link together lots of examples with different explanations within a paragraph.

However you structure your paragraphs, make sure you include all the parts of P.E.E.D. in your answer.

3) Linking your paragraphs together smoothly makes your writing sound confident and considered. You could use linking words like these to help you do this:

- However...
- In the same way...
- In contrast...
- In addition...
- On the other hand...
- Alternatively...
- Equally...
- Conversely...

Your answer needs to have a clear structure...

Organise your ideas into paragraphs, and use the phrases on this page to link them together smoothly.
A clear structure will show the examiner that you've thought about your answer, and make it easier to read.

Reading with Insight

To get the top grades, you need to show that you can 'read with insight' — you've got to make it clear that you understand more than just the obvious things. You can think of it as 'reading between the lines'.

You need to look **Beyond** what's **Obvious**

Looking beyond what's obvious will help you to make sure you've done the 'D' part of P.E.E.D. — look back at p.3 for more on this.

1) You may understand what <u>happens</u> in a text, or what it's <u>about</u>, but you'll need to write about <u>more</u> than just that in your answers.

2) You can show <u>insight</u> if you work out what the writer's <u>intentions</u> are and how they want the reader to <u>feel</u>.

3) Here's an <u>example</u> of the kind of thing you could write:

> *In 'Checking Out Me History', Agard uses a double negative in the phrase "no dem never tell me bout dat" to sound angry, which suggests he wants the reader to feel ashamed about the lack of diversity in British history teaching.*

 Think about the reasons <u>why</u> the writer has included certain features — show you've understood their <u>intended effect</u> on the reader.

4) Remember to include <u>examples</u> from the text to <u>support</u> your interpretation:

> *Darcy is portrayed as an unlikeable character in this extract. He is described as "above being pleased", hinting at his arrogance and haughtiness. However, the swiftness with which the ball-goers change their opinion of him shows their fickleness and hints that their judgement is not to be trusted.*

 Try to explain <u>how</u> the writer creates a particular impression of a character or event. Examiners love it if you can give <u>alternative interpretations</u> that go beyond the obvious.

Inference means working things out from Clues

1) Writers don't usually make things obvious — but you can use <u>evidence</u> from the text to make an <u>inference</u> about what the writer <u>really</u> wants us to think.

2) You need to analyse <u>details</u> from the text to show what they <u>reveal</u> about the writer's intentions:

> *The narrator of 'Pride and Prejudice' uses the words "self-conceit" and "self-importance", which imply disdain for Mr. Collins.*

 The writer's <u>language</u> indicates their <u>emotions</u> and <u>attitude</u>.

> *In 'The Emigrée', Rumens uses irony when describing the "free city" she has moved to, emphasising that, for her, it is a restrictive place.*

 The writer will often use <u>tone</u> to <u>imply</u> what they really mean — look out for <u>irony</u> or <u>sarcasm</u>.

3) You could use <u>phrases</u> like these to show that you've made an <u>inference</u>:

| The writer gives a sense of... | The writer appears to be... | This suggests that... |

Think about the effect the writer wants to create...

Everything in a text has been carefully crafted by the writer, so look for clues that reveal their intentions. Demonstrate that you understand what the writer is showing you, not just what they're telling you.

Spelling, Punctuation and Grammar

There are lots of marks available in these exams for correct use of spelling, punctuation and grammar, or SPaG for short. These pages should help you to avoid the most common SPaG errors...

You can **Gain Marks** for **SPaG**

1) It's important that you use correct <u>spelling</u>, <u>punctuation</u> and <u>grammar</u> in all of your answers.

2) However, it's particularly important in <u>Section A</u> of each paper, where some of the marks will be for your ability to write <u>accurately</u> and <u>clearly</u> — which includes good <u>SPaG</u>.

3) Here are some tips to help keep your writing as <u>accurate</u> as possible.

Here are some **Spelling** hints

1) Avoid <u>common spelling mistakes</u>, like 'their', 'they're' and 'there' or 'where', 'were' and 'wear'.

2) Remember that '<u>affect</u>' is a <u>verb</u>, e.g. 'the simile affects the mood of the text', but '<u>effect</u>' is a <u>noun</u>, e.g. 'the interruption has a shocking effect on the reader'.

3) Always <u>write</u> words out in <u>full</u> — avoid <u>abbreviations</u> like 'etc.' and 'e.g.', and <u>don't</u> use text speak.

4) Make sure any <u>technical terms</u>, like 'metaphor' or 'onomatopoeia', are spelt correctly.

5) Make sure any <u>information</u> taken from the <u>extract</u>, including the writer's name, is spelt correctly.

Use **Full Stops**, **Colons** and **Semi-colons** correctly

1) Make sure you've used <u>full stops</u> at the <u>end of sentences</u> and <u>question marks</u> at the <u>end of questions</u>.

2) Don't confuse <u>colons</u> and <u>semi-colons</u>:

- <u>Colons</u> can be used to introduce a <u>list</u> or if you want to add a piece of information that <u>explains</u> your sentence.

- <u>Semi-colons</u> can separate longer phrases in a <u>list</u>, or they can be used to <u>join</u> two sentences together — as long as both sentences are about the <u>same thing</u> and <u>make sense</u> on their own.

Use **Commas** properly

1) Use <u>commas</u> to separate items in a <u>list</u> or when you've used <u>more than one adjective</u>. E.g. 'The writer uses a series of short, emotive phrases to describe the scene.'

2) Use a <u>comma</u> when you use a <u>joining word</u> like 'and', 'so' or 'but' to link <u>two points</u> together. E.g. 'Jeremy says he isn't bothered by Mandy's behaviour, but his body language suggests otherwise.'

3) You should also use a pair of <u>commas</u> to separate <u>extra information</u> in a sentence. E.g. 'Ranjita, who is much calmer than Ashanti, does not respond to her father's taunting.'

Spelling, Punctuation and Grammar

Follow this **Grammar** advice

1) Don't change <u>tenses</u> in your writing by mistake.

2) Don't use <u>double negatives</u>, e.g. 'There wasn't no reason' should be 'There wasn't any reason'.

3) Remember '<u>it's</u>' (<u>with</u> an apostrophe) is short for '<u>it is</u>' or '<u>it has</u>'.
   '<u>Its</u>' (<u>without</u> an apostrophe) means '<u>belonging to it</u>'.

4) Never write 'should of' — it's always '<u>should have</u>', '<u>would have</u>', '<u>could have</u>'.

5) Start a <u>new paragraph</u> for each <u>new point</u>. Show that it's a new paragraph by
   starting a <u>new line</u> and leaving a gap or <u>indent</u> before you start writing.

Check over your **Work** when you've finished

1) Try to leave a few minutes at the <u>end</u> of the exams to <u>check</u> your work.

2) There might not be <u>time</u> to check everything thoroughly. Look for
   the <u>most obvious</u> spelling, punctuation and grammar mistakes.

3) Start by checking your answers to <u>Section A</u> in each paper,
   as there are <u>marks</u> for <u>accuracy</u> available in these sections.

This is how you should **Correct** any **Mistakes**

1) If you find a <u>spelling mistake</u>, put <u>brackets</u>
   around the word, <u>cross it out</u> neatly with <u>two
   lines</u> through it and write the correction <u>above</u>.

> Pigeon
> In '(~~Pijeon~~) English', Kelman presents
> Harri as a determined character.

2) If you've written something which isn't clear,
   put an <u>asterisk</u> (*) at the end of the sentence.
   Put another asterisk at the end of your
   work, and write what you mean beside it.

> Neptune is powerful*, so by linking himself with the figure,
> Browning's speaker in 'My Last Duchess' shows his control.
> * because he is the Roman god of the sea

3) If you realise you should have started a
   <u>new paragraph</u>, put // to show where it
   <u>starts</u> and write "(para)" in the margin.

> In this way, the setting of 'Great Expectations'
> creates fear in the reader. // The description   (para)
> of Magwitch also builds suspense.

4) If you find you've <u>missed out</u> a word or
   two, put a "∧" where the words should
   go, then write them in <u>above</u> the line.

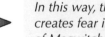

> In Act 3, Scene 5, Juliet feels more and isolated.
>   ∧

Make sure you can spell subject-specific words...

Some of the marks in your exams are for using subject terminology (e.g. metaphor, onomatopoeia). When
you're using these, you need to get the spelling correct — so make sure you learn those pesky words.

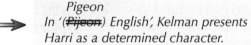

Revision Summary

Most of the sections in this book finish with a page like this one. It'll help you check you really know your stuff from the section. But don't worry — everything you need to know is covered on the previous pages.

- Try the questions below and <u>tick off each one</u> when you <u>get it right</u>.
- When you've done <u>all the questions</u> under a heading and are <u>completely happy</u> with it, tick it off.

Planning Answers (p.2) ☑

1) Is the following statement true or false?
   "If the question comes with an extract from a text, you
   should read the extract before reading the question." ☑

2) What are the two main things that you should include in a plan?
   a) your main ideas   b) lots of detailed evidence from the text
   c) the exact wording of your answer   d) the structure of your answer ☑

3) Give one way that you can save time when writing a plan. ☑

P.E.E.D. and Using Examples (p.3-4) ☑

4) What does P.E.E.D. stand for? ☑

5) Give three ways that you could develop a point. ☑

6) In your answers, how many of your points should be backed up with evidence from the text?
   a) a few of them b) about half of them c) some of them d) all of them ☑

7) Quotes from the text should usually be: a) short   b) long ☑

8) Choose two answers. When using a longer quote, make sure that you:
   a) copy it correctly   b) include a capital letter
   c) don't include quotation marks   d) use the correct punctuation ☑

Writing Well and Reading with Insight (p.5-6) ☑

9) Which of these words and phrases could you use to link paragraphs in an exam answer?
   a) secondly b) safe to say c) in addition to this d) conversely ☑

10) Give two examples of things you could comment on to show that you are reading with insight. ☑

11) What does 'inference' mean? ☑

12) Give an example of a phrase you could use to show that you've made an inference. ☑

Spelling, Punctuation and Grammar (p.7-8) ☑

13) Which of the following sentences is correct?
    a) I think the writer's use of metaphors in this extract is very effective.
    b) I think the writer's use of metaphors in this extract is very affective. ☑

14) Does the following sentence use a semi-colon correctly?
    Gazing out of the open window; Tomek dreamt of the day when he would be free from revision. ☑

15) Give three uses of commas. ☑

16) What is a double negative? ☑

17) Where is the grammatical error in the following sentence?
    You could of used a better paragraph structure to improve your answer. ☑

18) Write down the correction symbols for the following situations:
    a) when a new paragraph should start   b) when a word or two is missing
    c) when something isn't clear ☑

Writing About Prose and Drama

Prose and drama are similar in lots of ways, so this section covers some of the common features found in the two types of text. Sections Three (Drama) and Four (Prose) deal with issues specific to each type of writing.

Think about what the **Question** is **Asking**

1) Read the question <u>carefully</u> to make sure you're clear on <u>what</u> it is asking you to focus on. This could be:

- the <u>personality</u> of a <u>character</u>
- a specific <u>mood</u> or <u>atmosphere</u>
- a specific <u>theme</u> or <u>message</u>
- <u>attitudes</u> towards a theme or issue
- <u>relationships</u> between <u>characters</u>

2) Most questions will ask you to <u>comment</u> on <u>how</u> the writer <u>presents</u> something to the reader. This means that you need to focus on <u>language</u>, <u>structure</u> and <u>form</u>. Here are some <u>examples</u> of the <u>types</u> of question that might come up in the exam:

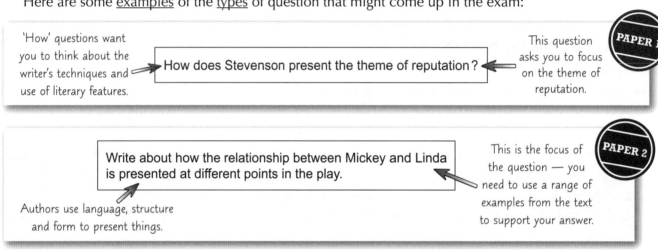

'How' questions want you to think about the writer's techniques and use of literary features.

How does Stevenson present the theme of reputation?

This question asks you to focus on the theme of reputation.

PAPER 1

Write about how the relationship between Mickey and Linda is presented at different points in the play.

Authors use language, structure and form to present things.

This is the focus of the question — you need to use a range of examples from the text to support your answer.

PAPER 2

Some questions ask about an **Extract** from the **Text**

1) You'll always have to write about a <u>whole text</u> in your answer.

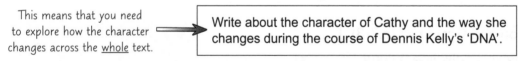

This means that you need to explore how the character changes across the <u>whole</u> text.

Write about the character of Cathy and the way she changes during the course of Dennis Kelly's 'DNA'.

PAPER 2

2) Some questions will also ask you to <u>focus</u> on a particular <u>extract</u>.

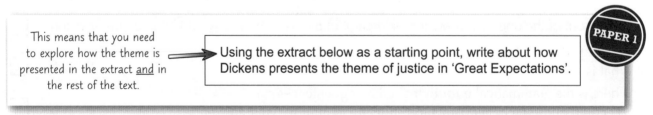

This means that you need to explore how the theme is presented in the extract <u>and</u> in the rest of the text.

Using the extract below as a starting point, write about how Dickens presents the theme of justice in 'Great Expectations'.

PAPER 1

3) If you're asked to write about an extract, it's <u>doubly important</u> to focus on things like <u>language</u>, <u>structure</u> and <u>form</u>. The examiner knows that you've got the text in front of you, so they're expecting you to <u>pick out</u> and <u>explain</u> some of the features in it.

Writing About Prose and Drama

Make sure you **Answer** the **Question** you're given

1) It's important to focus on the question — read it carefully a couple of times before planning your answer.

2) Some questions might give you bullet points of things to consider when writing your essay.

> Write about life in a new country and the way it is presented in 'Pigeon English'.
>
> Write about:
>
> - ideas about life in a new country in the novel
> - how these ideas are presented.

 These bullet points give you some ideas about things you should write about in your answer.

 PAPER 2

3) Make sure everything you write in your essay answers the question — irrelevant points won't get you any marks.

> *Harri moves from Ghana to London, where he lives in a tall building called Copenhagen House.*

→ This is too general — it doesn't tell you anything about how Kelman presents life in a new country.

> *Kelman uses comparisons to present Harri's experience of London. The description of his tower block being "as high as the lighthouse at Jamestown" shows that there are links between his old and new lives.*

→ This is much better — it comments on the presentation of life in a new country and uses a quote from the text to support the point.

Make sure you **Know** the text in **Detail**

1) You need to show the examiner that you know the text really well, and that you understand what happens and the order it happens in.

2) Make sure you're familiar with all the characters in the text — the examiner will be impressed if you make references to the minor characters as well as the major ones.

See pages 12-13 for more on writing about characters.

3) Learn some key quotes from the text that you can use in your essay to support your points.

Introduce some of your **Own Ideas**

1) Write about your personal response to the text. Think about what emotions it evokes and whether you like or empathise with certain characters.

> *The reader feels sympathetic towards Pip as he reads the names of his dead parents on the gravestone.*

 Don't use "I" when you're talking about your personal response — use "the reader" when you're writing about prose and "the audience" for plays.

2) To get a top grade, you need to find something original to say about the text. You can make whatever point you like, as long as you can back it up with evidence from the text.

The best way to keep focused on the question is to write a plan...

Take a couple of minutes at the start of each question to plan how you're going to write your answer. It will help you get all of your ideas down before you begin and keep you focused on the question.

Writing About Characters

You need to know about something called 'characterisation' — this means the methods that an author uses to convey information about, or make the reader feel a certain way about, a character in the text.

Characters are always there for a **Reason**

1) When you're answering a question about a character, bear in mind that characters always have a <u>purpose</u>.

2) This means that you can't talk about them as if they're real people — make it clear that the author has <u>created</u> them to help get a message across.

3) A character's <u>appearance</u>, <u>actions</u> and <u>language</u> all help to get this message across.

Find bits where the writer **Describes** the characters

Find descriptions of how the characters <u>look</u>, and then think about what this might <u>say</u> about them.

> *In 'Lord of the Flies', Golding's description of Jack's face as "crumpled" and "ugly without silliness" implies that he might have a sinister and unpleasant personality.*

Look at the way characters **Act** and **Speak**

1) Look at what characters do, and then consider <u>what that says about them</u>.

2) Try to work out <u>why</u> a character does something. Most characters are motivated by a <u>variety</u> of things, but there's usually one main <u>driving force</u> behind what they do.

> *In 'Romeo and Juliet', Tybalt's confrontational and violent actions (e.g. stabbing Mercutio) are ultimately driven by his fierce loyalty to the Capulets.*

3) The way characters, including the narrator, <u>speak</u> tells you a lot about them.

4) <u>Remember</u> to think about why the author is making their characters speak the way they do. Think about how the author wants you, the reader, to <u>perceive</u> the character.

> *In 'An Inspector Calls', Birling repeatedly shouts "Rubbish!" to dismiss what other people have said. But he finishes his own sentences with "of course", to make his own claims seem obvious and matter-of-fact. This means that the audience perceives him to be arrogant and opinionated.*

Look at how the characters treat **Other People**

The writer can tell you a lot about their <u>characters</u> by showing you how they get on with others. It can reveal sides to their character that they keep <u>hidden</u> from the other main characters.

> *My rage was without bounds; I sprang on him, impelled by all the feelings which can arm one being against the existence of another.*

⟹ In 'Frankenstein', Victor is kind and polite to most of the characters in the novel, but his attack on the monster reveals his concealed anger and violence.

Writing About Characters

Make sure you're **Prepared** for **Character Questions**

Characters are <u>key elements</u> of any text, so it's not really a surprise that examiners <u>enjoy</u> asking about them in exams. Here are some <u>important questions</u> to think about when you're <u>studying</u> or <u>revising</u> characters:

Why is the character important?

- How do they affect the <u>plot</u>?
- Do they represent a particular <u>point of view</u>?
- What would <u>happen</u> if they <u>weren't there</u>?

Madame is a key character in 'Never Let Me Go' — she provides a link with the world outside Hailsham, and her apparent disgust with the children hints at the wider world's perception of them.

Does the character change over the course of the story?

- Does the character <u>learn anything</u>?
- Does their <u>personality</u> or <u>behaviour</u> change?
- Are the changes <u>positive</u> or <u>negative</u>?
- How do these changes <u>affect</u> the character?

Over the course of 'A Christmas Carol', Ebenezer Scrooge becomes more charitable, generous and empathetic thanks to his experiences with the ghosts. This contrasts with the miserly and selfish character the reader meets at the start of the book.

How does the writer reveal the character's personality?

- <u>How</u> are the character's actions and experiences <u>presented</u> to the reader?
- Is the <u>reader's view</u> of the character the <u>same</u> as other <u>characters' view</u> of them?

The cold-hearted nature of Estella in 'Great Expectations' is revealed by her frequent attempts to "deceive and entrap" men. The reader is able to see her true nature more clearly than Pip, who is blinded by his love for her.

How is the character similar or different to other characters?

- How does the character <u>relate</u> to <u>other characters</u>?
- Do <u>differences</u> between characters <u>impact</u> on the <u>plot</u>?
- What is the writer <u>showing</u> us through these differences?

In some ways, Linda turns into Mrs Johnstone in 'Blood Brothers', becoming a housewife at a young age whilst also having to provide for the family.

Does the reader like or sympathise with the character?

- <u>Why</u> does the reader <u>feel</u> that way about the character?
- <u>How</u> does the writer <u>shape</u> the reader's feelings about the character?
- How does the reader's <u>opinion</u> of the character <u>affect</u> their opinion of the <u>text</u> as a whole?

The reader sympathises with Meena in 'Anita and Me' because her loyalty and trust is betrayed by Anita. Having the narrative in Meena's voice helps create empathy, as it means that Meena's viewpoint is heard throughout.

Get to know the main characters in your texts...

Draw a mind map for each key character in your texts. Add branches for each main aspect of their character — you can use this page to start off. Don't forget to add quotes to back up your ideas.

The Writer's Techniques

There are lots of marks available in English Literature for commenting on the way writers use language.

Analysing the writer's use of **Language** is key

1) Writers <u>select</u> the <u>language</u> they use carefully — it's up to you to work out <u>why</u> they've chosen a particular <u>word</u> or <u>phrase</u>, and to explain the <u>effect</u> that it has.

2) Look out for any <u>interesting</u>, <u>unusual</u> or <u>specialist vocabulary</u> — think about why it's been used. Take note of any <u>repeated</u> words and phrases too — they will have been repeated for a <u>reason</u>.

> *Anita Rutter laughs "in reverberated echo as the heavens slowly crumbled and fell".* ⟶ In 'Anita and Me', Syal uses <u>mythological</u> language to show how <u>powerful</u> Anita is in relation to Meena — she is described as if she were a <u>god</u>.

3) Examining the language used by <u>characters</u> is really important — think about the <u>way</u> characters speak, <u>why</u> they speak in that way and whether the way they speak is <u>different</u> to other characters.

> *"D' they call y' Eddie?"*
>
> *"Gis a sweet"* ⟶ In 'Blood Brothers', Russell uses <u>informal</u>, <u>colloquial</u> language for the Johnstone family — they <u>omit letters</u> off the end of words and use <u>non-standard pronouns</u>. This language is used to reflect their <u>social class</u>.

> *Hyde speaks "with a flush of anger" and makes inhuman noises, e.g. he screams in "animal terror".* ⟶ In 'Dr Jekyll and Mr Hyde', Stevenson uses language to reinforce Hyde's <u>incivility</u> — Hyde does not speak as gentlemen were expected to, suggesting to other characters that something is <u>not right</u>.

Look out for **Imagery**

Imagery is particularly common in prose texts, but it does crop up in plays too — Shakespeare uses lots of it.

1) <u>Imagery</u> is when an author uses <u>language</u> to create a <u>picture</u> in the reader's mind, or to describe something more <u>vividly</u>. It can add to the reader's or the audience's <u>understanding</u> of the story.

2) <u>Similes</u> describe something by saying that it's <u>like</u> something else:

> *No one can conceive the variety of feelings which bore me onwards, <u>like a hurricane</u>, in the first enthusiasm of success.* ⟶ In 'Frankenstein', Shelley uses the simile "like a hurricane" to <u>emphasise</u> the <u>power</u> of Victor's <u>feelings</u>.

3) <u>Metaphors</u> describe something by saying it <u>is</u> something else:

> *The <u>instruments of darkness</u> tell us truths.* ⟶ In 'Macbeth', Banquo's <u>suspicion</u> of the three Witches is shown by his use of the metaphor "instruments of darkness" to describe them.

4) <u>Personification</u> describes something (e.g. an animal, object or aspect of nature) as if it were <u>human</u>:

> *It was a wild, cold, seasonable night of March, with a pale moon, <u>lying on her back</u>...* ⟶ In 'Dr Jekyll and Mr Hyde', the <u>personification</u> of the moon makes it seem that the whole world has been <u>turned upside down</u> by Jekyll's secret.

The Writer's Techniques

Comment on **Sentence Structure**

1) It's not just particular words and phrases that you can comment on — you should also look at how writers use <u>sentences</u> and <u>paragraphs</u> to reinforce their points.

> *And among us animals let there be perfect unity, perfect comradeship in the struggle. All men are enemies.*

> In 'Animal Farm', Old Major uses a mix of <u>long</u> and <u>short sentences</u>, as well as <u>rhetoric</u>, to make his speech <u>persuasive</u>.

2) Different <u>sentence lengths</u> create different <u>effects</u>, e.g. a succession of <u>short</u> sentences could build <u>tension</u> or <u>excitement</u>, whereas <u>long</u> sentences might show a character getting <u>carried away</u> with their <u>emotions</u>.

> *"Seen him?" repeated Mr Utterson. "Well?"*
>
> *"That's it!" said Poole. "It was this way."*

> At the climax of 'Dr Jekyll and Mr Hyde', the characters talk in <u>short bursts</u>. This creates <u>suspense</u> by suggesting that events are happening at a <u>fast pace</u>.

> *There were great round, pot-bellied baskets of chestnuts, shaped like the waistcoats of jolly old gentlemen, lolling at the doors, and tumbling out into the street in their apoplectic opulence.*

> In 'A Christmas Carol', Dickens uses <u>long sentences</u> to describe the activity on the streets when Scrooge walks through London. This gives the Christmas scenes a sense of <u>endless</u> cheer, emphasising the joy Scrooge has excluded himself from.

Pay attention to **Descriptions** and **Settings**

1) Writers use <u>settings</u> to influence the way you <u>feel</u> about what's happening.

2) In the exam, you could get a passage that <u>describes</u> one of the settings from the text and be asked to talk about how the author has used it to create <u>atmosphere</u>.

3) You need to look at the writer's <u>descriptions</u> and think about <u>why</u> they have been included and <u>what effect</u> they have.

> *Alleys and archways, like so many cesspools, disgorged their offences of smell, and dirt, and life, upon the straggling streets.*

> In 'A Christmas Carol', Dickens uses descriptive language to present his reader with a <u>realistic</u>, <u>harsh</u> vision of <u>poverty</u> in London.

> *I did not dare return to the apartment which I inhabited, but felt impelled to hurry on, although drenched by the rain which poured from a black and comfortless sky.*

> In 'Frankenstein', this <u>bleak</u> and <u>dismal</u> setting reflects Victor's <u>hopeless and gloomy mood</u>.

> *When shall we three meet again?*
> *In thunder, lightning, or in rain?*
>
> *Hover through the fog and filthy air.*

> In 'Macbeth', the Witches repeatedly describe the <u>bad weather</u>. This reflects the <u>sinister atmosphere</u> created by the Witches' arrival.

The Writer's Techniques

Writers can present their ideas using **Symbolism**

1) Symbols can be used to reinforce the <u>themes</u> that run through a text. Look out for things that could be a <u>symbol</u> for something else, e.g. a <u>thunderstorm</u> could be a symbol for <u>destruction</u>.

> *In 'An Inspector Calls', Priestley uses Eva Smith as a symbol. Her first name sounds like 'Eve', the first woman (in the Biblical account of creation), which suggests she symbolises all women. Her surname is very common and it's also the word for a tradesman, which implies that she represents all ordinary, working-class women.*

> *In 'Great Expectations', the size and splendour of Satis House symbolises the wealth and grandeur of the upper classes. However, it is crumbling and run-down, which could symbolise their decay.*

2) Symbols are often used to create <u>additional meanings</u>. If the literal meaning of a sentence sounds strange, try to work out whether there's another layer of meaning.

> *This boy is Ignorance. This girl is Want. Beware them both...* In 'A Christmas Carol', Dickens uses the characters of Ignorance and Want to <u>symbolise</u> the <u>problems</u> caused by society's neglect of the <u>poor</u>.

Structure is always important

There's more information about the structure of plays on p.26 and prose texts on p.41.

1) <u>Structure</u> is the <u>order</u> that events happen in. Make sure you think about how a writer has put a text together, and what the <u>effect</u> of this is.

2) Structural devices can be used to make a text more <u>interesting</u>. For example:

- <u>Foreshadowing</u> gives <u>hints</u> about what will happen <u>later on</u> in the story.

> *In 'Never Let Me Go', Kathy frequently hints at how significant the character of Madame is to the students' lives, but her exact role in the system is not revealed until near the end of the novel. This creates suspense, as the reader waits for the mystery of the students' existence and Madame's role in their lives to be resolved.*

- <u>Flashbacks</u> temporarily <u>shift</u> the story back in time, often showing something from the <u>past</u> that is significant in the <u>present</u>.

> *The opening of 'The History Boys' shows Irwin in a wheelchair, before Bennett moves time backwards twenty years and Irwin is able to walk. The audience is therefore left wondering what happens to Irwin and expects that something is going to occur during the course of the play to explain his disability.*

Remember to write about the effect on the reader...

It's important to refer to the techniques that the writer uses, but if you want the top marks you'll also need to mention how those techniques affect the reader (or the audience if it's a play).

Context

Texts are influenced by the time and place they're written and set in, as well as by the person who wrote them. You need to consider these influences for each text you study.

Texts are shaped by the **Context** they were written in

1) Think about the <u>setting</u> of the <u>text</u> and <u>what was happening</u> when it was written.

2) Here are a few <u>questions</u> you should ask yourself when thinking about <u>context</u>:

Where is the text set?
Did the writer base the <u>setting</u> on their own experiences?

When was the text written?
- <u>What was happening</u> at the time the text was written?
- What was <u>society</u> like?

When does the story take place?
Did the writer base the story in the <u>time</u> in which they lived or a different time?

What do you know about the writer?
- Where is the writer <u>from</u>?
- What is their <u>background</u>?

What genre is the text part of?
- Is the text part of a <u>literary movement</u>?
- Was the writer <u>influenced</u> by other texts?

Show you're aware of the **Issues** the text raises

1) You need to show the examiner that you're aware of the <u>wider issues</u> raised by the text, and <u>comment</u> on how these issues are <u>portrayed</u> in the text.

2) Here are some of the <u>issues</u> that you should look out for:

Social or cultural issues
Authors often <u>comment</u> on the <u>society</u> they're living in, particularly the <u>faults</u> they associate with it. *'Blood Brothers' examines social class, and how it can determine the course of people's lives.*

Historical or political issues
Writers may focus on a particular <u>historical situation</u> or <u>political issue</u>. *George Orwell wrote 'Animal Farm' in 1945 as an allegory for events which took place around that time in Communist Russia.*

Moral issues
Sometimes a text aims to challenge the reader with a <u>moral message</u>. *'Frankenstein' raises the question of whether advances in science are beneficial or dangerous for mankind.*

Philosophical issues
Some writers explore a <u>philosophical question</u> through their texts. ⟶ *In 'Romeo and Juliet', Shakespeare questions what romantic love actually is.*

Reactions to texts can change over time...
When writing about context, think about whether attitudes toward certain issues have changed over time. The original audience of a text may have viewed a text very differently to how an audience would today.

Themes and the Writer's Message

Texts don't just tell a story — they explore significant issues and questions.

Think about the **Themes** of the text

1) Texts usually have something to say about the <u>society</u> in which they were <u>written</u> or <u>set</u>.

2) Think carefully about the <u>themes</u> of the text, and what the writer might have been <u>saying</u> about them.

Fate

- Do we control our own lives or are they controlled by fate?

Characters in 'Romeo and Juliet' blame fate for their problems. This makes the audience question whether what is happening is indeed down to fate or whether the characters should take responsibility for their actions.

Gender

- How do the lives of men and women differ?
- What is the impact of gender inequality?

In 'Pride and Prejudice', the Bennet sisters cannot inherit their father's estate because they are female. Their best chance of independence and financial security is to marry well.

Social Class

- What is the impact of social class on characters' lives?
- Is it right that social class is so important?

In 'An Inspector Calls', Priestley contrasts the actions and qualities of the working-class characters with those of the middle classes to highlight the unfairness of the class system.

Ambition

- Is ambition healthy or destructive?
- How can we control our ambition?

By showing Macbeth's downfall, Shakespeare gives the audience a warning about the destructive nature of ambition.

Love

- What is the true nature of love?
- How far will we go to pursue love?

In 'Much Ado About Nothing', Shakespeare contrasts Claudio's shallow, fickle feelings for Hero with the deep love that develops between Beatrice and Benedick.

Work out the writer's **Overall Message**

1) Think about <u>why</u> the writer might have <u>written</u> the book or play.

2) Look at the <u>issues</u> and <u>questions</u> the text raises.

Dickens' message in 'A Christmas Carol' is that the rich have a duty to help those less fortunate than themselves.

The central message of 'Lord of the Flies' is that all humans have evil inside them and are capable of committing terrible deeds.

You need to study the text carefully to work out the message...

It might take a while to work out the writer's overall message, so make sure you read the text carefully. The fates of characters, significant passages of speech and the ending of the text are all worth examining.

Using Quotations

You're not allowed to take any of your texts into the exam, so you're going to need to learn some quotations...

Learn **Key Quotations** that are relevant to **Characters** and **Themes**

1) When you're reading a text, make a <u>note</u> of some <u>good quotes</u> to learn. Examiners aren't expecting you to memorise big chunks of text, so the quotes you pick out should be <u>short</u> and <u>snappy</u>.

2) You need to use the quotes to <u>back up</u> the <u>points</u> in your essay, so make sure the quotes you choose are <u>relevant</u> to things you're likely to write about in the exam, e.g. a <u>key character</u> or <u>theme</u>.

3) When you're <u>revising</u>, it's a good idea to make <u>lists</u> of <u>key quotes</u> for each theme or character.

'Anita and Me': THEME — FAMILY

The Rutters — "Tell me mom. I don't care." (Anita)
— "Where's me mum?" (Tracey)

The Kumars — Meena says she will "never leave" Mama
— "the English... kick their elders in the backside" (Mama)

It's a good idea to learn quotes that relate to different aspects of a theme — in this example there are some quotes from different characters. Quotes can be as short as a word or phrase — don't try to learn long sentences.

Embed **Short Quotations** into your sentences

Quoting from Shakespeare is covered on page 33.

1) The <u>best</u> way to use quotes is to <u>embed</u> (insert) them into your <u>sentences</u>. This just means that they should be a <u>natural part</u> of a sentence, allowing you to go on to <u>explain</u> how the quote <u>supports</u> your <u>point</u>.

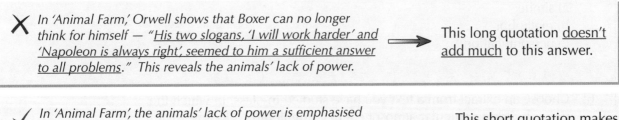

In 'An Inspector Calls', the Inspector describes Eva positively, calling her "<u>pretty</u>" and "<u>lively</u>", which makes the audience feel more sympathetic towards her.

2) Using shorter quotations allows you to explain the <u>same point</u> in <u>fewer words</u>.

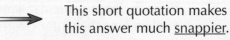

✗ *In 'Animal Farm,' Orwell shows that Boxer can no longer think for himself — "<u>His two slogans, 'I will work harder' and 'Napoleon is always right', seemed to him a sufficient answer to all problems.</u>" This reveals the animals' lack of power.*

→ This long quotation <u>doesn't add much</u> to this answer.

✓ *In 'Animal Farm,' the animals' lack of power is emphasised by Boxer's repetition of "<u>Napoleon is always right</u>", which shows that he can no longer think for himself.*

→ This short quotation makes this answer much <u>snappier</u>.

3) If you get an <u>extract question</u> (see page 10) make sure you quote <u>accurately</u> from the text you're given. But <u>don't be tempted</u> to quote huge chunks of text — always be <u>selective</u> with the quotes you use and make sure you explain their <u>significance</u> or <u>effect</u>.

Don't try to learn very long quotes...

When you're revising quotes, don't memorise long chunks of text — short phrases or single words are easier to learn. They'll also help keep your answers concise, which will please the examiners.

Warm-Up Questions

You'll need your set texts to hand when you're answering these questions, but don't worry — you don't need to write any long answers (yet). If you don't know what texts you're studying, now would be a good time to find out from your teacher.

Warm-Up Questions

1) Look at the different types of question in the box and read the sample questions below. For each sample question, write down what type of question you think it is.

> • **theme**   • **characterisation**   • **mood/atmosphere**

   a) Beginning with this extract, explore how Shakespeare presents Anthony as a resourceful character in 'Julius Caesar'.
   b) How does Austen present ideas about class in 'Pride and Prejudice'?
   c) Explore how Kelly creates tension in 'DNA'.

2) Choose one of the texts you have studied.
   Write a paragraph describing your personal response to the text.

3) Choose a character from one of the texts you have studied.
   Find five key quotations which illustrate something about their personality.
   Write a sentence explaining what each quotation tells you about them.

4) For the character you chose in question 3, explain how you feel about that character and how the author has made you feel that way.
   Use evidence from the text to back up your argument.

5) Using one of your set texts, find one example of:
   a) simile
   b) metaphor
   c) personification

6) Choose an extract from a text you have studied in class, in which the writer builds a particular atmosphere (e.g. frightening, gloomy, joyful).
   Explain how the writer creates that atmosphere, and what effect it has on the reader.
   Remember to use evidence from the text to back up your argument.

7) Using a text you have studied in class, identify an unusual structural feature (e.g. an instance of foreshadowing, a flashback or a jump in time).
   Write a short paragraph describing the feature and explaining its effect.

Warm-Up Questions

8) Read the passages below. For each one, write a sentence or two stating what you think each object or action in bold is a symbol for, and explaining your view.

   a) | *In 'Lord of the Flies', the boys use the **conch shell** to bring order to their meetings — whoever is holding it is allowed to speak, while everyone else has to keep quiet and listen.*

   b) | *In 'Jane Eyre', Mr Rochester proposes to Jane underneath the old **chestnut tree** in the grounds of Thornfield. That night, the tree is struck by lightning and split down the middle. Later, Jane discovers that Mr Rochester is already married, so she refuses to marry him and runs away.*

   c) | *In 'Never Let Me Go', the students are forced into a particular way of life over which they have very little control. When they discuss their futures, many of them claim that they would like to have jobs that involve **driving**.*

9) Choose a text you have studied in class and answer the following questions about it.
  a) When was the text written? Is it set at this time or in a different period?
  b) How does the writer portray the time in which the text is set?
  c) Do the characters encounter any problems related to the text's context, e.g. based on class, race or gender?

10) Choose a text you have studied in class. Write down three of the text's key themes (e.g. social class, gender, power). For each theme, write down an example from the text and explain how it relates to the theme.

Your examples for this question could be events in the story, characters' reactions to events, or quotes from the text.

11) Think about two of your set texts. What do you think the message of each one is?

12) Which of the following paragraphs shows a better use of quotations? Explain your answer.

   a) | *In 'Anita and Me', Meena has unrealistic, childish dreams of what her future holds. She describes winning a talent show and becoming a "major personality" as her "most realistic escape route" from her current life.*

   b) | *In 'Anita and Me', Meena has unrealistic, childish dreams of what her future holds. She watches a talent show and says "I knew that this could be my most realistic escape route from Tollington, from ordinary girl to major personality in one easy step."*

Exam-Style Questions

Writing about texts is an acquired skill — you can only get better at it by practising. The next two sections go into more detail about drama and prose, and you'll find some practice exam questions at the end of each section. To get you into the swing of it, have a go at answering these.

Q1   Choose a character from a Shakespeare play you have studied. Starting with one scene, explain how Shakespeare presents the character in that scene and in the play as a whole.

Q2   Choose a passage from a prose text you have read which you find particularly tense **or** exciting. Write about the methods the author has used to create tension **or** excitement in the passage and in the text as a whole.

Q3   Choose a modern (post-1914) text that you have studied.
Explore how the author presents **either** power **or** love **or** childhood **or** social class.

Q4   Choose a key theme from a 19th-century text that you have studied.
Starting with a short extract from the text, write about how the author explores the theme in that extract and in the text as a whole.

Revision Summary

Congratulations — you've reached the end of the section. All in the brain? Have a go at these to check...

- Try these questions and <u>tick off each one</u> when you <u>get it right</u>.
- When you've done <u>all the questions</u> under a heading and are <u>completely happy</u> with it, tick it off.

Writing About Prose and Drama (p.10-11) ☑

1) What should you always do when making a point in an answer?
   a) Make sure it answers the question you've been given.
   b) Add as many extra details about the text as you can. ☑

2) Which of the following sentences is better to include in an essay?
   a) The foreshadowing in 'Never Let Me Go' meant I was intrigued about the story —
      I wanted to keep reading.
   b) The use of foreshadowing in 'Never Let Me Go' creates intrigue, and makes the reader
      want to find out more. ☑

Writing About Characters (p.12-13) ☑

3) What is characterisation? ☑

4) Give three examples of things you could write about when answering a question
   about a particular character. ☑

The Writer's Techniques (p.14-16) ☑

5) What is the difference between a simile and a metaphor? ☑

6) What is the word given to the type of imagery where something (like an animal or object)
   is described as if it were human? ☑

7) Why might a writer choose to use a shorter sentence instead of a longer sentence? ☑

8) Write a brief explanation of what authors can use settings for. ☑

9) Explain what symbolism is. Give an example of a symbol from a text you have studied. ☑

10) What is foreshadowing? ☑

11) What are flashbacks?
    a) Times when a character's vision goes blank for a couple of seconds and then returns.
    b) Moments when the writer describes something as if it were a human.
    c) Parts where the story shifts to an earlier time. ☑

Context (p.17) ☑

12) Give three questions to ask yourself when thinking about the context of a text. ☑

13) Write down two examples of wider issues that might be raised by a text. ☑

Themes and the Writer's Message (p.18) ☑

14) Give three examples of themes that are often addressed in texts. ☑

15) Is the following statement true or false?
    "To work out the overall message, you should consider why the writer may have written the text." ☑

Using Quotations (p.19) ☑

16) When quoting from a text, why should you try to include short rather than long quotations? ☑

17) Give two examples of things you need to be especially careful of when quoting
    from the text to answer an extract question. ☑

Reading Plays

Writers use stage directions to show what's happening on stage. Different types of speech give clues about a character's personality, their relationships with other characters and their innermost thoughts.

Stage Directions describe the action on stage

Stage directions are usually written in italics or put in brackets to distinguish them from things that are said.

1) When you're reading a play, look out for the <u>stage directions</u>.
   These are <u>instructions</u> from the <u>playwright</u> to the director and the actors
   — they can tell you a lot about <u>how</u> the playwright wants the play to be <u>performed</u>.

2) There are lots of things to look out for in the stage directions. For example, <u>music</u> and <u>sound effects</u> might be used to create a specific <u>mood</u>, or the <u>set</u> may be designed to create a certain <u>atmosphere</u>.

A bass note, repeated as a heartbeat.	In 'Blood Brothers', Russell uses <u>music</u> to build <u>tension</u>. This stage direction emphasises the significance of the moment, and highlights Mrs Johnstone's <u>fear</u>.

3) Stage directions can also describe the characters' <u>actions</u> and the use of <u>props</u>.

Christopher puts his hands over his ears. He closes his eyes... He starts groaning.	In 'The Curious Incident of the Dog in the Night-Time', Stephens uses stage directions to <u>tell</u> the actor playing Christopher <u>how to act</u>, and to give the audience an insight into the character's <u>personality</u>.

Stage directions reveal what the writer Wants

You should write about how the stage directions reveal the playwright's <u>intentions</u>.

Action

We see Mickey comb the town, breaking through groups of people, looking, searching, desperate... *('Blood Brothers' — Willy Russell)*	These stage directions <u>describe</u> what's happening on stage — Mickey's desperate search makes this scene <u>dramatic</u>.

Staging

The dining-room of a fairly large suburban house... It has good solid furniture... *('An Inspector Calls' — J. B. Priestley)*	In these opening stage directions, Priestley establishes <u>how</u> he would like the <u>set</u> to <u>look</u>. The set reflects the <u>class</u> and <u>status</u> of the Birlings.

Characterisation

Jo dances on dreamily. *('A Taste of Honey' — Shelagh Delaney)*	This stage direction occurs after Jo has agreed to <u>marry</u> her boyfriend. It hints at her <u>longing to escape</u> and her <u>dreams</u> of a better life.

Dialogue

Irwin *(thoughtfully) That's very true.* *('The History Boys' — Alan Bennett)*	The stage direction here tells the actor playing Irwin <u>how</u> he should <u>deliver</u> his line.

Reading Plays

Plays contain **Different** types of **Speech**

1) <u>Dialogue</u> is when two or more characters are speaking.
It shows how characters <u>interact</u> with each other.

> **Eric** *If you think that's the best she can do —*
> **Sheila** *Don't be an ass, Eric.*
> **Mrs Birling** *Now stop it, you two.*
>
> *('An Inspector Calls' — J.B. Priestley)*

This dialogue hints at the <u>tensions</u> that exist between the characters.

2) A <u>monologue</u> is when <u>one character</u> speaks for a long time and the other characters on stage <u>listen</u> to them.

> **Benedick** *O, she misused me past the endurance of a block! An oak but with one green leaf on it would have answered her...*
>
> *('Much Ado About Nothing' — William Shakespeare)*

After Beatrice offends him, Benedick gives a <u>monologue</u> in which he conveys his <u>frustration</u> to Don Pedro. His <u>exaggerated</u> complaints emphasise the <u>strength</u> of his emotions.

3) In a <u>soliloquy</u>, a <u>single character</u> speaks their <u>thoughts out loud</u> — other characters can't hear them. This reveals to the audience something of the character's <u>inner thoughts</u> and <u>feelings</u>.

> **Mrs Johnstone** *Only mine until*
> *The time comes round*
> *To pay the bill*
>
> *('Blood Brothers' — Willy Russell)*

Mrs Johnstone's song 'Easy Terms' acts as a <u>soliloquy</u> about how she can't keep the things she has bought. Her sorrow is made more <u>poignant</u> by the fact that Mrs Lyons has pressured her into giving up one of her children.

4) An <u>aside</u> is like a soliloquy, but it is usually a <u>shorter comment</u> which is only heard by the <u>audience</u> — other characters don't hear it.

> **Macbeth** *(aside)* *Glamis, and Thane of Cawdor:*
> *The greatest is behind. (To Rosse and Angus)*
> *Thanks for your pains.*
>
> *('Macbeth' — William Shakespeare)*

Macbeth's first remarks are heard only by the <u>audience</u>, then he returns to addressing <u>other characters</u>. This allows the audience to see what he is <u>thinking</u>, and emphasises that he is <u>hiding</u> things from the other characters.

Some playwrights use stage directions more than others...

Different writers use different methods. Shakespeare didn't use many stage directions — he relied instead on characters' speech to tell the story. Modern writers tend to use more stage directions than Shakespeare.

Writing About Plays

When you're writing about a play, keep in mind the fact that it's intended to be watched by an audience.

Write about the **Language** of the play

1) You need to write in <u>detail</u> about the <u>language</u> used in the play.

2) Writers often use <u>imagery</u>, like <u>similes</u>, <u>metaphors</u> and <u>personification</u>.

> *My bounty is as boundless as the sea,*
> *My love as deep; the more I give to thee*
> *The more I have, for both are infinite.*
>
> *('Romeo and Juliet' — William Shakespeare)*

Juliet uses a <u>simile</u> to compare her love for Romeo to the sea, saying that it is both as endless and as deep.

> *Life's but a walking shadow, a poor player*
> *That struts and frets his hour upon the stage*
> *And then is heard no more.*
>
> *('Macbeth' — William Shakespeare)*

Macbeth <u>personifies</u> life, comparing it to an <u>actor</u> whose influence is limited to his time on stage. This shows that Macbeth thinks life is brief and pointless.

3) You also need to write about how playwrights use <u>dialogue</u>, for example how particular scenes are used to develop <u>characters</u>, reveal the <u>plot</u> and explore wider <u>issues</u> and <u>themes</u>.

> **Mrs Lyons** *When are you due?*
> **Mrs Johnstone** *Erm, well, about... Oh, but Mrs...*
> **Mrs Lyons** *Quickly, quickly, tell me...*
>
> *('Blood Brothers' — Willy Russell)*

This <u>dialogue</u> shows that Mrs Lyons is more <u>powerful</u> than Mrs Johnstone — her interruption and use of <u>imperatives</u> like "tell me" show that she controls the conversation.

4) Think about the <u>effects</u> the language and dialogue have on the <u>audience</u>.

> *In the opening scene of 'DNA' by Dennis Kelly, Jan and Mark constantly speak over and interrupt one another. This increases the pace of the scene and makes it more difficult for the audience to follow, which helps to convey a sense of the stress and confusion that Jan and Mark are experiencing.*

A play's **Structure** is important too

You need to think about how the play is <u>structured</u>. For example:

1) How does the playwright use <u>act</u> and <u>scene breaks</u>?

> *Each act of 'An Inspector Calls' ends on a cliffhanger, and at the beginning of the next act, the "scene and situation are exactly as they were" at the end of the previous act. This builds the tension and sense of pressure that the Birlings are under.*

2) How does the playwright show <u>changes</u> in <u>time</u>?

> *In 'Blood Brothers', Russell uses a montage (a series of short scenes) to move time forwards four years. The speed at which time passes on stage symbolises the fleetingness of youth, and gives the audience the sense that the play is moving rapidly towards its tragic ending.*

Writing About Plays

Show you know that plays are intended to be **Watched** not **Read**

Plays are written to be <u>acted on stage</u>, not read silently from a book. This means that you shouldn't refer to the '<u>reader</u>' — talk about the '<u>audience</u>' instead.

> *Siobhan acts as a kind of narrator in 'The Curious Incident of the Dog in the Night-Time' — she reads segments of Christopher's work, which helps the audience make sense of what's happening, and gives them an insight into Christopher's mind.*

 You should comment on how the play works on <u>stage</u> and how this <u>impacts</u> on the <u>audience</u>.

Show you appreciate **Stagecraft**

1) You also need to show that you appreciate the writer's <u>stagecraft</u> — their <u>skill</u> at writing for the <u>stage</u>. Playwrights use features like <u>silences</u>, <u>actions</u> and <u>sound effects</u> to create a mood, reveal something in a certain way or add drama to a situation — these things are usually mentioned in <u>stage directions</u> (see p.24).

2) Appreciating the stagecraft means asking yourself a few <u>key questions</u>:

- How would this scene <u>look on stage</u>?

- How would the <u>audience react</u>?

- Is it <u>effective</u>?

3) Writers might use stagecraft to vary the <u>pace</u> of the play to keep it interesting for the audience. For example, in Act Two of 'Blood Brothers', Russell uses <u>simultaneous conversations</u> to create a fast-paced scene:

> *Mickey and Sammy are speaking on one side of the stage whilst Edward and Linda are speaking on the other side. Both conversations have life-changing consequences, and the combination of the two dialogues emphasises the fact that both twins are at a crossroads in their lives.*

4) Writers can also use stagecraft to increase the <u>tension</u>, particularly at a <u>climactic moment</u> in the play. In the final act of 'Romeo and Juliet', Shakespeare uses <u>dramatic irony</u> to build up the suspense:

> *Romeo fights Paris in the tomb while the audience, knowing that Friar Lawrence is on his way, hope he'll arrive and avert the tragedy. He arrives too late: Romeo has already killed Paris and committed suicide. These events happen in a very short space of time, and the tension is incredible. Even though the audience knows from the start of the play that Romeo and Juliet will both die, we still hope that they won't.*

Dramatic irony is where the audience knows something that a character on stage doesn't know.

Reading the play aloud will help you understand it...

Try reading bits of the play out loud. Some lines have a particular rhythm to them that is more obvious when they're spoken. Reading aloud can also help you remember quotes from the play.

Writing About Modern Plays

If you're studying a modern play (that's one written after 1914), read on — this is important stuff...

You might have to write about a Modern Play

1) For Paper 2, you'll have to study either a modern play or a modern prose text. Your teacher will be able to tell you which you're doing.

See p.41-43 for information on writing about modern prose texts.

2) The modern plays you might study are:

- An Inspector Calls by J.B. Priestley
- Blood Brothers by Willy Russell
- The History Boys by Alan Bennett
- A Taste of Honey by Shelagh Delaney

- DNA by Dennis Kelly
- The Curious Incident of the Dog in the Night-Time by Simon Stephens

Modern plays are often Realistic

1) Many modern plays try to be realistic, featuring characters who lead ordinary lives. They often include:

- Everyday settings. The setting could be real, e.g. Liverpool in 'Blood Brothers', or made-up but realistic, e.g. Brumley in 'An Inspector Calls'.
- Characters who are ordinary people, rather than kings or heroes.
- Characters who speak in a realistic way — for example, they might use slang or a regional accent.

2) Realistic plays tend to feature issues that affect ordinary people in society, e.g. living in poverty in 'A Taste of Honey'.

3) The writer might use their play to encourage the audience to think about these issues in their own lives — and even change their behaviour as a result.

Modern playwrights often criticise Social Divides

1) Modern British plays often focus on social class divides in Britain.

2) They might write about situations when middle and upper-class people have more opportunities than working-class people. This might be reflected in things like education, job prospects and wealth.

In 'Blood Brothers', one twin is raised in a middle-class family, while the other is raised in a working-class family. The play shows how social class affects the boys' lives. Edward goes to university and becomes a councillor, while Mickey struggles with a low-paid, insecure job from which he is eventually laid off.

3) Some modern writers have used their plays to encourage people to treat everyone equally, regardless of their social class or background.

In 'An Inspector Calls', the working-class character Eva Smith/Daisy Renton is mistreated by all the members of the middle-class Birling family. Priestley uses the play to criticise prejudiced attitudes towards poor or working-class people, and to encourage people to take responsibility for one another in society.

Writing About Modern Plays

Being a **Young Person** is explored in many modern plays

1) Modern plays often present the lives of <u>young people</u> or <u>teenagers</u>,
   showing a young person <u>growing up</u> and trying to <u>understand</u> the world.

> *One of the themes of 'The Curious Incident of the Dog in the Night-Time' is Christopher coming to terms with the changes in his family, after discovering that his father killed a neighbour's dog. Christopher's journey into London on his own represents him gaining independence and dealing with the changes in his life.*

2) Some writers explore concerns in <u>society</u> about teenagers who commit <u>crime</u>
   or <u>behave antisocially</u>. E.g. 'DNA' explores how a group of teenagers <u>react</u>
   after a bullying incident goes wrong and someone is <u>killed</u>.

Some modern plays explore **Gender** and **Sexuality**

1) Modern plays often explore the <u>experiences</u> of <u>different groups</u> in society.

2) Some plays focus on issues that <u>women</u> face, e.g. the expectation that
   a woman would get <u>married</u> and have <u>children</u> instead of <u>working</u>.

> *In 'A Taste of Honey', Jo becomes pregnant without being married and wants to work to support the baby. The play shows some of her efforts to become independent.*

3) Other plays might explore how people with <u>different sexualities</u>
   face <u>prejudice</u> or <u>discrimination</u> by others in society.

> *In 'The History Boys', Bennett explores how Posner comes to understand his sexuality, as well as some of his fears about how he will be treated in society because he is gay.*

Think about how the play might be **Staged**

1) Modern writers often use <u>stage directions</u> (see p.24) to show how they want a scene to be <u>performed</u>.

> *In 'DNA', Kelly writes that Phil "puts his Coke carefully on the ground" before explaining his plan to cover up Adam's murder. This slow, careful movement shows how undisturbed he is by the incident.*

2) The use of <u>lighting</u>, <u>music</u> and <u>special effects</u> can affect the way the play is <u>interpreted</u>.

> *At the end of 'The Curious Incident of the Dog in the Night-Time', Christopher demonstrates a maths problem. Stephens gives stage directions for this scene that include the use of lights and projections. By using technology to make Christopher's demonstration more visually impressive, Stephens emphasises Christopher's achievement in his maths A-level and in overcoming adversity.*

Modern plays often address social issues...

Modern plays deal with some pretty tricky themes. Finding out a bit about when and where a play is set can really help to understand the problems the writer is addressing and the messages they want to give out.

Writing About Shakespeare

You'll need to know a bit about Shakespeare for your exam. The next few pages will give you a hand.

Shakespeare's plays can be Serious or Funny

1) You'll have to study a <u>Shakespeare play</u> as part of your course. The plays you might study are:

- Macbeth
- The Tempest
- Much Ado About Nothing
- Romeo and Juliet
- The Merchant of Venice
- Julius Caesar

2) Shakespeare's plays are often split into different <u>genres</u> based on the <u>features</u> they have in common.

Tragedy

- Tragedies (e.g. '<u>Macbeth</u>' and '<u>Romeo and Juliet</u>') often focus on <u>big topics</u> — e.g. love, death, war, religion. They can be <u>emotionally powerful</u> and often have a <u>moral message</u>.
- Some of Shakespeare's tragedies are set in an <u>imaginary</u> or <u>historical</u> world. The characters are often <u>kings</u>, <u>queens</u> or other <u>rulers</u>.

Comedy

- Comedies (e.g. '<u>Much Ado About Nothing</u>' and '<u>The Merchant of Venice</u>') are written to be <u>funny</u>.
- They feature events and characters that are often <u>exaggerated</u> for humorous effect.
- They can still have a <u>moral message</u> though, and often include <u>serious</u> or <u>emotional</u> elements.

Romance

- <u>Romances</u> are similar to <u>comedies</u> but have <u>darker elements</u>.
- '<u>The Tempest</u>' is often described as a romance.

History

- <u>Histories</u> are based on <u>real historical events</u>.
- '<u>Julius Caesar</u>' has sometimes been considered a history play.

3) Some plays might fit into <u>more than one</u> genre, e.g. '<u>The Tempest</u>' has elements of both <u>romance</u> and <u>comedy</u>, and '<u>Julius Caesar</u>' has been described as both a <u>tragedy</u> and a <u>history</u>.

Shakespeare's plays share Similar Themes

Shakespeare's plays tend to have <u>similar themes</u>. Some of the most <u>common</u> ones are:

Power & Ambition

'Macbeth' explores the title character's ambition to be king. The play shows his downfall after this desire leads to murder, suggesting that too much ambition can be a bad thing.

Fate & Free Will

The events of 'Romeo and Juliet' suggest that a person's fate is unavoidable. The couple's love is described as "death-marked" in the Prologue, and they are unable to escape their families' conflict.

Love & Relationships

In 'Much Ado about Nothing', Shakespeare contrasts the relationship between Hero and Claudio (shallow and immature) with that between Beatrice and Benedick (deeper and more mature) to explore the real meaning of love.

Justice & Revenge

In 'The Merchant of Venice', two different ideas of justice are shown. Portia believes it would be just for Shylock to show mercy to Antonio, while Shylock thinks he deserves revenge. The play debates whether revenge is ever justified.

Writing About Shakespeare

Show you're aware that Shakespeare was writing **400 Years Ago**

1) Shakespeare (1564-1616) wrote his plays about 400 years ago, so it's not surprising that some of the language, themes and ideas can seem a bit strange to us.

2) He lived at the end of a period of European history known as the Renaissance — a time when there were lots of developments in the arts, politics, religion and science. The theatre was very popular at this time.

3) Shakespeare was aware of his audience when writing his plays. A wide range of people went to watch his plays, from the very rich to servants and labourers. Shakespeare tended to include complex imagery and puns for the educated nobles, and slapstick for the uneducated poor.

4) Many people in Shakespeare's Britain believed in the supernatural — people were executed for witchcraft, and superstitious behaviour was common. Several of Shakespeare's plays have supernatural elements, e.g. the Witches in 'Macbeth' and the spirits in 'The Tempest'. The audience would usually have taken these supernatural characters seriously.

5) Shakespeare was keen to keep the British king or queen of the day happy. His plays often had a royal audience — both Elizabeth I and James I enjoyed performances of his plays.

> *There are many features in 'Macbeth' which could have been included to please King James I. For example, the events following Duncan's murder show the negative consequences for those who try to seize power from the reigning king. James was also obsessed with stamping out witchcraft — Shakespeare's portrayal of the Witches as wholly evil would have pleased the king.*

Learn about **Theatrical Performances** in Shakespeare's time

Knowing a bit about theatrical performances in Shakespeare's time will help you to write top answers about his plays. Here are some of the key features:

1) Only men were allowed to act on stage — all the female roles were played by boys. Shakespeare's comedies include lots of jokes about girls dressing up as boys.

2) Most of the actors wore elaborate costumes that were based on the fashions of when the play was written, and that reflected the status of the character. Plays set overseas, e.g. in ancient Rome or Greece, used costumes appropriate to the location.

3) Musicians helped to create atmosphere in the theatre. They also made sound effects, such as the thunder at the beginning of 'Macbeth'.

4) Plays didn't use much scenery — sets were simple so that they could show different locations in a play, and could be adapted easily to be used for several different plays.

Think about how Shakespeare kept his audience entertained...

When writing about Shakespeare's plays, remember that he meant them to be performed on stage. Mentioning how a particular method could affect the audience is a great way to pick up marks.

Shakespeare's Language

When you're writing about a Shakespeare play, you need to take a close look at the language, and think about the effect it would have on someone watching the play.

Shakespeare uses lots of **Imagery**

Shakespeare's <u>imagery</u> includes similes, metaphors and personification.

> *Now does he feel his title*
> *Hang loose about him, like a giant's robe*
> *Upon a dwarfish thief.*
>
> *'Macbeth' Act 5, Scene 2*

Angus uses a <u>simile</u> to suggest that Macbeth's duties as King are too much for him, like clothes that are too big.

> *Pardon me, Julius! Here wast thou bayed, brave hart;*
> *Here didst thou fall; and here thy hunters stand...*
>
> *'Julius Caesar' Act 3, Scene 1*

Antony uses a <u>metaphor</u> to describe Caesar as a hunted deer (a hart) and his killers as hunters. This suggests that he thinks Caesar was wrongly killed.

Look out for **Striking Words** and **Phrases**

When you read through the text, make a note of any words that <u>jump out at you</u>.
Think about why they're important, and what effect they have.

> *If you tickle us, do we not laugh? If you poison us, do*
> *we not die? And if you wrong us, shall we not revenge?*
>
> *'The Merchant of Venice' Act 3, Scene 1*

Shylock's <u>emotive speech</u> uses <u>rhetorical questions</u> to show that as a Jew he's no different to Christians. The mention of <u>revenge</u> hints at his <u>anger</u>.

> *When the battle's lost and won.*
> *'Macbeth' Act 1, Scene 1*

The Witches use <u>paradox</u> — this hides their motives from the other characters and the audience, and emphasises that <u>nothing is as it seems</u>.

Humour is also important in Shakespeare's plays

Shakespeare uses lots of <u>puns</u> and <u>jokes</u>. They can help to <u>relieve tension</u>, <u>lighten the mood</u> and highlight <u>key themes</u>.

> *Ask for me tomorrow, and you shall*
> *find me a grave man.*
>
> *'Romeo and Juliet' Act 3, Scene 1*

Mercutio makes a joke about his own <u>death</u>, playing on the <u>double meaning</u> of "<u>grave</u>" ('serious', and 'a place to put dead bodies').

> **Messenger**   *I see, lady, the gentleman*
> *is not in your books.*
> **Beatrice**   *No — an he were, I would*
> *burn my study.*
>
> *'Much Ado about Nothing' Act 1, Scene 1*

Beatrice plays on the meaning of the word "books" — the Messenger means that Benedick is not in Beatrice's <u>favour</u>, but Beatrice deliberately <u>misinterprets</u> him, replying as if he had meant <u>actual books</u>.

Section Three — Drama

Shakespeare's Language

Look at Shakespeare's **Verse Forms**

1) Shakespeare wrote his plays in a mixture of <u>poetry</u> and <u>prose</u>.
   You can tell a lot about a <u>character</u> by looking at the <u>way</u> they <u>speak</u>.

2) The majority of Shakespeare's lines are written in <u>blank verse</u> (unrhymed iambic pentameter). Blank verse sounds <u>grander</u> than prose and can be used by almost any characters, but <u>lower-class</u>, <u>comic</u> and <u>mad</u> characters generally <u>don't</u> use it.

A line written using iambic pentameter usually has 10 syllables (five unstressed and five stressed).

Come I to speak in Caesar's funeral.
He was my friend, faithful and just to me.

'Julius Caesar' Act 3, Scene 2

Antony is a <u>powerful Roman</u>, so it is suitable that he speaks in <u>blank verse</u>. It also sounds <u>formal</u>, which is fitting for the funeral speech he is giving at this point.

3) Sometimes Shakespeare uses <u>rhymed iambic pentameter</u> to make speech sound <u>dramatic</u> and <u>impressive</u>, e.g. at the beginning and end of a scene, or when a posh character is speaking.

From forth the fatal loins of these two foes
A pair of star-cross'd lovers take their life,
Whose misadventur'd piteous overthrows
Doth with their death bury their parents' strife.

'Romeo and Juliet' Prologue

The Prologue acts as an introduction to the play, when the audience are told that Romeo and Juliet are doomed to die. The <u>importance</u> of this message is emphasised by the fact that it is in <u>rhymed iambic pentameter</u>.

4) The rest of Shakespeare's writing is in <u>normal prose</u>. <u>Funny bits</u> and dialogue between more minor or lower-class characters are usually written in prose.

Come hither, neighbour Seacole. God hath blest you with a good name: to be a well-favoured man is the gift of fortune, but to write and read comes by nature.

'Much Ado About Nothing' Act 3, Scene 3

Dogberry is a <u>lower-class</u> and <u>comical</u> character. He therefore speaks in <u>prose</u> rather than verse. This makes his speech sound <u>natural</u> and <u>informal</u>.

Look out for switches between **Poetry** and **Prose**

1) Check for when characters <u>change</u> between verse and prose. You can tell from the lines — if each <u>new line</u> starts with a <u>capital letter</u>, it's <u>verse</u>, but if it <u>carries on</u> from the last line <u>without</u> a capital, it's <u>prose</u>.

2) The switch can give you clues about a character's <u>state of mind</u>, e.g. Lady Macbeth speaks in <u>prose</u> when she is sleep-walking, which shows her <u>loss of control</u>.

3) You need to <u>quote</u> your play correctly. For <u>prose</u> quotes, just quote as you would from a <u>novel</u>. But if it's <u>verse</u>, and the quote goes over <u>more than one line</u> in the <u>original text</u>, show this using a <u>slash</u> — '<u>/</u>'.

The epilogue to 'The Tempest' is written in rhyming couplets, for example, "<u>Now my charms are all o'erthrown, / And what strength I have's mine own</u>".

This answer uses a quote that's in <u>verse</u> and goes over <u>two lines</u>, so it uses a '<u>/</u>' to show where the <u>line break</u> is in the original text.

Get to grips with the Shakespeare play you're studying...

It's important that you know your Shakespeare text really well. If there are any bits of the play that you don't understand, take the time to reread them carefully and work out what they mean before the exam.

The Structure of Shakespeare's Plays

A text's structure has a big impact on how it's understood. Shakespeare's plays are no different...

Shakespeare **Structured** his plays in **Different Ways**

1) You need to think about the <u>overall structure</u> of your Shakespeare play.

2) Most of Shakespeare's <u>tragedies</u> have a <u>tragic structure</u>. In these plays, the first part <u>builds</u> up to a <u>turning point</u> and the second part deals with the <u>consequences</u> of this.

<u>Mercutio's death</u> in 'Romeo and Juliet' is the play's main turning point. The rest of the play shows the <u>aftermath</u> of this event.

3) Some of Shakespeare's plays have a <u>cyclical structure</u>. This means they <u>start</u> and <u>end</u> with the <u>same situation or setting</u>.

'Macbeth' begins and finishes with a <u>battle</u> to defeat a <u>merciless tyrant</u>. This shows that the events have come <u>full circle</u> and <u>order</u> is restored at the end of the play.

4) Some plays feature <u>repetition</u>, with <u>similar</u> <u>images</u> or <u>ideas</u> appearing at different points in the play. This is can create <u>suspense</u> or emphasise <u>important themes</u>.

Several <u>omens</u> appear in the early scenes of 'Julius Caesar', which <u>hint</u> at what will happen later in the play and increase the <u>tension</u>.

Look at the **Order** of **Scenes** in a play

1) Shakespeare often uses the <u>order</u> of scenes within a play to create particular <u>effects</u>.

- Some scenes are put near the <u>start</u> of the play to emphasise a key <u>theme</u> — e.g. the fight between the two families at the start of 'Romeo and Juliet' shows how <u>violent</u> the feud is.
- Putting a scene at the <u>start</u> of an <u>act</u> can also <u>set the mood</u> for the rest the act — e.g. Act 2 of 'Macbeth' has a <u>dark atmosphere</u> after Macbeth goes to murder Duncan at the start of the act.

2) Shakespeare's plays have <u>key scenes</u> and <u>minor scenes</u>. <u>Key</u> scenes are usually about the <u>main plot</u> or <u>characters</u> of the play, whereas <u>minor</u> scenes typically feature <u>less important</u> characters or develop a <u>sub-plot</u> of the play.

3) Shakespeare often <u>follows</u> a key scene with a minor scene, or vice versa. This is used to:

- change the <u>pace</u> — for example, a <u>humorous</u> minor scene coming before or after an <u>emotional</u> key scene can provide <u>light relief</u> for the audience.
- <u>reflect</u> or <u>contrast</u> different <u>characters</u>, <u>relationships</u> or <u>ideas</u> — e.g. in 'The Tempest', Caliban, Trinculo and Stephano's plot to kill Prospero <u>mirrors</u> Antonio and Sebastian's plot to kill Alonso. Since these characters often have a <u>comedic</u> role and spend a lot of time <u>drinking</u>, their scenes show how <u>silly</u> the arguing between noblemen is.
- develop important <u>themes</u> — e.g. in 'The Merchant of Venice', Launcelot's jokes about Jews converting to Christianity highlight the <u>split</u> between <u>Jews</u> and <u>Christians</u>, which is part of the <u>main plot</u> of the play.

Work out the structure of your Shakespeare play...

Make a graph of your play's structure. Draw a line that goes up as the tension increases and down as it lessens. Mark any turning points, key and minor scenes and anything else important.

Warm-Up Questions

Plays come in different shapes and sizes, but the way you study them should be pretty much the same — pay close attention to the play's language, structure and stagecraft and you'll be scoring marks all over the place. These questions should get you in the mood for the exam. Take a look at the suggested answers on page 111 when you're done.

Warm-Up Questions

1) In one of the plays you have studied, find an example of how the writer uses stage directions to create a specific mood or atmosphere.

2) Write a brief definition of each of the terms below.
   Then, using a set play you have studied, find an example of each term.

   Monologue   Aside   Soliloquy

3) Find one example of each of the following dramatic techniques in a play you have studied:
   a) imagery
   b) repetition
   c) the rhythm of a character's words having a powerful effect.

4) Find an example of humour in a Shakespeare play you have studied.
   What effect does it have on the scene?

5) Choose a Shakespeare play you have studied in class. Pick a passage you find particularly effective (e.g. frightening, funny or tense) and write two or three paragraphs explaining how Shakespeare makes it so effective. Hint: think about form, structure and language.

6) Read the following extracts, and then complete the tasks below.

   | Don Pedro: | My love is thine to teach. Teach it but how, |
   And thou shalt see how apt it is to learn
   Any hard lesson that may do thee good.

   Much Ado About Nothing Act 1, Scene 1

   Trinculo:

   Here's neither bush nor shrub to bear off any weather at all, and another storm brewing. I hear it sing i' th' wind. Yond same black cloud, yond huge one, looks like a foul bombard that would shed his liquor.

   The Tempest Act 2, Scene 2

   | Prince: | A glooming peace this morning with it brings, |
   The sun, for sorrow, will not show his head.
   Go hence, to have more talk of these sad things;
   Some shall be pardoned, and some punishèd.

   Romeo and Juliet Act 5, Scene 3

   a) For each extract, write down whether it is in verse, blank verse or prose.
      Write a sentence explaining how you can tell.
   b) What effect do the form and rhyme scheme of the Prince's speech have?

Worked Exam-Style Question

Here's an example of how to write a top-notch essay about a play. Give it a read through, even if you aren't studying 'Macbeth' — it shows you the kind of thing you'll need to include in any exam answer.

Q1 Read Act 4, Scene 3 of 'Macbeth', from the beginning of the scene to "Yet grace must still look so." Using this extract as a starting point, discuss how far Shakespeare presents Macbeth as a cruel tyrant.

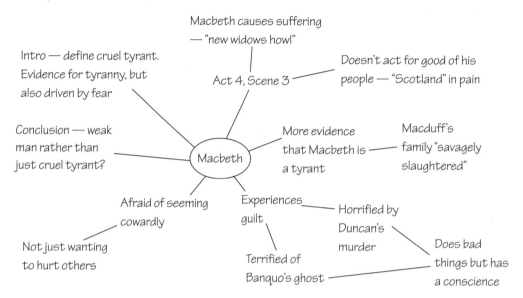

A cruel tyrant could be defined as someone who uses their power to oppress and cause pain to others, has no remorse, and acts for themselves rather than for the good of their people. In 'Macbeth', there is evidence that the main character is a tyrant, including his killing of innocent people to keep his position as king. However he does feel guilt about his bad deeds, and he often acts through fear, suggesting he is not wholly selfish or cruel. <u>He is not simply a cruel tyrant, therefore, but is also a flawed character who is easily controlled by his fears.</u>

← Outline your argument in the <u>introduction</u>.

Don't forget to write about the <u>extract</u> you've been given. →

<u>In Act Four, Scene Three</u>, Malcolm and Macduff describe Macbeth as a "tyrant" and discuss his cruelty, saying that <u>"Each new morn, / New widows howl, new orphans cry"</u>. <u>This shows that Macbeth is causing misery and suffering to his subjects.</u> The repetition of "new" emphasises that the murders are happening regularly. Macbeth seems prepared to go to any length to hold power and is willing to cause suffering to do so. At this point in the play he is therefore behaving as a cruel tyrant.

Remember to include <u>quotes</u>, and <u>explain</u> how they support your points. →

Macduff shows how Scotland as a whole is suffering under Macbeth's rule. He uses <u>personification</u> when describing how heaven "yelled" in pain "As if it felt with Scotland". The word "with" implies that Scotland is also able to feel pain and sadness. This emphasises how the whole country is being oppressed by Macbeth. Macbeth is clearly causing distress rather than acting for the good of the country he rules, reinforcing the reader's impression of him as a tyrannical ruler.

← Naming the <u>technique</u> the writer uses will impress the examiner.

Worked Exam-Style Question

Try to pick out the examples that illustrate your point best, rather than just listing the events of the play.

Remember to talk about other parts of the play as well as the extract.

The most clear-cut example of Macbeth's tyranny elsewhere in the play is when he hires two murderers to ensure that Macduff's wife and children are "Savagely slaughtered", because the witches' apparition warns him to "beware Macduff". The alliteration of "Savagely slaughtered" gives the phrase a harsh tone that makes the murders seem especially aggressive and cruel, suggesting that Macbeth's decision to have them killed was inhumane. This shows how far he is driven by his selfish desire to be king and by his need to destroy any threat to his power.

However, although some of the acts that Macbeth commits are undoubtedly tyrannical, he is deeply troubled by what he has done. After murdering Duncan, it is clear that Macbeth feels very guilty. He says "Methought I heard a voice cry, 'Sleep no more! / Macbeth does murder sleep,' the innocent sleep". His rambling speech, with its repetition of "sleep", shows that he is confused, upset and plagued by guilt. The theme of hallucination and imagination, shown here in the voice Macbeth hears, recurs throughout the play, usually as a sign of his troubled conscience. For example, after having Banquo murdered, Macbeth sees his ghost at the banquet, showing that he is horrified at what he has done. Macbeth's remorse and regret suggest that he is not entirely a cruel tyrant.

Keep referring back to the question to make sure you stay focused.

Good analysis of how the writer uses language to achieve an effect.

It's great to show that you've thought about the broader themes of the play.

Think carefully about why characters act they way they do.

Furthermore, as a brave man, unused to feeling fear, Macbeth is frightened of being thought weak, cowardly or unmanly. It is this fear, at least in part, that drives him to acts of tyranny, rather than just a desire to hurt others. At first, this is because Lady Macbeth questions his bravery and manliness, and later because he questions it himself, and feels the need to prove himself. When Macbeth is killed, the audience feels a mixture of relief, pity and regret. If he was purely a tyrant, his death would come as a relief, so the audience's reaction at this point demonstrates that his character is more complex than this.

This is a good personal response to the play.

In summary, Macbeth often behaves in a cruel and tyrannical way. However, his guilt about his acts of tyranny and the fact that he is driven to some of these acts through fear show that he is not a straightforward cruel tyrant. Instead, he is a complicated character, driven by a mixture of motives that are not always cruel or oppressive in their nature. These things together show that, ultimately, Macbeth is merely very human.

Write a strong, memorable conclusion to sum up your argument.

Worked Exam-Style Question

This is an example answer to a question on a modern play — it's got some good tips on writing about modern drama, even if you're not studying 'An Inspector Calls', so give it a good read.

Q1 How does Priestley show the importance of the Inspector to the play as a whole in 'An Inspector Calls'?

Write about:

- how the Inspector is important to the play as a whole
- how Priestley presents the character of the Inspector.

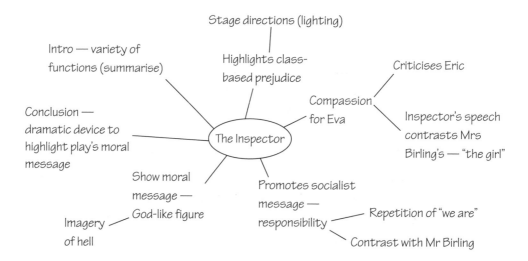

The Inspector in 'An Inspector Calls' serves a variety of important functions within the play. He makes the Birlings recognise their faults and the consequences of their actions; highlights the importance of people taking responsibility for one another; and also serves as an all-seeing, God-like figure, giving the impression that those who do not take responsibility for their crimes will be punished. Priestley presents these aspects of the Inspector's role through the use of stage directions, contrasts, repetition and imagery.

Makes sure you address the question in your introduction.

One of the most important functions of the Inspector is to highlight problems within the Birling family and, by extension, within the class-obsessed social system of the early twentieth century. This is illustrated by the stage directions. When the Inspector arrives, the lighting changes from "pink and intimate" to "brighter and harder". This suggests that the Inspector will shine a light on the true nature of the Birling family, shattering their illusion of the 'perfect' family and forcing them to 'see' things more clearly. This includes the reality of how their actions have affected other, less fortunate people.

Show you know about the play's context.

Don't forget to consider the writer's stagecraft.

Worked Exam-Style Question

Priestley also uses the Inspector as a contrasting figure to the Birlings, which helps him to show how wrong class-based prejudice is. The Inspector shows compassion for Eva Smith, criticising Eric for treating her "as if she was an animal, a thing, not a person". In contrast, most of the other characters do not show any kindness towards Eva because she is of a lower class. For instance, Mrs Birling repeatedly refers to her as "the girl", as if she cannot bear to mention her name or as if she does not matter as a person. The contrast in the way Mrs Birling and the Inspector talk about Eva, and the Inspector's insistence on treating Eva as a person, makes Mrs Birling appear narrow-minded and shows the audience that it is wrong to look down on the working classes.

> This uses <u>other characters</u> in the play to make a point about the Inspector's character.

Another important function of the Inspector is to promote Priestley's socialist message: that we should all take responsibility for one another. This is shown most clearly at the end of the play, when the Inspector says "We are members of one body. We are responsible for each other". The repetition of "We are" includes both the other characters and the audience, making it clear that this is how everyone should behave. This contrasts directly with Birling's belief that a man has to "look after himself and his own". The difference in the two characters' views highlights the selfishness and cruelty of some middle-class attitudes at the time.

> It's impressive if you can show you understand the play's <u>overall message</u>.

> This is a <u>good analysis</u> of the writer's <u>technique</u>.

In his final speech, the Inspector's language has an almost God-like quality, suggesting that his main role is as a dramatic device to promote a moral message. He states that if people do not take responsibility for others, then they will learn to do so in "fire and blood and anguish". This imagery is reminiscent of Hell, implying that the suffering experienced will be particularly painful, and portraying the Inspector as a God-like figure who can judge others. As the Inspector's language in this speech is out of keeping with the rest of his language in the play, it is implied that the audience is supposed to view him as a dramatic device, rather than a convincing character. In this way Priestley uses the Inspector as a vessel for his own views, and to represent the main moral of the play.

> This shows an awareness of the <u>effects</u> of different techniques.

> <u>Comparing different parts</u> of the play shows you understand it as a whole.

In conclusion, the character of the Inspector is used by Priestley to show the class-based prejudice of other characters. Stage directions show his pivotal role in highlighting the Birling family's flaws, and his compassion contrasts their unkindness. His god-like language in his final speech shows that he used by Priestley to express the play's key messages. His function as a dramatic device therefore makes him the most important character in the play.

> <u>Summarise</u> your <u>main points</u> in your conclusion.

Exam-Style Questions

Now that you've revised drama, have a go at these practice exam questions. You don't have to answer them all, but you'll find it useful to at least write a plan for any that are relevant to your set plays.

Q1 Read **either** the prologue of 'Romeo and Juliet' **or** Act 1 Scene 3 of 'Macbeth', from "Glamis, and Thane of Cawdor" to "Commencing in a truth?", **or** Act 1 Scene 2 of 'Julius Caesar', from the beginning of the scene to "Let us leave him. Pass!".

Using one of these extracts as a starting point, write about how Shakespeare explores fate and free will in the play.

Q2 Read **either** Act 3 Scene 5 of 'The Merchant of Venice', from the beginning of the scene to "on the coals for money.", **or** Act 2 Scene 1 of 'Much Ado About Nothing', from "Come, lady, come" to "his conceit is false."

Using one of these extracts as a starting point, discuss Shakespeare's use of comedy in the play.

Q3 With reference to a post-1914 play you have studied, discuss how the writer presents ideas about gender **or** growing up.

Write about:

- the ideas about gender or growing up in the play
- how these ideas are presented.

Q4 Read Act 2 Scene 1 of 'The Tempest', from "It was a torment" to "Go, hence with diligence!", **or** Act 1 Scene 1 of 'Macbeth'.

Using one of these extracts as a starting point, explore how Shakespeare presents the supernatural in the play.

Q5 With reference to a post-1914 play you have studied, discuss how the relationship between two central characters changes during the course of the play.

Write about:

- how the relationship between the two characters changes
- the techniques the writer uses to present the relationship between the two characters.

Writing About Prose

You'll have to study a 19th-century prose text for your course, and you might study a modern prose text too.

You might have to write about two different types of Prose

1) For Paper 1, you'll have to study <u>one</u> of these <u>prose texts</u> from the <u>19th century</u>:

- <u>The Strange Case of Dr Jekyll and Mr Hyde</u> by Robert Louis Stevenson
- <u>A Christmas Carol</u> by Charles Dickens
- <u>Great Expectations</u> by Charles Dickens
- <u>Jane Eyre</u> by Charlotte Brontë
- <u>Frankenstein</u> by Mary Shelley
- <u>Pride and Prejudice</u> by Jane Austen
- <u>The Sign of Four</u> by Sir Arthur Conan Doyle

2) For Paper 2, you might have to study some <u>modern prose</u> — the texts you might study are:

- <u>Lord of the Flies</u> by William Golding
- <u>Telling Tales</u> — the AQA Anthology of short stories
- <u>Animal Farm</u> by George Orwell
- <u>Never Let Me Go</u> by Kazuo Ishiguro
- <u>Anita and Me</u> by Meera Syal
- <u>Pigeon English</u> by Stephen Kelman

If you're not studying a modern prose text, you'll study a modern play instead
— see Section Three (p.24-40) for more on writing about drama.

Form and Structure both have an impact on a text

1) The <u>form</u> of a prose text affects how the story is told — e.g. short stories might have <u>simple</u>, <u>dramatic plots</u>, whereas novels are longer, so the plot can be more <u>detailed</u> or take place over a <u>longer period of time</u>.

2) The <u>structure</u> of a prose text is also important — different structures can have different <u>effects</u> on the reader.

- Texts can be split into <u>chapters</u> or <u>sections</u>. This can create <u>cliffhangers</u> or <u>switch</u> the <u>focus</u> of the plot.

'Jane Eyre' is divided into three separate volumes — original readers of the book had to buy each volume separately. Brontë used cliffhangers at the end of the first two volumes, which would have encouraged readers to buy the next volume.

- Think about how the novel <u>starts</u> and <u>ends</u>, and what the impact of this may be on the <u>reader</u>.

'Animal Farm' has a cyclical structure — elements at the start of the book repeat themselves at the end, but under Napoleon's rule rather than Farmer Jones'. For example, by the end of the book Napoleon has become a drunk, just like Jones. This shows that the new regime is mirroring the old one.

- Some plots move forwards <u>chronologically</u> (in time order). Others are non-chronological.

'A Christmas Carol' includes three episodes set in different time periods, each of which jumps between different times and places. This gives them a dreamlike quality.

- The novel may have <u>one main plot</u>, or <u>several plots</u> that link together.

'Pride and Prejudice' has several different stories which interlink. The revelations about Wickham, the romance between Bingley and Jane, and Mr Collins' search for a wife all make the novel more interesting. They also allow Austen to further explore themes such as social class and gender.

Writing About Prose

Writers sometimes use **Structural Devices**

For more on flashbacks and foreshadowing, see page 16.

1) The author may use structural devices such as flashbacks, foreshadowing and different narrative structures.

2) A frame narrative is where the main story is told within the frame of another story.

> 'Frankenstein' uses a frame narrative — Walton's letters frame Frankenstein's story, which in turn acts as a frame for the monster's account. This prompts the reader to question their judgement of events — Walton presents Frankenstein as a "wonderful man", but this is undermined by events in Frankenstein's own narrative.

3) An embedded narrative is where several different stories are told within the main story.

> 'Dr Jekyll and Mr Hyde' has several embedded narratives in the form of written documents (Lanyon's letter, Jekyll's statement) and testimonies from characters. These make the story appear more authentic and make the reader curious — each narrative adds more evidence as the reader starts to form a picture of who Mr Hyde is.

Comment on the writer's choice of **Language**

1) Authors love using descriptive language, including similes, metaphors and personification.

> "bloodthirsty snarling"
> "the tearing of teeth and claws" $\longrightarrow$ In 'Lord of the Flies', Golding uses animal imagery to describe the boys, showing that they are becoming more savage.

2) Particularly keep an eye out for any language or imagery that's repeated — there's usually a reason for this.

> "he locked the note into his safe"
> "he turned to examine the door in the by-street. It was locked" $\longrightarrow$ In 'Dr Jekyll and Mr Hyde', there are numerous images of locked doors. These are used to symbolise secrecy, and the way that humans try to hide their dual nature.

3) The language used by characters is also really important. For example:

> "Yow can come with uz, right, but don't say nothin'" $\longrightarrow$ In 'Anita and Me', Meena uses Midlands dialect words, slang and non-standard grammar to try to fit in and impress Anita.

Characters' Thoughts are often described

You can find more information about analysing characters on pages 12-13.

1) Novels and short stories give descriptions of characters' thoughts and behaviour.

2) Look out for those bits, quote them, and comment on how they help answer the question.

> The head, he thought, appeared to agree with him. Run away, said the head silently... $\longrightarrow$ The narrator of 'Lord of the Flies' describes Simon's thoughts and imagined conversation with the pig's head. This allows the reader to experience Simon's hallucinations.

Don't be afraid to be original...

When it comes to language and structure, there are no wrong points (as long as you have evidence to back them up). If you think of something original about a text, remember it in case you can use it in the exam.

Analysing Narrators

The narrator is the person telling the story — they are the link between the reader and the plot.

There are **Different Types** of **Narrator**

1) All <u>prose</u> texts have a <u>narrator</u> — a <u>voice</u> that's telling the story.

2) A <u>first-person</u> narrator is a character who tells the story from their <u>perspective</u>, e.g. Pip narrates 'Great Expectations' and Kathy narrates 'Never Let Me Go'. You get a first-hand description of exactly what the character <u>sees</u>, <u>does</u> and <u>thinks</u> all the way through the story.

> *In what ecstasy of unhappiness I got these broken words out of myself, I don't know. The rhapsody welled up within me, like blood from an inward wound, and gushed out.*

In 'Great Expectations', Pip's narration is very <u>personal</u> and appeals to the reader's <u>emotions</u>. This helps the reader to <u>empathise</u> with him.

3) A <u>third-person</u> narrator is a separate voice, created by the author to tell the story — this type of narrator is used in 'A Christmas Carol' and 'Pride and Prejudice'. They usually describe the thoughts and feelings of several <u>different characters</u>, making them more of a <u>storyteller</u> than a <u>character</u>.

4) Third-person narrators can be <u>omniscient</u> (all-knowing) or <u>limited</u> (only aware of the thoughts and feelings of one character). They may also describe only what can be <u>seen</u> or <u>heard</u> — for example, in 'Animal Farm', the narrator usually just presents the reader with <u>factual information</u>.

> *To Catherine and Lydia, neither the letter nor its writer were in any degree interesting.*

The <u>omniscient</u>, <u>third-person</u> narrator of 'Pride and Prejudice' gives the reader an insight into the <u>thoughts</u> of many of the characters, even though the story follows Elizabeth most closely.

Not all narrators are **Reliable**

1) Don't automatically <u>trust</u> what a narrator says — they may be <u>unreliable</u>. This is particularly common with first-person narrators, who see things from their <u>own point of view</u>.

> *I have recorded in detail the events of my insignificant existence...*

The first-person narrator of 'Jane Eyre' calls herself "insignificant", but the fact that she's the <u>main character</u> in the book suggests this <u>isn't true</u>.

2) The narrator is <u>not</u> the <u>same</u> person as the author, but watch out for examples of the writer's <u>viewpoint</u> being <u>revealed</u> through the narrator. For example:

> *Scrooge! a squeezing, wrenching, grasping, scraping, clutching, covetous old sinner!*

The third-person narrator of 'A Christmas Carol' has <u>strong opinions</u> on Scrooge, which seem to be <u>Dickens's views</u>.

EXAM TIP

The narrator and the writer are not the same person...

In the exam, keep in mind that what the narrator thinks isn't necessarily the same as what the writer thinks. Refer to how the writer uses the narrator, rather than just what the narrator says.

19th-Century Fiction

You have to study a 19th-century novel, so the next three pages contain some useful background information on life in the period. This will help you understand the texts better, and to write more informed essays.

There was a **Big Gap** between the **Upper** and **Lower Classes**

1) <u>Class</u> was <u>important</u> in the 19th century — your class <u>determined</u> what <u>kind</u> of life you had.

2) Early 19th-century society was divided between the <u>rich upper classes</u> (who <u>owned</u> the <u>land</u>, didn't need to <u>work</u> and so <u>socialised</u> a lot) and the <u>poorer working classes</u> (who <u>relied</u> on the upper classes for work, and were often <u>looked down on</u> because of it).

3) The <u>Industrial Revolution</u> created opportunities for more people to <u>make money</u>, meaning that the <u>middle classes</u> grew in <u>size</u> and <u>influence</u> throughout the century.

4) However, the fact that the <u>middle classes</u> relied on a <u>profession</u> or <u>trade</u> for their wealth meant that they were <u>looked down on</u> by the <u>upper classes</u>.

> In the Industrial Revolution, technological advances meant that goods could be produced by machines in factories, rather than by hand in people's homes. This resulted in many people moving from working in farming (and living in the countryside) to working in manufacturing (and living in cities).

> *'Pride and Prejudice' examines and criticises judgements based on social status. Austen mocks 19th-century class prejudices by showing that characters' behaviour is down to personality, not class.*

Many cities were **Overcrowded** and had **Terrible Living Conditions**

1) In the 19th century, millions of people moved from the countryside to the <u>cities</u> in search of <u>work</u> in the new factories. As a result, the <u>population</u> of cities grew rapidly and uncontrollably.

2) Most of these people ended up living in <u>slums</u> of cheap, overcrowded housing. There was often no proper drainage or <u>sewage</u> system, and many families had to share one tap and toilet. Overcrowding led to <u>hunger</u>, <u>disease</u> and <u>crime</u>.

> *Dickens uses 'A Christmas Carol' to highlight the problems and poverty of working-class London. He contrasts the wealth of Scrooge with the poverty of the Cratchit family.*

Women were often **Dependent** on men

1) During the 19th century, <u>women</u> were normally <u>dependent</u> on the <u>men</u> in their family, especially in the <u>upper classes</u>. It was usually men who <u>earned a living</u> or <u>owned land</u> which generated income from rent.

2) A woman's best chance of a <u>stable future</u> was a good <u>marriage</u> — there were very few <u>job</u> options available for upper and middle-class women, and women often weren't allowed to <u>inherit</u> land or money.

3) Women didn't have the <u>vote</u>, and generally had to do what their <u>husband told them</u> — they were expected to stay at home and look after children.

> *'Jane Eyre' was unusual at the time of publication not only because it was written by a woman, but also because its main character is a determined and sometimes outspoken woman. By the end of the novel, Jane is both emotionally and financially independent.*

19th-Century Fiction

Education was Not Compulsory until the late 19th century

1) Education was a privilege — only wealthy families could afford to send children away to school, or to hire a governess to live with them and teach the children.

2) Boys' education was more of a priority, and many girls weren't educated at all. An academic education was seen as unnecessary for women — girls from rich families were taught art, music and dance as this would help them to get a husband, and girls from poorer families were expected to go straight into a job that didn't require an education.

3) Many schools were run by the Church and supported by charity donations. The government began funding schools in 1833, but the funding was very limited.

4) School wasn't compulsory until 1880, when an Education Act finally made it compulsory for children between the ages of five and ten to attend school.

> In 'Great Expectations', Pip receives hardly any formal education as a child. He is desperate to gain an education, believing this is key to becoming a gentleman, and attempts to improve his education throughout the novel.

Reputation was important

1) In middle and upper-class society, it was important to be respectable.

2) The middle and upper classes were expected to have strong morals and to help others. They were also expected to keep their emotions under strict control and to hide their desire for things like sex and alcohol.

3) If someone was seen doing anything which wasn't considered respectable, their reputation could be ruined. To protect their reputation, people often kept their sinful behaviour and desires secret.

> The gentlemen in 'Jekyll and Hyde' are concerned with their reputations. Jekyll creates Hyde in order to hide his sins and preserve his reputation, and Utterson consistently tries to protect Jekyll's reputation. The book explores how this obsession with reputation can actually be destructive.

Many texts were influenced by Romanticism and the Gothic genre

1) 'Romanticism' had a big impact on literature and art in the late 18th century and the early 19th century.

2) The 'Romantics' tried to capture intense emotions and experiences in their work, and were especially influenced by nature. They saw nature as a powerful force that could inspire and restore people.

3) Many 19th-century writers were influenced by the Gothic genre — this generally involved a mysterious location, supernatural elements, troubling secrets and elements of madness.

4) The double (or doppelgänger) is another key feature of Gothic novels — it's where two characters are presented as if they are each a version of the other.

> 'Frankenstein' includes aspects of the 'Romantic' and the Gothic. Frankenstein travels to the Alps in the hope that the "magnificence" of nature will help him to forget his "sorrows", but it is there that he meets the monster, who is presented as the other side of him.

19th-Century Fiction

Victorian society was very **Religious**

1) <u>Christianity</u> had a strong influence on life in Victorian Britain. To be good Christians, many people believed they should live by a strict <u>moral code</u> — attending church regularly, avoiding alcohol and exercising sexual restraint.

2) However, others believed that being a good Christian meant being <u>charitable</u> and <u>forgiving</u>.

> *At the end of 'A Christmas Carol', Scrooge resolves to "honour Christmas" and to continue his generosity and goodwill "all the year". This appears to be Dickens's view of being a good Christian.*

Darwin's theory of **Evolution** was **Controversial**

1) In the early 1800s, Christianity taught that <u>God</u> created every species to be <u>perfectly adapted</u> to its environment. The Book of Genesis also taught that humans were made in <u>God's image</u>, different from all <u>other animals</u> and ruling over them.

2) In contrast, some scientists, including Charles Darwin, claimed that all creatures <u>evolved</u> from common ancestors through a process called '<u>natural selection</u>'.

3) Darwin also claimed that humans shared a <u>common ancestor</u> with <u>apes</u>. This went against the Christian idea that man's nature was <u>different</u> from that of other animals. People found this <u>unsettling</u> because it means there may be an <u>animalistic</u> side to everyone, capable of <u>uncivilised</u> acts and <u>violent</u> crimes.

> *In 'Dr Jekyll and Mr Hyde', Hyde is described as the "animal within" Jekyll. Utterson describes him as "hardly human", and Poole says he is "like a monkey". Stevenson may be hinting that Hyde is a less evolved version of Jekyll.*

Scientists were **Investigating** where **Life** comes from

1) Many 19th-century scientists were fascinated with the <u>origins of life</u>. Some believed that studying <u>electricity</u> might reveal what gives life to people and animals.

2) Scientists experimented with passing <u>electric currents</u> through animal and human bodies. The current made the bodies <u>move</u>, which led some to conclude there was a type of 'animal electricity' (later called '<u>galvanism</u>') within <u>living things</u>.

> *In 'Frankenstein', Shelley implies that Victor uses electricity to animate the monster — he infuses a "spark of being" into a "lifeless thing". This suggests Shelley was influenced by contemporary science.*

Make sure you understand the text's context...

Make a list of relevant context points for the 19th-century prose text you've studied (use these pages to get you started). Then jot down a sentence explaining <u>why</u> each point is relevant to the text.

Warm-Up Questions

When you're writing an exam answer about prose texts, always think about the language, the structure and the issues raised in the texts. You also need to remember to focus on the detail and to choose your quotes wisely. Start with the questions on this page, and the exam questions on p.52 should be no problem at all.

Warm-Up Questions

1) Choose a prose text that you have studied. Open it at the first page and read the opening paragraph. Write down three things that you notice about the way the author has written the paragraph.

2) Using a prose text you have studied in class, find a passage that uses descriptive language to set the scene. Write a short paragraph explaining how the writer makes this description vivid. (Hint: think about their use of imagery, interesting vocabulary and appeals to the senses.)

3) Think about a central character in one of the prose texts you have studied, and write a short paragraph for each of the following questions.
   a) Why is this character important to the novel?
   b) Do you sympathise with this character? Why or why not?
   c) How does this character change over the course of the text?

4) Choose a prose text you have studied. Does the text have a first-person or third-person narrator? Write a short paragraph about the effect this narrator has on the text.

5) Read the passage below.
   a) Make a list of all of the words and phrases that are about reputation.
   b) Using your list from part a), write a short paragraph about the importance of reputation for women in 19th-century Britain.

> *"This is a most unfortunate affair, and will probably be much talked of. But we must stem the tide of malice, and pour into the wounded bosoms of each other the balm of sisterly consolation."*
>
> *Then, perceiving in Elizabeth no inclination of replying, she added, "Unhappy as the event must be for Lydia, we may draw from it this useful lesson: that loss of virtue in a female is irretrievable; that one false step involves her in endless ruin; that her reputation is no less brittle than it is beautiful; and that she cannot be too much guarded in her behaviour towards the undeserving of the other sex."*

Worked Exam-Style Question

Take a look at this worked answer for an essay about 'A Christmas Carol'. It will give you some ideas for how to structure your own answers, as well as the sort of points you could include.

Q1 Read the passage from Chapter 1 of 'A Christmas Carol' which begins "At this festive season of the year, Mr. Scrooge" and ends "Good afternoon, gentlemen!", then answer the question.

Using this extract as a starting point, write about Scrooge and the way he changes throughout the novel.

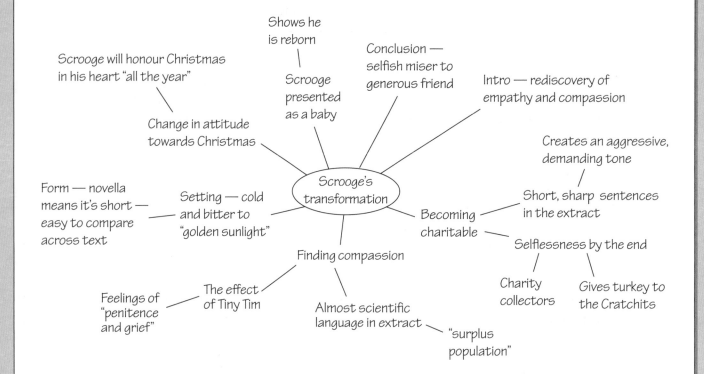

Charles Dickens's 'A Christmas Carol' shows the transformation of Scrooge. The text's structure follows Scrooge as he undergoes a fundamental change of character, rediscovering empathy, compassion and human emotion. He is transformed from a "covetous, old sinner" into someone who keeps the Christmas spirit "all the year". This change is emphasised through Dickens's use of language, setting and structure, as well as how he presents Scrooge's attitude towards Christmas.

This question is all about how Scrooge changes — refer to the techniques Dickens uses to show this.

One of the most obvious changes in Scrooge is his discovery of charity. His conversation with the charity collectors in the extract highlights his selfishness and greed. When asked to make a "slight provision" to help the poor, he responds with a series of short, sharp questions. These give his speech an aggressive and demanding tone, which highlights his lack of sympathy for other people. However, after the visitation of the three ghosts, Scrooge makes active choices to share his wealth, such as making a generous donation to the charity collectors and buying a "prize Turkey" for Bob and his family. The fact that Scrooge sends the turkey anonymously shows that he doesn't expect anything in return, emphasising his newfound selflessness.

Comparing how Scrooge differs in different parts of the novel is key to writing about how he has changed.

It's important to write about the extract given in the question.

Worked Exam-Style Question

Use <u>quotes</u> from the <u>extract</u> in your answer.

Scrooge is presented as uncompassionate towards the poor in the extract, saying that if the poor would rather die than go to the workhouses then they should "do it" and "<u>decrease the surplus population</u>". <u>Dickens's use of cold, almost scientific language shows how cold-hearted and distanced Scrooge is from the poor.</u> However, this attitude changes over the course of the novel. For example, when the Ghost of Christmas Present tells Scrooge that Tiny Tim may die, he repeats Scrooge's exact words. Hearing his own words applied specifically to Bob's son causes Scrooge to feel "penitence and grief", showing that he regrets his earlier lack of compassion, and contrasting his cold-hearted behaviour at the beginning of the story.

This sentence <u>explains</u> the <u>effect</u> that Dickens's language has.

Dickens uses the setting of the text to reinforce the changes in Scrooge's character. In the first chapter, the narrator describes Scrooge as carrying "his own low temperature always about with him", implying that his heart is as cold as the "biting" weather outside. However, by the end of the text the fog and mist have been replaced with "golden sunlight". This change in the weather reflects the change Scrooge has gone through; from a cold-hearted miser to a man of warmth and generosity. By changing elements of the setting for different effects at the start and end of the text, Dickens invites the reader to make a direct comparison across the story about how Scrooge has changed. <u>The text's form makes it even more likely that readers would draw these comparisons, because as a novella it would often have been read from beginning to end in one sitting.</u>

Don't forget to mention how the <u>form</u> of the text is relevant.

A further change in Scrooge is his attitude to Christmas. In Chapter 1, Scrooge represents solitude and frugality. His repeated shouts of "Humbug" in response to his nephew's festivity show that he denounces Christmas and therefore the values it represents. However, his attitude in the final chapter is a strong contrast: he says that he will honour Christmas in his heart "all the year". By keeping it in his "heart", an organ that is not only associated with love but that is also crucial for life, it suggests that he will make the positive values of Christmas a vital part of who he is. <u>By the end of the nineteenth century, Christmas had come to represent family and feasting</u>; in showing that Scrooge has embraced Christmas, Dickens further emphasises that Scrooge's solitude and frugality have been overcome.

Use <u>context</u> to support your points where possible.

At the end of the text, Dickens presents Scrooge as if he has been reborn. He refers to himself as "quite a baby", and <u>this is emphasised by his enthusiastic language, such as his shouts of "Whoop" and "Hallo", which make him sound young and excited.</u> This emphasis on youth and rebirth shows that Scrooge has changed so much that it is as though he has begun a new life.

When writing about <u>language</u>, make sure you write about the <u>effect</u> it has.

The conclusion should <u>sum up</u> the <u>main points</u> of the answer.

In conclusion, the main focus of 'A Christmas Carol' is Scrooge's journey from selfish miser to generous friend. <u>Dickens uses language, setting and the structure of the text to show that Scrooge has learnt to be compassionate to the poor, and has fully embraced the Christmas spirit and the values of kindness, charity and family that it represents.</u>

Worked Exam-Style Question

It can be tricky to fit language, structure, form and context into just one answer. Luckily, these pages show how to include all these things in an answer about a modern prose text.

Q1 How does Golding present civilisation and savagery in 'Lord of the Flies'?
Write about:
- ideas about civilisation and savagery in the novel
- how these ideas are presented.

Initially a paradise — The island — Becomes hellish

Represents democracy, law etc

Intro — battle between civilisation and savagery, Golding's message

Civilisation — the conch

Destroyed — just like civilisation

Conclusion — the conflict represents human nature

Civilisation and savagery

Savagery — pig's head

Wider world parallels — backdrop of war, Golding's beliefs

Represents evil and the 'beast within'

Simon's understanding and resulting death — breakdown of civilisation

---

Commenting on the <u>type</u> of novel is a good way to write about <u>form</u> in your answers.

<u>'Lord of the Flies' is an allegorical novel that explores the battle between civilisation and savagery.</u> Throughout the novel, the boys start to lose their sense of civilisation and descend into savagery. The characters, settings, objects and events in the novel act as an allegory for society as a whole, ultimately <u>conveying the author's message that all humans, no matter how civilised, have savagery within them.</u>

It's good to think about how the question relates to the novel's <u>message</u>.

<u>The setting of the island helps to illustrate the conflict between civilisation and savagery throughout the novel.</u> At the beginning it is a paradise, with plenty of fresh water, fruit and firewood, where the boys can "have fun" until they are rescued. By the end, the island is "burning wreckage", with more in common with hell than paradise. This mirrors the boys' loss of innocence and their descent into chaos and savagery. <u>The loss of innocence is particularly evident in Ralph</u> who, at the beginning of the novel, is excited at the prospect of living without adults and "savoured the right of domination", but by the end of the novel has become aware of "the darkness of man's heart" — the evil that exists inside everyone.

This paragraph gives a good introduction to the subject by discussing <u>large-scale</u> points such as setting, before the essay goes into more <u>detail</u>.

This makes it <u>obvious</u> what the paragraph will be about and gives the answer a <u>clear structure</u>.

<u>The conch is a clear symbol of civilisation in the novel.</u> At first, it is used to summon the boys to meetings, and because only the boy holding it is allowed to speak, it comes to represent democracy and the rules of society. It is one of the major reasons for the boys voting for Ralph as leader: "The being that had blown that... was set apart". <u>The description of Ralph's "stillness" and calling him a "being" rather than a boy give him an almost God-like quality, meaning that</u>

You need to think about the <u>language</u> the writer uses and the <u>effect</u> it has.

Think about how objects and characters <u>change</u> through the novel, and what these changes <u>mean</u>.

<u>the conch becomes a powerful sign of authority.</u> As civilisation is eroded and replaced by savagery, so too the conch begins to lose its power for all of the boys except Piggy and Ralph, who continue to use it even when their group consists only of them, Sam and Eric. The other boys do have respect for the conch, but it is easily overwhelmed by their newfound savagery: "Piggy held up the conch and the booing sagged a little, then came up again to strength." This hesitation highlights the conflict between this and their more civilised start on the island. <u>The conch is finally shattered "into a thousand white fragments" by the same rock that kills Piggy. This marks the end of civilisation on the island.</u> From this point forward, Jack's tribe lose any semblance of humanity and even Ralph acts like an animal, obeying <u>"an instinct that he did not know he possessed"</u> to escape, running and hiding from the hunt.

Don't forget to put in <u>quotes</u> to support your points.

The pig's head, the Lord of the Flies, is the opposite of the conch — it represents chaos, savagery and the evil inside each human being. Originally intended as an offering to "the Beast", the pig's head is most powerfully symbolic when it 'talks' to Simon, telling him that the beast is inside them: "You knew, didn't you? I'm part of you?". Its words foreshadow Simon's death because, when he tries to explain what he has learned to the others, they fear that he is the beast, which drives them to kill him with "teeth and claws". This marks a major turning point in the boys' descent from civilisation to savagery. <u>At the end of the novel, the conch is destroyed in Jack's camp, and Ralph uses the stick from the Lord of the Flies as a weapon. This shows that civilisation has been completely overcome by savagery, and that even Ralph has become corrupted by the power of evil.</u>

Details like this show that you know the text <u>really well</u> and have given it a lot of <u>thought</u>.

Shows that you know about the writer's <u>background</u> and <u>beliefs</u>.

The naval officer who rescues the boys can be seen as an adult representation of the conflict between civilisation and savagery. Despite his smart uniform and politeness, he is still associated with war, which shows the reader that civilisation and savagery are also in conflict in the adult world. <u>This is in keeping with Golding's beliefs about society. His experiences during World War II led him to realise that even 'civilised' people are capable of committing evil acts.</u>

Golding explores the conflict between civilisation and savagery throughout the entire novel. He uses the characters, setting and events in the novel to show how civilisation gives way to savagery, and that anybody can become savage and commit evil acts if the rules of civilisation are removed. In this way, Golding draws parallels with historical events and questions the assumption that people can be fully 'good' or that society can be completely 'civilised'.

Remember to write a brief <u>conclusion</u> to sum up your answer.

Exam-Style Questions

Answering the questions on this page should give you a good chance to practise what you've learned ready for the exam. Whatever text you've studied, there's at least one question for you.

Q1 Discuss how the theme of prejudice is presented in **either** 'Anita and Me' **or** 'Frankenstein' **or** 'Pride and Prejudice'.

Q2 Choose one of the following themes, and explore how it is presented in a prose text you have studied.
a) marriage and relationships
b) power
c) reputation
d) social class

Q3 What methods does the writer use to create a sense of fear in a prose text you have studied?

Q4 How does the writer present ideas about the nature of evil in **either** 'Lord of the Flies' **or** 'The Strange Case of Dr Jekyll and Mr Hyde'?

Q5 Analyse the extent to which the main character is shown to change or stay the same during the course of a prose text you have studied.

Poetry — What You Have To Do

Poetry is an important part of your English Literature GCSE. The next three sections will get you up to speed with what you need to do to write cracking poetry essays.

You'll write about poetry in **One** of your Literature exams

The poetry aspect of your GCSE English Literature course is divided into <u>two</u> main sections:

1) <u>Poetry anthology</u> (see Section Six) — you'll study a group (or '<u>cluster</u>') of poems in class. The poems will share common themes.

2) <u>Unseen</u> poetry (see Section Seven) — in the exam, you have to write about two poems that you've never seen before. You'll get a copy of them in your exam paper and have to <u>analyse</u> them on the spot.

You could be asked about any of the poems from the group you've studied, so you need to know them all well.

Think about **Language**, **Structure** and **Form**

For more about form, structure and language, see pages 54-59.

You should always write about <u>language</u>, <u>structure</u> and <u>form</u> in your answers on poetry.

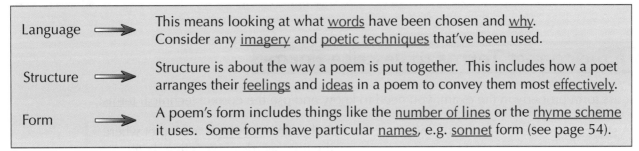

Language ⟹ This means looking at what <u>words</u> have been chosen and <u>why</u>. Consider any <u>imagery</u> and <u>poetic techniques</u> that've been used.

Structure ⟹ Structure is about the way a poem is put together. This includes how a poet arranges their <u>feelings</u> and <u>ideas</u> in a poem to convey them most <u>effectively</u>.

Form ⟹ A poem's form includes things like the <u>number of lines</u> or the <u>rhyme scheme</u> it uses. Some forms have particular <u>names</u>, e.g. <u>sonnet</u> form (see page 54).

You must show you **Appreciate** what the **Poet** is doing

1) Once you've identified points about language, structure and form, think about the <u>effects</u> that these features create.

2) To get the top marks, you need to consider what these effects <u>suggest</u> about the <u>speaker</u>, or how they <u>make</u> the <u>reader</u> feel.

3) You're the reader, so you should include your <u>personal opinion</u> — you can be as creative as you like, as long as you <u>back up</u> your idea with a <u>relevant quote</u> from the poem.

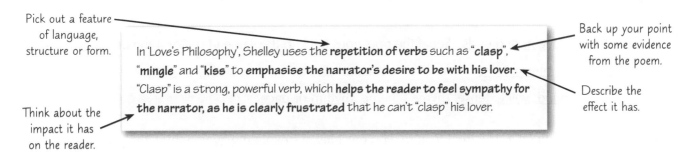

Pick out a feature of language, structure or form.

Think about the impact it has on the reader.

In 'Love's Philosophy', Shelley uses the **repetition of verbs** such as "**clasp**", "**mingle**" and "**kiss**" to **emphasise the narrator's desire to be with his lover**. "Clasp" is a strong, powerful verb, which **helps the reader to feel sympathy for the narrator, as he is clearly frustrated** that he can't "clasp" his lover.

Back up your point with some evidence from the poem.

Describe the effect it has.

Go over the poem several times to properly understand it...

Don't be put off if you feel like you don't understand a poem. Go over it a few more times and start to look at language, structure and form — they often give you a clue about the poem's meaning.

Form and Structure

Form and structure are all about the way a poem is put together. Have a look at this page to find out more.

Poetry comes in **Different Forms**

Different forms (or <u>types</u>) of poems follow different rules. You need to be able to <u>recognise</u> common forms of poetry for your exam.

Sometimes poets use a certain form but break some of its rules for effect.

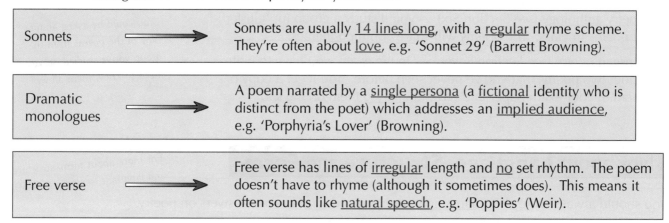

| Sonnets ⟶ | Sonnets are usually <u>14 lines long</u>, with a <u>regular</u> rhyme scheme. They're often about <u>love</u>, e.g. 'Sonnet 29' (Barrett Browning). |

| Dramatic monologues ⟶ | A poem narrated by a <u>single persona</u> (a <u>fictional</u> identity who is distinct from the poet) which addresses an <u>implied audience</u>, e.g. 'Porphyria's Lover' (Browning). |

| Free verse ⟶ | Free verse has lines of <u>irregular</u> length and <u>no</u> set rhythm. The poem doesn't have to rhyme (although it sometimes does). This means it often sounds like <u>natural speech</u>, e.g. 'Poppies' (Weir). |

Learn the correct **Terms** to describe **Form**

To discuss form properly in the exam, you need to <u>know</u> and <u>use</u> the correct <u>technical terms</u>:

- A <u>stanza</u> (or verse) is a group of lines.
- A <u>tercet</u> is a three-line stanza.
- A <u>quatrain</u> is a four-line stanza.
- A <u>couplet</u> is a <u>pair of lines</u>, usually with the same <u>metre</u> (see p.57).

- A rhyming <u>couplet</u> is a couplet where the <u>final words</u> of each line <u>rhyme</u>.
- A <u>rhyming triplet</u> is where the <u>final words</u> of <u>three</u> successive lines <u>rhyme</u> with each other.

Structure is how a poem is arranged

Structure is how the poet <u>arranges</u> their <u>feelings</u> or <u>ideas</u> in a poem to convey them most effectively. Two poems with the <u>same form</u> can be structured very differently.

Think about:

1) How a poem <u>begins</u> and <u>ends</u>. See if the poet <u>goes back</u> to the same ideas, or if the poem <u>progresses</u>.

2) Any <u>pauses</u> or <u>interruptions</u> in ideas in the poem.

3) Changes in <u>mood</u>, <u>voice</u>, <u>tense</u>, <u>rhyme scheme</u>, <u>rhythm</u> or <u>pace</u>.

Once you've <u>identified</u> a structural feature, you must always explain <u>why</u> you think the poet has used it.

Don't ignore form and structure...

It can be easy to concentrate on language, but you need to write about structure and form as well to get top marks. You can write about any poem's form, even if it's to say that it doesn't have a regular one.

Poetic Techniques

Poets use lots of techniques to get their message across. Here are the ones you need to know.

A poem's **Voice** is **Who's Speaking** and **How**

1) A poem's <u>voice</u> can affect how the poet's <u>message</u> is <u>conveyed</u>.

2) The narrator might speak in the <u>first person</u> ('<u>I</u>') or the <u>third person</u> ('<u>he</u>' or '<u>she</u>').

3) A <u>first-person voice</u> gives you one person's <u>perspective</u>. It often makes the poem <u>more personal</u>.

> The use of a <u>first-person voice</u> in Rumens's 'The Emigrée' allows the narrator to speak <u>personally</u> about her childhood. Phrases such as "I am branded" show her continued <u>connection</u> with her place of birth.

4) A <u>third-person voice</u> is often <u>more detached</u> from the action. It can give an <u>outside perspective</u>.

> The narrator of Tennyson's 'Charge of the Light Brigade' uses the <u>third person</u> to describe the battle from a <u>distance</u>. This allows him to portray the <u>large number</u> of soldiers who fought there and show how the whole battle <u>occurred</u>, e.g. "Into the valley of Death / Rode the six hundred".

Think about who the poem is **Addressed To**

1) Some poems are written as if the speaker is talking to a <u>specific person</u> — this is called <u>direct address</u>.

2) Direct address can often give the reader <u>hints</u> about the speaker's <u>relationship</u> with <u>another person</u>.

> In Dooley's poem 'Letters from Yorkshire', the narrator <u>directly addresses</u> a man whose lifestyle she admires. The direct address used throughout the poem emphasises the <u>connection</u> between the two characters, and suggests they have a <u>close relationship</u> despite the distance between them.

Some poems include features of **Spoken Language**

1) Poems can reproduce <u>spoken language</u>, e.g. dialect words or phonetic spellings.

2) Some poets use features of spoken language to make the poem more <u>natural</u> and <u>personal</u>.

> In 'Remains', Armitage uses <u>contractions</u> such as "he's" and <u>colloquial language</u> like "mates" to represent how the soldier might actually <u>speak</u>. Using an <u>authentic</u> voice makes the war seem more <u>real</u> and <u>frightening</u> by emphasising that the soldier is just like any other person.

3) Other poets use <u>spoken language features</u> to convey a speaker's <u>accent</u>.

> Agard's poem 'Checking Out Me History' reflects the speaker's <u>Caribbean accent</u> by using <u>phonetic spellings</u> such as "Dem" and "ole", as well as <u>non-standard grammar</u>, e.g. "she volunteer to go". This implies that the speaker is <u>rebelling</u> against the standard English <u>grammar</u> taught in schools as a way of showing his <u>pride</u> in his Caribbean <u>heritage</u>.

Poetic Techniques

Rhyme can add Power to the poet's message

1) Rhyme helps a poem develop its beat or <u>rhythm</u>. Poets can also use it to reinforce the poem's <u>message</u>.

2) Rhyme can be <u>regular</u> (occurring in a set pattern), <u>irregular</u> (with no pattern) or <u>absent</u> from a poem.

3) This creates different <u>effects</u> — regular rhyme schemes can create a sense of <u>control</u>, whereas an irregular rhyme scheme might show <u>chaos</u> or <u>unpredictability</u>. These effects can link to the poem's <u>themes</u> or message.

> *"We stood by a pond that winter day,*
> *And the sun was white, as though chidden of God,*
> *And a few leaves lay on the starving sod;*
>   *– They had fallen from an ash, and were grey."*
>
> *('Neutral Tones' — Thomas Hardy)*

The <u>ABBA rhyme scheme</u> mirrors the <u>cyclical structure</u> of the poem — the 'A' rhyme returns at the end of each stanza, just as the image of the pond returns at the end of the poem. This reflects the way that the <u>narrator's memory</u> of the break-up returns to affect him.

4) Sometimes rhymes occur within lines, too. These are called <u>internal rhymes</u>.

> *"The reader's eyeballs prick*
> *with tears between the bath and pre-lunch beers."*
>
> *('War Photographer' — Carol Ann Duffy)*

Duffy uses an <u>internal rhyme</u> to <u>emphasise</u> how quickly readers will <u>forget</u> the photos of suffering in war that they have seen in newspapers — the "<u>tears</u>" they cry will soon be replaced by "<u>beers</u>".

Rhythm alters the Pace and Mood of a poem

1) Rhythm is the <u>arrangement</u> of beats within a line. It's easier to <u>feel</u> a rhythm than to see it on the page.

2) Like rhyme, rhythm can be <u>regular</u> or <u>irregular</u>. A <u>strong</u> rhyme scheme often creates a <u>regular</u> rhythm.

3) Rhythm can affect the <u>pace</u> (speed) and <u>mood</u> of a poem — a fast rhythm can make a poem seem <u>rushed</u> and <u>frantic</u>, whereas a slow and regular rhythm can make a poem seem <u>calm</u>.

4) Sometimes poets use rhythm to <u>imitate</u> sounds related to the poem, e.g. a heartbeat or beating drums.

> *"Half a league, half a league,*
>   *Half a league onward"*
>
> *('The Charge of the Light Brigade'*
> *— Alfred Tennyson)*

Tennyson uses a <u>regular</u>, <u>relentless rhythm</u> in these lines to create a <u>fast pace</u>. This imitates the sound of the <u>galloping horses</u>.

5) The rhythm often reflects the poem's <u>themes</u>, how the narrator is <u>feeling</u> or the overall <u>message</u>.

> *"Oh! my God! the down,*
> *The soft young down of her"*
>
> *('The Farmer's Bride' — Charlotte Mew)*

Mew uses <u>monosyllabic</u> words to <u>break down</u> the poem's <u>rhythm</u>. This draws attention to the narrator's loss of <u>self-control</u>.

Poetic Techniques

Metre is the Pattern of Syllables in a line

1) In poetry, the rhythm of a line is created by <u>patterns</u> of <u>syllables</u>. If the patterns are <u>consistent</u>, then the poem's rhythm is <u>regular</u>.

A syllable is a single unit of sound, for example, 'beat' has one syllable and 'sonnet' has two syllables.

2) <u>Metre</u> is the technical term for these patterns. There are different types of metre, depending on which syllables are <u>stressed</u> (emphasised) and which are <u>unstressed</u>.

<u>Iambic pentameter</u> is a metre that's commonly used in poetry. It has 10 syllables in a line — an <u>unstressed</u> syllable followed by a <u>stressed</u> syllable, repeated five times over.

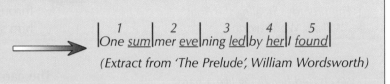

| 1 | 2 | 3 | 4 | 5 |
| One <u>sum</u> | mer <u>eve</u> | ning <u>led</u> | by <u>her</u> | I <u>found</u> |

(Extract from 'The Prelude', William Wordsworth)

Punctuation affects how a poem Flows

Punctuation can affect the <u>pace</u> of a poem, emphasise <u>specific words</u>, or <u>interrupt</u> a poem's <u>rhythm</u>.

1) When punctuation creates a <u>pause</u> during a line of poetry, this is called a <u>caesura</u>.

"Happy and proud; at last I knew
Porphyria worshipped me; surprise"

('Porphyria's Lover' — Robert Browning)

The semi-colons create <u>caesurae</u> which make the poem sound <u>fragmented</u>, reflecting the narrator's <u>unstable mind</u>.

2) <u>Enjambment</u> is when a <u>sentence</u> or <u>phrase</u> runs over from <u>one line</u> of poetry into the <u>next one</u>. Often enjambment puts emphasis on the <u>last word</u> of the first line or on the <u>first word</u> of the next line.

"two days of rain and then a <u>break</u>
in which we walked,"

('Winter Swans' — Owen Sheers)

The <u>enjambment</u> puts stress on the <u>final word</u> of the first line, <u>emphasising</u> that there is a <u>pause</u> in the <u>weather</u>, and suggesting a pause in the couple's <u>arguing</u>.

"when it blows full
<u>Blast</u>*"*

('Storm on the Island'
— Seamus Heaney)

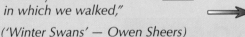

When describing the storm, Heaney uses <u>enjambment</u> to <u>emphasise</u> the word "<u>Blast</u>" by putting it on a <u>new line</u>. This hints at the storm's <u>strength</u> and <u>energy</u>.

3) An <u>end-stopped line</u> is a line of poetry that ends in a <u>definite pause</u>, usually created by <u>punctuation</u>. End-stopped lines can help to maintain a <u>regular rhythm</u> and can also affect the <u>pace</u> of a poem.

"I wander through each chartered street,
Near where the chartered Thames does flow,"

('London' — William Blake)

Blake uses <u>repeated end-stopped lines</u>. This helps to give the poem a <u>strong rhythm</u> but also makes his version of London feel <u>restrictive</u>.

Poetic Techniques

Similes and Metaphors add power to Descriptions

1) Similes <u>compare</u> one thing to another — they often contain the words '<u>like</u>' or '<u>as</u>'.

2) Similes are frequently used to <u>exaggerate</u> — the poet usually wants to <u>emphasise</u> something.

> "my boat
> Went heaving through the water <u>like a swan</u>"
> ('The Prelude: Stealing the Boat'
> — William Wordsworth)

The narrator compares his boat to a "swan" to emphasise how it <u>moves easily</u> through the water. This simile makes him seem <u>confident</u> and <u>in control</u>.

> "<u>We chased her, flying like a hare</u>"
> ('The Farmer's Bride' — Charlotte Mew)

The narrator uses a simile that links his wife with <u>prey</u> being <u>hunted</u>. This shows that she is <u>vulnerable</u> and <u>frightened of men</u>.

3) Metaphors describe something as though it <u>is</u> something else.

4) They take an object or person and give it the <u>qualities</u> of something else. This means that the poet can put a lot of <u>meaning</u> into a few words.

> "a <u>healing star</u>
> among the wounded"
> ('Checking Out Me History' — John Agard)

The narrator uses the metaphor of a "<u>star</u>" to describe Mary Seacole — the image suggests she brings <u>hope</u>, <u>light</u> and <u>warmth</u> to her patients.

> "<u>porcelain</u> over the stilling water"
> ('Winter Swans' — Owen Sheers)

The narrator uses a metaphor to describe the swans as "<u>porcelain</u>", emphasising their <u>strength</u> and <u>beauty</u>.

Personification gives an object Human Qualities

1) Personification means describing an <u>object</u> as if it feels or behaves in a <u>human way</u>.

2) It can add <u>emotion</u> or alter the <u>mood</u> of a poem — this can really help the poet convey their <u>message</u>.

> "The <u>sullen</u> wind was soon <u>awake</u>"
> ('Porphyria's Lover' — Robert Browning)

Browning personifies the wind as "<u>sullen</u>", stating it was "<u>soon awake</u>". This sets a <u>threatening mood</u>, as the bad-tempered wind has been disturbed.

> "My city <u>takes me dancing</u> through the city of walls."
> ('The Emigrée' — Carol Rumens)

Rumens personifies the speaker's place of birth as a <u>dancing partner</u>, reflecting her love for and close connection with the city.

Poetic Techniques

Imagery isn't just visual

1) Poets often appeal to all the senses (touch, sight, sound, smell and taste)
   — this is called <u>sensory imagery</u>.

2) Sensory imagery helps to create a <u>vivid image</u> in the reader's mind.

> *"the skin of his finger is <u>smooth</u> and <u>thick</u> like <u>warm ice</u>."*
>
> ('Climbing My Grandfather' — Andrew Waterhouse)

Waterhouse uses sensory imagery such as "smooth", "thick" and "like warm ice" to show the <u>close bond</u> between the narrator and their grandfather.

> *"<u>Our brains ache</u>, in the merciless iced east winds that knive us...
> Wearied we keep awake because <u>the night is silent</u>...
> <u>Low, drooping flares</u> confuse our memory of the salient..."*
>
> ('Exposure' — Wilfred Owen)

The poem uses three senses (<u>touch</u>, <u>sound</u> and <u>sight</u>) to describe how the soldiers feel. The use of so many senses emphasises their pain and confusion.

Poets use the Sounds of words for effect

Mood is the atmosphere of a poem, and tone is the feeling the words are spoken with.

The sounds words create can alter the <u>mood</u>, <u>pace</u> and <u>tone</u> of a poem. Here are some of the most common <u>techniques</u> that use sound for effect:

1) <u>Alliteration</u> is where words that are close together <u>start</u> with the <u>same sound</u>.

> *"me with my <u>h</u>eartful of <u>h</u>eadlines"*
> ('Letters from Yorkshire' — Maura Dooley)

The repeated 'h' sound creates a sense of <u>heaviness</u>, which reflects the narrator's <u>discontent</u> with her life.

2) <u>Assonance</u> is when <u>vowel</u> sounds are <u>repeated</u>.

> *"How should I gr<u>ee</u>t th<u>ee</u>?"*
> ('When We Two Parted' — Lord Byron)

The <u>assonant long 'ee'</u> sounds <u>draw out</u> each word — this reflects the <u>long-lasting</u> nature of the narrator's <u>pain</u>.

3) <u>Sibilance</u> is when sounds create a '<u>hissing</u>' or '<u>shushing</u>' effect.

> *"My mother <u>sh</u>ade<u>s</u> her eye<u>s</u> and look<u>s</u> my way"*
> ('Eden Rock' — Charles Causley)

The 's' and 'sh' sounds create a <u>hushed tone</u>, reflecting the <u>tranquillity</u> of the scene.

4) <u>Onomatopoeia</u> is when a word <u>mimics</u> the sound it's describing.

> *"To get out of that blue <u>crackling</u> air"*
> ('Bayonet Charge' — Ted Hughes)

The word "crackling" makes the air sound <u>electric</u>, emphasising the <u>danger</u> of the battlefield.

REVISION TASK

Try to learn some technical terms...

Write down some technical terms on separate pieces of card, and write the meaning on the back of each one. Then, for each card, read the meaning and guess what the technical term is without looking.

Comparing Poems

In the exam you'll have to compare poems — they could be seen or unseen. Here are some general tips.

Compare both poems in Every Paragraph

1) When you're asked to compare poems, you need to find <u>similarities</u> and <u>differences</u> between them.

2) This means you need to discuss <u>both poems</u> in <u>every paragraph</u>. There's a lot to squeeze in, so it's important to <u>structure</u> your paragraphs well.

3) <u>Comparative words</u> help you to do this. They clearly show the examiner if the point you're making is a <u>similarity</u> or <u>difference</u> between the two poems. Here are a few examples:

| similarly | equally | in contrast | however | conversely |

Compare Language, Structure and Form

When you plan your answer, make sure you consider <u>language</u>, <u>structure</u> and <u>form</u> — that way you won't forget to write about them in your essay.

Language

* Think about the <u>language techniques</u> the poets have used, e.g. <u>rhyme</u>, <u>imagery</u>, <u>sound</u>.

* Comment on how the language used in each poem is <u>similar</u> or <u>different</u>, and explain <u>why</u>.

Both 'Before You Were Mine' and 'Sonnet 29' use <u>onomatopoeia</u> to emphasise <u>strong emotions</u>. Duffy's verb "stamping" reflects the mother's <u>frustration</u> about her loss of freedom. Similarly, Barrett Browning's use of "burst" and "shattered" emphasise the narrator's <u>passion</u>.

Structure

* Compare the <u>beginnings</u> and <u>endings</u> of the poems, and how the ideas and feelings presented are developed.

* Comment on changes in <u>mood</u>, <u>voice</u>, <u>tense</u> and <u>tone</u> — think about <u>the effect</u> this has.

In 'London', the narrative <u>begins</u> and <u>ends</u> on the dismal streets of London, suggesting that its inhabitants are <u>unable to escape</u> the suffering found there. In contrast, 'War Photographer' <u>ends</u> in a different place to where it <u>begins</u>. However, the fact that the photographer is starting another assignment highlights the <u>unending cycle</u> of war and violence.

Form

* See if the poems have a specific <u>form</u> and explain <u>why</u> you think the poet has made that choice.

* Compare the <u>effects</u> of form in each poem. Think about how they relate to the <u>themes</u>.

* Check if any rules are broken for <u>effect</u>, e.g. a sonnet with 15 lines instead of 14.

'Mother, Any Distance' is written loosely in the form of a <u>sonnet</u>. By choosing a form that is normally used for <u>love poems</u>, Armitage emphasises how the speaker <u>still loves his mother</u>. On the other hand, 'Letters from Yorkshire' is written in <u>free verse</u> — the <u>irregular line lengths</u> make the poem flow like <u>natural speech</u> or a <u>letter</u>.

Compare the poems in every paragraph...

The examiner wants to see you're comparing both poems. Make it easy for them — write one point of comparison in each paragraph and use comparative words to show your comparisons clearly.

Warm-Up Questions

When it comes to poetry, you need to look at the overall message of the poem — but don't forget to focus on smaller things too, such as line endings, punctuation and even the vowel sounds in the middle of words. They all have a part to play. To see if you've got to grips with this section, have a go at these questions.

Warm-Up Questions

1) Write a brief definition of each of the following poetic techniques:
   a) Onomatopoeia b) Caesura c) Enjambment

2) Write out the sentences below. For each sentence, underline the letters or words that are used to create the effect in brackets.
   Write a sentence for each example explaining the effect of the technique used.

   "the fizzy, movie tomorrows / the right walk home could bring." (**onomatopoeia**)
   (Before You Were Mine, Carol Ann Duffy)

   "They accuse me of absence, they circle me." (**sibilance**)
   (The Emigrée, Carol Rumens)

   "Slowly our ghosts drag home" (**assonance**)
   (Exposure, Wilfred Owen)

   "a blockade of yellow bias binding around your blazer." (**alliteration**)
   (Poppies, Jane Weir)

3) The extract below personifies dawn on a battlefield. Write two paragraphs describing the impression you get of the speaker's feelings and how this impression is created.

   > Dawn massing in the east her melancholy army
   > Attacks once more
   >
   > *Exposure*, Wilfred Owen

4) Read the extract below. Write a sentence explaining the effect of each of the following features of the extract:
   a) The rhyme scheme.
   b) The use of direct address.
   c) Enjambment.

   > That's my last Duchess painted on the wall,
   > Looking as if she were alive. I call
   > That piece a wonder, now: Frà Pandolf's hands
   > Worked busily a day, and there she stands.
   > Will't please you sit and look at her? I said
   > 'Frà Pandolf' by design, for never read
   > Strangers like you that pictured countenance,
   > The depth and passion of its earnest glance,
   > But to myself they turned (since none puts by
   > The curtain I have drawn for you, but I)
   >
   > *My Last Duchess*, Robert Browning

Revision Summary

This section should give you a <u>good basic knowledge</u> of the things you need to cover when you <u>write</u> about poems. So, if you can <u>answer the questions</u> on this page you should be well on the way to getting some <u>great marks</u> in your exam. If not, <u>look back over</u> the section until you get them right.

*   Try these questions and <u>tick off each one</u> when you <u>get it right</u>.
*   When you've done <u>all the questions</u> under a heading and are <u>completely happy</u> with it, tick it off.

Poetry — What You Have To Do (p.53) ☑

1) There are three main elements of a poem that you have to write about in the exam. One is the language of the poem. What are the other two? ☑
2) What should you include to back up each of your ideas about the poem? ☑

Form and Structure (p.54) ☑

3) What is the difference between form and structure? ☑
4) Write a sentence describing each of these forms of poem: a) dramatic monologue b) sonnet c) free verse ☑
5) What is: a) a stanza? b) a couplet? c) a quatrain? ☑

Poetic Techniques (p.55-59) ☑

6) Write down whether each of these descriptions refers to the first- or third-person narrative voice: a) is more detached b) gives you one person's point of view ☑
7) Why might a poet include features of spoken language in their poem? Give one reason. ☑
8) Write a brief explanation of what an irregular rhyme scheme is. ☑
9) What two aspects of a poem does the rhythm alter? ☑
10) Below are two lines from a poem. What is the metre? How can you tell?

   Shall I compare thee to a summer's day?
   Thou art more lovely and more temperate.
   (Sonnet 18 — William Shakespeare) ☑
11) What is the difference between enjambment and end-stopping? ☑
12) Explain the difference between a simile and a metaphor. Give an example of each from the poems you have studied. ☑
13) Find two examples of sensory imagery from the poems you have studied. Explain their effect on the reader. ☑
14) Write a sentence explaining what each of these technical terms means: a) alliteration b) sibilance c) assonance ☑
15) What are "boom", "splash" and "crunch" all examples of? ☑

Comparing Poems (p.60) ☑

16) Give two examples for each of the following:
   a) comparative words you could use when explaining the similarity between two poems.
   b) comparative words you could use when explaining the difference between two poems. ☑
17) Is the following statement true or false?
   "It's best to compare two poems by writing several paragraphs about one
   and then several paragraphs about the other." ☑

The Poetry Anthology

You'll have to study a collection of poems in class, which you'll write about in Paper 2, Section B of your exam.

This is what you'll have to do in the Exam

1) You'll be given a copy of <u>one poem</u> from your anthology, and asked to compare it with <u>another</u> poem of your <u>choice</u> from the anthology.

2) Your comparison will based on something the two poems have in common, e.g. a particular <u>theme</u>. Choose your second poem carefully so you'll have lots of <u>comparison points</u> to make in your answer.

3) You'll need to know about <u>all the poems</u> in <u>one</u> of these clusters:

Power and Conflict

- The poems in this cluster explore <u>different types of power and conflict</u> in the world.

- Some poems focus on <u>human power</u> (e.g. 'Ozymandias') or the <u>power of nature</u> (e.g. 'Storm on the Island'). You might also have to write about themes like <u>memory</u>, <u>identity</u> or the <u>effects of conflict</u>.

Love and Relationships

- This cluster is all about <u>different types of relationships</u> between people.

- Some of the poems are about <u>romantic relationships</u> (e.g. 'Winter Swans') or <u>family relationships</u> (e.g. 'Follower'). <u>Desire</u>, <u>distance</u>, and <u>memory</u> are also common themes.

4) You <u>won't</u> have a copy of the anthology in the exam, so make sure you know <u>all</u> the poems in your cluster really well.

Read the Question carefully and Underline key words

Make sure you're looking at the <u>right poetry cluster</u> (see above if you're unsure which one). Read the question carefully. Underline the <u>theme</u> and any other <u>key words</u> — like so:

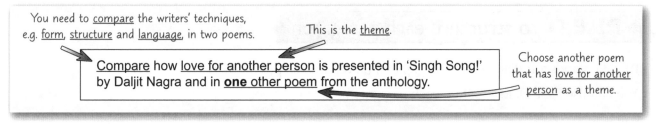

You need to <u>compare</u> the writers' techniques, e.g. <u>form</u>, <u>structure</u> and <u>language</u>, in two poems.

This is the <u>theme</u>.

<u>Compare</u> how <u>love for another person</u> is presented in 'Singh Song!' by Daljit Nagra and in **one** other poem from the anthology.

Choose another poem that has <u>love for another person</u> as a theme.

There are Three Main Ways to get marks

There are <u>three main things</u> to keep in mind when you're <u>planning</u> and <u>writing</u> your answer:

- Give your own <u>thoughts</u> and <u>opinions</u> on the poems and support them with <u>quotes</u> from the text.

- <u>Explain</u> features like <u>form</u>, <u>structure</u> and <u>language</u>.

- Describe the <u>similarities</u> and <u>differences</u> between poems and their <u>contexts</u>.

Make sure you have a good knowledge of all your poems...

Draw a mindmap for every poem you've studied — add branches for relevant themes and then add short quotes to each branch. You can then use these quotes to back up your points in the exam.

How to Structure Your Answer

A solid structure is essential — it lets the examiner follow your argument nice and easily.

Start with an **Introduction** and end with a **Conclusion**

1) Your introduction should begin by giving a clear answer to the question in a sentence or two. Use the rest of the introduction to briefly develop this idea — try to include some of the main ideas from your plan.

2) The main body of your essay should be three to five paragraphs of analysis.

3) Finish your essay with a conclusion — this should summarise your answer to the question. It's also your last chance to impress the examiner, so try to make your final sentence memorable.

Compare the two poems throughout your answer

1) Don't just write several paragraphs about one poem, followed by several paragraphs about the other.

2) Instead, structure each paragraph of your essay by writing about one poem and then explaining whether the other poem is similar or different.

3) Every paragraph should compare a feature of the poems, such as their form, their structure, the language they use or the feelings they put across.

4) Link your ideas with words like 'similarly', 'likewise' or 'equally' when you're writing about a similarity. Or use phrases such as 'in contrast' and 'on the other hand' if you're explaining a difference.

Remember to start a new paragraph every time you start comparing a new feature of the poems.

Use **P.E.E.D.** to structure each paragraph

1) P.E.E.D. stands for: Point, Example, Explain, Develop. See p.3 for more.

2) You can use P.E.E.D. to structure each paragraph of your answer, like this:

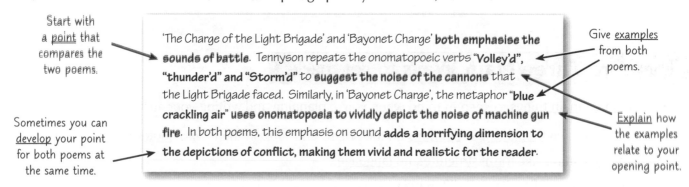

Start with a point that compares the two poems.

Sometimes you can develop your point for both poems at the same time.

'The Charge of the Light Brigade' and 'Bayonet Charge' **both emphasise the sounds of battle.** Tennyson repeats the onomatopoeic verbs "Volley'd", "thunder'd" and "Storm'd" to **suggest the noise of the cannons** that the Light Brigade faced. Similarly, in 'Bayonet Charge', the metaphor "**blue crackling air" uses onomatopoeia to vividly depict the noise of machine gun fire.** In both poems, this emphasis on sound **adds a horrifying dimension to the depictions of conflict, making them vivid and realistic for the reader.**

Give examples from both poems.

Explain how the examples relate to your opening point.

P.E.E.D. is a good way to structure an essay, but it's not essential...

P.E.E.D. is a framework you can use to make sure your paragraphs have all the features they need to pick up marks — it's a useful structure to bear in mind, but you don't have to follow it rigidly in every paragraph.

How to Answer the Question

Now you're up to speed with how to structure your answer, there are a few other things you should keep in mind when answering an exam question on your anthology poems.

Look closely at **Language**, **Form** and **Structure**

1) To get <u>top marks</u>, you need to pay <u>close attention</u> to the <u>techniques</u> the poets use.

2) <u>Analyse</u> the <u>form</u> and <u>structure</u> of the poems, which includes their <u>rhyme scheme</u> and <u>rhythm</u>.

3) Explore <u>language</u> — think about <u>why</u> the poets have used certain <u>words</u> and <u>language techniques</u>.

4) You also need to <u>comment</u> on the <u>effect</u> that these techniques have on the <u>reader</u>. The examiner wants to hear what <u>you think</u> of a poem and how it makes <u>you feel</u>.

5) This is the kind of thing you could write about <u>language</u>:

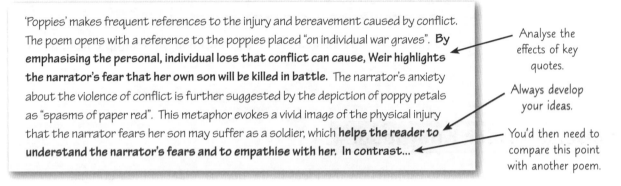

'Poppies' makes frequent references to the injury and bereavement caused by conflict. The poem opens with a reference to the poppies placed "on individual war graves". **By emphasising the personal, individual loss that conflict can cause, Weir highlights the narrator's fear that her own son will be killed in battle.** The narrator's anxiety about the violence of conflict is further suggested by the depiction of poppy petals as "spasms of paper red". This metaphor evokes a vivid image of the physical injury that the narrator fears her son may suffer as a soldier, which **helps the reader to understand the narrator's fears and to empathise with her. In contrast...**

Analyse the effects of key quotes.

Always develop your ideas.

You'd then need to compare this point with another poem.

Always **Support Your Ideas** with **Details** from the **Text**

1) You need to <u>back up your ideas</u> with <u>quotes</u> from or <u>references</u> to the text.

2) <u>Choose</u> your quotes <u>carefully</u> — they have to be <u>relevant</u> to the point you're making.

3) <u>Don't</u> quote <u>large chunks</u> of text — instead, use <u>short</u> quotes and <u>embed</u> them in your sentences.

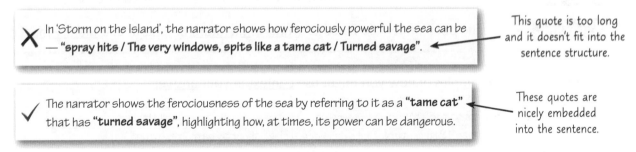

✗ In 'Storm on the Island', the narrator shows how ferociously powerful the sea can be — **"spray hits / The very windows, spits like a tame cat / Turned savage".**

This quote is too long and it doesn't fit into the sentence structure.

✓ The narrator shows the ferociousness of the sea by referring to it as a **"tame cat"** that has **"turned savage"**, highlighting how, at times, its power can be dangerous.

These quotes are nicely embedded into the sentence.

4) <u>Don't</u> forget to <u>explain</u> your quotes — you need to use them as <u>evidence</u> to support your <u>argument</u>.

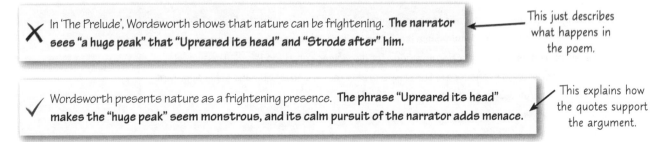

✗ In 'The Prelude', Wordsworth shows that nature can be frightening. **The narrator sees "a huge peak" that "Upreared its head" and "Strode after" him.**

This just describes what happens in the poem.

✓ Wordsworth presents nature as a frightening presence. **The phrase "Upreared its head" makes the "huge peak" seem monstrous, and its calm pursuit of the narrator adds menace.**

This explains how the quotes support the argument.

How to Answer the Question

Give Alternative Interpretations

1) You need to show you're aware that poems can be <u>interpreted</u> in <u>more than one</u> way.

2) If a poem is a bit <u>ambiguous</u>, or you think that a particular line or phrase could have several <u>different meanings</u>, then <u>say so</u>.

> In 'Ozymandias', Shelley refers to the sculptor as the "hand that mocked" the statue. On the surface, the word **"mocked"** shows only that the sculptor created the artwork. However, Shelley may also be playing on the second meaning of the word "mocked" (to make fun of); the **"wrinkled lip and sneer"** of the statue suggest that the sculptor disliked Ozymandias, hinting that he may have intended to ridicule the leader by his unflattering depiction.

Remember to support your interpretations with evidence from the poem.

3) Be <u>original</u> with your ideas — just make sure you can back them up with an <u>example</u> from the text.

Show some Wider Knowledge

1) To get a top grade, you need to <u>explain</u> how the <u>ideas</u> in the poems relate to their <u>context</u>.

2) When you're thinking about a particular poem, consider these aspects of <u>context</u>:

Historical — Do the ideas in the poem relate to the <u>time</u> in which it's <u>written</u> or <u>set</u>?

Geographical — How is the poem shaped and influenced by the <u>place</u> in which it's set?

Social — Is the poet <u>criticising</u> or <u>praising</u> the <u>society</u> or <u>community</u> they're writing about?

Cultural — Does the poet draw on a particular aspect of their <u>background</u> or <u>culture</u>?

Literary — Was the poet influenced by other <u>works of literature</u> or a particular <u>literary movement</u>?

3) Here are a couple of <u>examples</u> of how you might use <u>context</u> in your <u>answer</u>:

> In 'London', Blake's reference to the "chimney-sweeper's cry" creates a vivid picture of child labour, which was common in the late 18th century. Blake considered child labour to be morally wrong, and he may have included this emotive image in order to boost public sympathy for his views.

> Browning is thought to have based the speaker in 'My Last Duchess' on the Duke of Ferrara, an important nobleman in Renaissance Italy. The Italian Renaissance was a time of great artistic innovation, but it was also infamous for its violence and bloodshed. These dual aspects of society are reflected in the Duke's pride in his art collection and in his apparent lack of guilt about seemingly having had his wife killed.

How to Answer the Question

Use **Sophisticated Language**

1) Your writing has to sound <u>sophisticated</u> and <u>precise</u>.

> ✗ The narrator of 'Eden Rock' **seems to quite like** Eden Rock. — Not very sophisticated.
>
> ✓ Causley's narrator **presents a positive view** of Eden Rock. — This sounds much better.

2) It should be <u>concise</u> and <u>accurate</u>, with no <u>vague words</u> or <u>waffle</u>.

> ✗ Hardy uses **lots of depressing words and descriptions** to express his sorrow. — This is too vague.
>
> ✓ Hardy uses **a range of references to death and winter** to express his sorrow. — Use more specific language.

3) Your writing should also show an <u>impressive range</u> of <u>vocabulary</u>.

Don't keep using the same word to describe something. →

> ✗ In 'Poppies', the narrator **feels cut off** from her son. The word "blockade" shows that she **feels cut off** from him. The idea that she **feels cut off** from her son is also shown by the description of his hair as "gelled blackthorns".

Vary how you say things — it sounds much more impressive. →

> ✓ In 'Poppies', the narrator **feels cut off** from her son. This **sense of separation** is emphasised by the metaphor describing his hair as "gelled blackthorns", which suggests that her son has become prickly and **unapproachable**.

4) However, make sure you <u>only</u> use words that you know the <u>meaning</u> of. For example, don't say that a poem has a '<u>volta</u>' if you don't know what it <u>really means</u> — it will be <u>obvious</u> to the examiner.

Use **Technical Terms** where possible

1) To get top marks, you need to use the <u>correct technical terms</u> when you're writing about poetry.

2) Flick back to Section Five (p.53-62) for more on these terms, or have a look at the <u>glossary</u> at the back of the book.

Don't write

> ✗ Simon Armitage uses <u>good images</u>.
>
> ✗ The poet uses <u>words that are also sounds</u>.
>
> ✗ The <u>sentences run on from line to line</u>.

Write

> ✓ Simon Armitage uses <u>effective metaphors</u>.
>
> ✓ The poet uses <u>onomatopoeia</u>.
>
> ✓ The poet uses <u>enjambment</u>.

It's not just what you write...

... it's also how you write it. In the exam, think about your writing style — you should be clear and precise, and you'll need to use the correct terms to show the examiner you know your stuff.

How to Write a Top Grade Answer

If you're aiming for a grade 9, you're going to have to do a little bit extra. Here are a few tips...

Know the Poems inside out

You have to know the poems, their key themes and techniques like the back of your hand. Everyone has their own ways of understanding poetry, but here are a few ideas of how to get to grips with them:

- Read the poems again and again, highlight bits, jot down notes — whatever works for you.
- Make a list of the key themes, and note down plenty of quotes that relate to each one.
- List the major techniques that the poet uses, along with their effect.

Memorise your lists in time for the exam.

Be as Original as you can

1) There are no wrong interpretations of a poem, so come up with your own ideas.

2) Make sure you can back up your interpretations with evidence from the text. For example:

> In 'Follower' by Seamus Heaney, the narrator describes how his father has become the one who follows and that he "will not go away". As well as describing the physical actions of his father, this statement could also be symbolic of his father's legacy, hinting at the narrator's sadness that he did not learn to plough like his father and suggesting that this feeling "will not go away".

Write about the poems Critically

1) Being critical means giving your own opinions about the poems — e.g. how effective you think the poet's techniques are, and why you think this.

2) You need to phrase your opinions in a sophisticated way. For example:

> In 'Neutral Tones', the phrase "God-curst sun" compels the reader to experience the scene as Hardy's narrator does: a bleak, lifeless landscape, devoid of hope and forsaken by God.

Get to grips with Context

It's not enough just to mention a link to context — you need to really explore the effect it has on the poem, or on your understanding of it. For example:

> In common with other Romantic poets, Wordsworth viewed nature as a powerful force that could inspire and transform people. This is evident in the extract from his autobiographical poem 'The Prelude'; the encounter with the "huge peak" leaves him in a "grave / And serious mood", seemingly forcing him to contemplate his own mortality and place in the Universe.

For a top grade, think originally and critically...

When it comes to grade 9, the examiner wants your interpretation and your opinion of the poems. Have a look at the sample answers on pages 70-73 for some ideas of how to write a great poetry essay.

Warm-Up Questions

For a poetry essay, you need to know what to write about and how to write it. When you answer the questions on this page, practise using sophisticated language so it becomes second nature by the time the exam comes round. Remember to use technical terms whenever possible as well.

Warm-Up Questions

1) In your anthology, find a poem that rhymes.
   What effect does the use of rhyme have in this poem?

2) Choose a poem from your anthology that is written in the first person and one that is written in the third person. Do you find it easier to empathise with the first-person narrator or the characters described by the third-person narration? Write a paragraph explaining your answer.

3) For each of the following aspects of form and structure, find an example from any of the poems in your anthology. Write a sentence explaining the effect each example has on the reader.
   a) End-stopping.
   b) Caesurae.
   c) Dramatic monologue.
   d) Enjambment.

4) Using two of your answers to question 3, write a paragraph comparing the form and structure of two of the poems, and explaining how the poets use form and structure to help convey their messages.

5) For each of the following language techniques, find an example from any of the poems in your anthology. Write a sentence explaining the effect each example has on the reader.
   a) Repetition.
   b) Onomatopoeia.
   c) Alliteration.
   d) Assonance.

6) Using two of your answers to question 5, write a paragraph comparing the language of two of the poems, and explaining how the poets use language to help convey their messages.

7) Pick one more poem from your anthology. How does the poet use imagery in the poem? Write a paragraph about your favourite image, explaining what effect it has on you.

Worked Exam-Style Question

Here's an example of how you might answer a question comparing two poems from 'Love and Relationships'.

Q1 Compare how childhood is presented in Seamus Heaney's 'Follower' and one other poem you have studied.

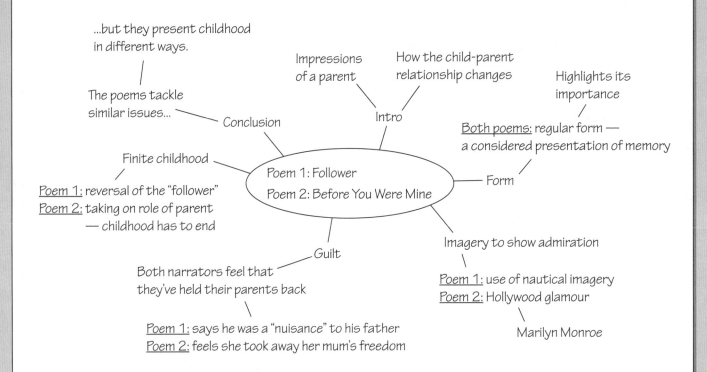

...but they present childhood in different ways.

The poems tackle similar issues...

Conclusion

Finite childhood

Poem 1: reversal of the "follower"
Poem 2: taking on role of parent — childhood has to end

Impressions of a parent

How the child-parent relationship changes

Intro

Poem 1: Follower
Poem 2: Before You Were Mine

Highlights its importance

Both poems: regular form — a considered presentation of memory

Form

Guilt

Both narrators feel that they've held their parents back

Poem 1: says he was a "nuisance" to his father
Poem 2: feels she took away her mum's freedom

Imagery to show admiration

Poem 1: use of nautical imagery
Poem 2: Hollywood glamour

Marilyn Monroe

Tell the examiner which <u>poems</u> you've chosen in your <u>first sentence</u>.

<u>Both Seamus Heaney's 'Follower' and Carol Ann Duffy's 'Before You Were Mine' present ideas about childhood through the narrators' impressions of a parent.</u> The narrator in 'Follower' recalls his childhood memories of his father and reflects on how their relationship has changed over time, whereas in 'Before You Were Mine' the narrator uses memories from her childhood to inform the description of her mother's life before she was born. Both poets use this relationship between child and parent to explore the idea of childhood and how this relationship changes as people get older and leave childhood behind.

It's important to write about <u>form</u> in your answers.

Make sure you <u>develop your points</u> clearly.

<u>Both poems have a regular form; these careful frameworks emphasise how precious the narrators' memories are to them.</u> 'Follower' has six four-line stanzas, and 'Before You Were Mine' consists of four five-line stanzas. In both poems, this creates an unhurried, steady rhythm that reflects the narrators' considered presentation of their memories. <u>This highlights the importance of these childhood memories and implies that both narrators consider the day-to-day activities of their childhoods to have been significant, even if they were just ordinary events at the time.</u>

Worked Exam-Style Question

Each paragraph should mark the start of a new point.

<u>The imagery used to describe the parents in both poems suggests that the narrators admired them as children.</u> In 'Follower', Heaney uses nautical imagery to emphasise the power and strength of the father, comparing his shoulders to a "full sail strung". <u>Similarly, the narrator in 'Before You Were Mine' describes her mother as "Marilyn", in reference to Marilyn Monroe, a famous actress and model from the 1950s.</u> By using the metaphor of an iconic Hollywood film star to describe her mother, the narrator compares the way that children admire their parents to the way that people admire famous people. In this way, both poets use imagery of strong, powerful and successful people to reflect the way that children often idolise their parents.

Show that you can apply <u>your own knowledge</u> to the poem.

Embedding <u>short quotes</u> helps to keep your sentences <u>clear</u> and <u>easy to understand</u>.

However, as adults, both narrators seem to feel a sense of guilt at holding their parents back. In 'Follower', the narrator describes himself as a "<u>nuisance</u>", using the onomatopoeic verb "Yapping" to suggest that he was irritating to his father. Similarly, in 'Before You Were Mine' the narrator describes her "loud, possessive yell". <u>The combination of forceful adjectives with the powerful verb "yell" emphasises how demanding the narrator was as a child.</u> Both narrators seem to have been unaware of the negative effect they had on their parents until they were older; this suggests that childhood is a time of innocence and unquestioning acceptance of a parent's love and attention.

It's good to show the examiner that you can analyse the effect of <u>specific words</u>.

Both poems also explore the idea that as children grow older they take on the characteristics of their parents. In 'Follower', the father, in whose "wake" the son once followed, is now "stumbling / Behind" the narrator, while the narrator is the one who leads. This happens in the final two lines of the poem, which highlights its significance. <u>This also creates a cyclical structure that reflects the way the roles between the narrator and his father have been reversed since his childhood.</u> The narrator in 'Before You Were Mine' also takes on the role of a parent, asking "whose small bites on your neck, sweetheart?" The word "sweetheart" makes it sound as if the narrator is affectionately mimicking the voice of a parent. <u>In this way, Duffy presents childhood as having an inevitable endpoint, after which the child begins to acquire the traits of their parent.</u>

This paragraph develops each point in a way that <u>links back to the theme</u> in the question.

Make sure you include <u>both similarities and differences</u> between the poems.

'Follower' and 'Before You Were Mine' both present ideas about childhood through the relationship between a child and their parent. <u>Although the way these relationships are presented differs, they both highlight similar issues: admiring a parent, the guilt that is eventually felt and the inevitable end of childhood.</u> Both poets use structure, vivid imagery and language to present these issues, as well as to convey the complex emotions that arise from them.

Worked Exam-Style Question

Here's another example answer, this time for the 'Power and Conflict' cluster. Have a good read of it, then when you're happy flick over to page 74 and try some exam-style questions for yourself.

Q1 Compare how the reality of conflict is presented in Ted Hughes's 'Bayonet Charge' and one other poem you have studied.

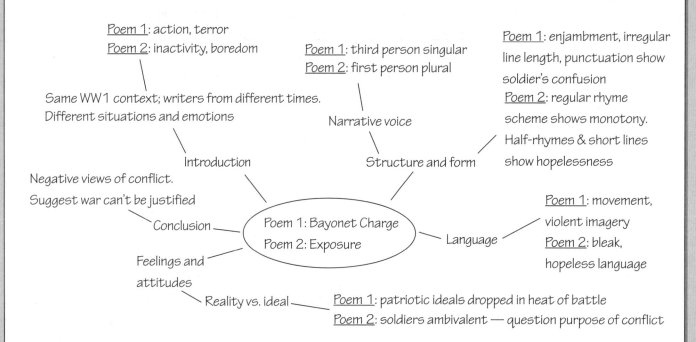

Poem 1: action, terror
Poem 2: inactivity, boredom

Same WW1 context; writers from different times.
Different situations and emotions

Poem 1: third person singular
Poem 2: first person plural

Narrative voice

Poem 1: enjambment, irregular line length, punctuation show soldier's confusion
Poem 2: regular rhyme scheme shows monotony.
Half-rhymes & short lines show hopelessness

Introduction

Structure and form

Negative views of conflict.
Suggest war can't be justified

Conclusion

Poem 1: Bayonet Charge
Poem 2: Exposure

Language

Poem 1: movement, violent imagery
Poem 2: bleak, hopeless language

Feelings and attitudes

Reality vs. ideal

Poem 1: patriotic ideals dropped in heat of battle
Poem 2: soldiers ambivalent — question purpose of conflict

Compare the poems in your <u>opening sentence</u>.

<u>Although the action of both 'Bayonet Charge' and 'Exposure' occurs on the battlefields of World War One, the poems offer two very different portrayals of the reality of conflict.</u> While 'Bayonet Charge' depicts the violent action and overwhelming terror experienced by a soldier going into battle, 'Exposure' focuses on the boredom and inactivity of men waiting in the freezing trenches of the Western Front while "nothing happens" on the battlefield. <u>Both poets present war as a profoundly negative experience, in which hope, faith and sense of self are overpowered by pain and fear.</u>

Sum up the <u>main argument</u> of your essay.

Try to <u>develop</u> your ideas.

The poems use different narrative voices. 'Bayonet Charge' is written in the third person. The anonymity of the subject, "he", and the fact that he is the only human mentioned in the poem make him seem isolated and alone, even though it is clear that he must be surrounded by other soldiers. <u>This sense of isolation heightens the feeling of terror in the poem by reflecting the soldier's acute focus on his own survival.</u> In contrast, 'Exposure' is written in the first person plural ("our memory", "we hear"), which creates a sense of the shared suffering experienced by the millions of soldiers who fought and died in the First World War. This emphasises the vast scale of misery and loss of life in the war.

Compare the poems' <u>form</u> and <u>structure</u>.

<u>The poets also use other aspects of form and structure to present the reality of conflict.</u> In 'Bayonet Charge', Hughes uses <u>enjambment</u> and uneven line lengths to create an irregular rhythm, echoing the confusion experienced by the soldier. The irregular rhythm is heightened by <u>caesurae</u> in lines 11 and 15. These

Use the correct <u>technical terms</u>.

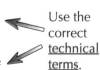

Worked Exam-Style Question

help to turn the second stanza into a pause in the action, which reflects the soldier's experience of time apparently standing still as he struggles to understand "the reason / Of his still running". In contrast, Owen uses a regular rhyme scheme (ABBAC) to emphasise the monotony experienced by the soldiers. Despite this regularity, half-rhymes such as "wire" / "war" create a sense of jarring discomfort that mirrors the soldiers' suffering.

The different experiences of conflict presented in 'Exposure' and 'Bayonet Charge' are conveyed through <u>the contrasting language the poets use</u>. Owen's language is bleak and hopeless — dawn is personified as a "melancholy army" "massing in the east", a metaphor which has a powerful effect on the reader by subverting their expectations — dawn is usually a symbol of hope, but here it only brings more "poignant misery". The soldiers' sense of hopelessness is also evident in the phrase "love of God seems dying", <u>which suggests that the horrific reality of conflict is causing them to lose their faith in God, or perhaps to believe that a God who can subject them to such suffering has lost faith in them</u>. In contrast to this bleak imagery, 'Bayonet Charge' is filled with frantic movement. Active verbs such as "running" and "stumbling" help to create a vivid image of the soldier's desperate actions as he races into battle. The sense of movement in the poem is also conveyed by the opening phrase, "<u>Suddenly he awoke</u>", which places the reader in the middle of the action from the start. <u>This gives the poem a nightmarish quality, highlighting the feelings of confusion and terror that are driving the soldier.</u>

Both poems suggest that the reality of conflict does not match up to the ideal. In 'Bayonet Charge', Hughes questions the patriotic ideals of "King, honour, human dignity, etcetera", arguing that in the heat of battle they are "Dropped like luxuries" as terror takes over. <u>Information about the horrors of World War One was readily available in the 1950s when Hughes wrote this poem, and there is a sense of pity for the soldiers who fought.</u> Similarly, in 'Exposure', the narrator questions whether anything is achieved by the soldiers' sacrifice. On the surface, the phrase "Since we believe not otherwise can kind fires burn" suggests the soldiers believe their sacrifice is necessary to protect the "kind fires" of home, but the complex, broken syntax reflects their lack of conviction that this is true. <u>This reveals the alienation many soldiers felt: they believed no-one at home appreciated their sacrifice.</u>

'Bayonet Charge' and 'Exposure' both present vividly negative views of the reality of conflict for soldiers on the front line. The experience of the soldiers in the two poems is very different: Hughes focuses on the raw terror and active suffering of a soldier going into battle, whereas Owen concentrates on the hopelessness and passive suffering of men dying from exposure. However, both poets use structure, form and vivid imagery to powerfully convey the soldiers' suffering. <u>Both narrators question the patriotic ideals used to justify war, suggesting instead that there can be no justification for the bleak and dehumanising reality of conflict.</u>

Compare the <u>language</u> used in the two poems.

You can give <u>more than one interpretation</u> in your answer.

Use <u>quotes</u> to support your argument.

Explain the <u>effect</u> of the examples you give.

Bring in some <u>contextual</u> details to your answer.

Your last sentence should <u>sum up your argument</u>, and it needs to be <u>memorable</u>.

Exam-Style Questions

Now it's time to put all you've learned about how to write a great answer into practice. Not all of these questions will be relevant to your cluster, but there should be at least one question you can answer.

Q1 Compare how feelings towards another person are presented in 'Sonnet 29' by Elizabeth Barrett Browning and one other poem from your poetry anthology.

Q2 Compare the ways in which time is presented in two poems from your poetry anthology.

Q3 Compare how war is presented in 'Remains' by Simon Armitage and one other poem from your poetry anthology.

Q4 Compare the way that a sense of place is created in two poems from your poetry anthology.

Q5 Compare how human power is presented in two poems from your poetry anthology.

Five Steps to Analysing a Poem

In the final section of Paper 2, you're going to have to analyse some unseen poetry — here's how to do it.

The examiner is looking for **Four Main Things**

You'll have to answer <u>two questions</u> in this section — one on an <u>unseen poem</u>, and one where you <u>compare</u> the poem with another unseen poem. To impress the examiner, you need to:

1) Show that you <u>understand</u> what the poems are <u>about</u>.

2) Write about the <u>techniques</u> used in the poems.

3) Use the <u>correct technical terms</u> to describe the techniques in the poems.

4) <u>Support</u> every point you make with <u>quotes</u> or <u>examples</u> from the poems.

Five Steps to analysing an unseen poem

Pick out the important bits of the poem as you read it — underline them or make notes.

1) Work out what the poem's about

- Work out the <u>subject</u> of the poem, e.g. the poem is about the narrator's relationship with his parents.

- Think about <u>who</u> is <u>speaking</u>, and <u>who</u> the poem is <u>addressing</u> — e.g. the narrator's lover, the reader...

2) Identify the purpose, theme or message

- Think about <u>what</u> the poet is saying, <u>why</u> they've written the poem, or what <u>ideas</u> they're using.

- The poem could be an <u>emotional response</u> to something. It might aim to <u>get a response</u> from the <u>reader</u>, or put across a message or an opinion about something.

3) Explore the emotions, moods or feelings

- Consider the <u>different emotions or feelings</u> in the poem and identify its <u>mood</u>.

- Look at how the poet <u>shows</u> these emotions (see step 4).

4) Identify the techniques used in the poem

- Find the <u>different techniques</u> the poet has used and how they create <u>emotions</u>, <u>moods</u> or <u>feelings</u>. Think about <u>why</u> the poet has used them, and what <u>effect</u> they create.

- Techniques can be related to <u>language</u> (<u>alliteration</u>, <u>onomatopoeia</u>, <u>imagery</u> etc.), <u>structure</u> (the order of <u>ideas</u> and any changes in <u>mood</u> or <u>tone</u>) and <u>form</u> (<u>line</u> and <u>stanza</u> length, <u>rhyme schemes</u> etc.).

5) Include your thoughts and feelings about the poem

- Examiners love to hear what <u>you think</u> of a poem and how it makes <u>you feel</u>. Think about how well the poem gets its <u>message</u> across and what <u>impact</u> it has on you.

- Try <u>not</u> to use "<u>I</u>" though — don't say "I felt sad that the narrator's brother died", it's much <u>better</u> to say "It makes the reader feel the narrator's sense of sadness at the death of his brother."

- Think about any <u>other ways</u> that the poem could be <u>interpreted</u>.

Always read the poem with the question in mind...

The first thing to do when you're analysing a poem is to read the question carefully and underline the key words. That'll help you to identify aspects of the poem that are directly relevant to the question.

Worked Exam-Style Question

On the next three pages is a step-by-step guide to answering an unseen poetry question in the exam. The first stage is to read the question carefully and annotate the relevant parts of the poem.

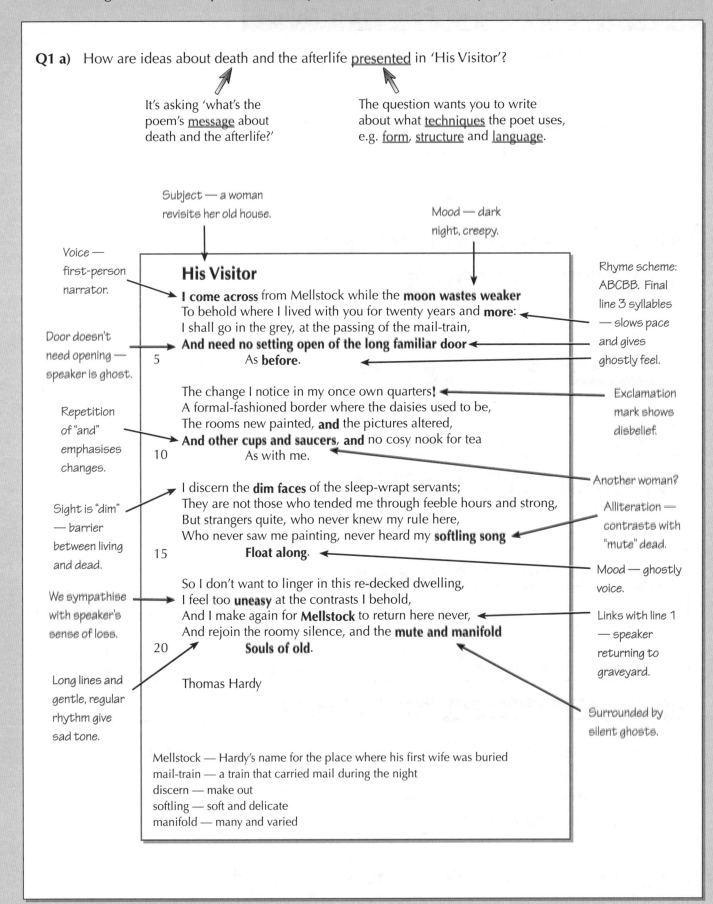

Q1 a) How are ideas about death and the afterlife <u>presented</u> in 'His Visitor'?

It's asking 'what's the poem's <u>message</u> about death and the afterlife?'

The question wants you to write about what <u>techniques</u> the poet uses, e.g. <u>form</u>, <u>structure</u> and <u>language</u>.

Subject — a woman revisits her old house.

Mood — dark night, creepy.

Voice — first-person narrator.

Rhyme scheme: ABCBB. Final line 3 syllables — slows pace and gives ghostly feel.

His Visitor

I come across from Mellstock while the **moon wastes weaker**
To behold where I lived with you for twenty years and **more**:
I shall go in the grey, at the passing of the mail-train,
And need no setting open of the long familiar door
5   As **before**.

Door doesn't need opening — speaker is ghost.

The change I notice in my once own quarters**!**
A formal-fashioned border where the daisies used to be,
The rooms new painted, **and** the pictures altered,
And other cups and saucers, and no cosy nook for tea
10   As with me.

Repetition of "and" emphasises changes.

Exclamation mark shows disbelief.

Another woman?

I discern the **dim faces** of the sleep-wrapt servants;
They are not those who tended me through feeble hours and strong,
But strangers quite, who never knew my rule here,
Who never saw me painting, never heard my **softling song**
15   **Float along**.

Sight is "dim" — barrier between living and dead.

Alliteration — contrasts with "mute" dead.

Mood — ghostly voice.

So I don't want to linger in this re-decked dwelling,
I feel too **uneasy** at the contrasts I behold,
And I make again for **Mellstock** to return here never,
And rejoin the roomy silence, and the **mute and manifold**
20   **Souls of old**.

We sympathise with speaker's sense of loss.

Links with line 1 — speaker returning to graveyard.

Thomas Hardy

Long lines and gentle, regular rhythm give sad tone.

Surrounded by silent ghosts.

Mellstock — Hardy's name for the place where his first wife was buried
mail-train — a train that carried mail during the night
discern — make out
softling — soft and delicate
manifold — many and varied

Worked Exam-Style Question

Once you've got to grips with the poem, spend five minutes planning your answer.
Then get writing your answer — just make sure you refer back to your plan as you write.

Plan:

1. Intro
- Subject — a ghost visits her former home.
- Sorrow of dead.

Don't spend too long on your plan. It's only rough work, so you don't need to write in full sentences.

2. Death isn't the end
- Ghost narrator.
- Ghost is sad, not scary — reader sympathises with her.

3. The dead are powerless
- She is "uneasy" at the changes, but can't do anything about them.
- Her only choice is to "rejoin the roomy silence".
- Sad tone (reinforced by gentle, regular rhythm) — living move on, dead don't.

Focus on three or four key points about the poem.

4. Separation between dead and living
- She doesn't need the door opened — she's formless.
- Living are unaware of her.
- Living are "dim faces" — indistinct.
- Living are vocal — "softling song". Dead are "mute".

Remember to write about what the poet says and how they say it.

5. Effect of death on the living
- Poet vs. narrator. He imagines her response.
- Guilt at the changes/new wife?

6. Conclusion
- Dead always with us.
- Living and dead are separate but impact on each other.

The poem 'His Visitor' describes the return of a ghost to the home she shared with her partner for "twenty years and more". In it, the poet imagines her resentment of the changes that have occurred since her death, indirectly revealing his own guilt at allowing these changes to take place. The poem suggests that although the living can affect the dead, and vice versa, ultimately they are separate states with no point of contact.

Clear start, showing that you've understood the poem.

Write about the poem's main messages early on in your essay.

The most obvious point the poet makes about death is that it is not the end. Although the narrator of the poem never explicitly states that she is a ghost, it is made clear when she says, for instance, that she arrives by night and needs "no setting open" of the door. The use of the first person makes the reader empathise with the sadness of the narrator, breaking down the stereotype of ghosts being frightening.

Always use quotes to back up points.

Give a personal response to the poem.

78

Worked Exam-Style Question

Write about
<u>feelings</u> and
<u>mood</u>, and use
quotes to back
up your points.

<u>The feeling of sorrow is emphasised by the powerlessness of the narrator. Although she is "uneasy" at the changes that have been made to her former home, the only way she can ease her discomfort is to leave and "return here never".</u> Death therefore involves giving up a loved home and all that is familiar, and instead accepting the loneliness that comes with joining the "roomy silence". The gentle rhythm of the poem reinforces the narrator's loneliness. <u>The three-syllable lines that end each stanza</u> are separated from the rest of the stanza by the change in rhythm, but they are linked to it by rhyme. They have the effect of making each stanza seem to tail off wistfully, reinforcing the narrator's sorrow, while their content shows her fixation on "before". This suggests that, while the living are able to move forward, the dead are trapped in the past.

<u>Comment</u> on
<u>form</u> and the
effect it has.

The poet also suggests that death divides the narrator from the living world. The colours of the poem are muted: <u>the "grey" of night and the moon that "wastes weaker" create a feeling of unreality</u> that contrasts with the "cosy nook" of the past. <u>The "dim faces" of the sleeping servants may be shadowy because it is night, or because the narrator exists in the spiritual world</u>, so to her, the material world is vague and unclear. Although the narrator is aware of her surroundings, she cannot interact with them, instead passing through the "long familiar door". <u>The silence of the dead is emphasised by the alliteration of "mute and manifold"</u>, which contrasts with the "softling song" of the narrator when she was alive.

Write about
any <u>imagery</u>
in the poem.

Think about
<u>different
interpretations</u>
to help you get
top marks.

Mention and
explain any
<u>poetic devices</u>
that you spot.

Think about
any <u>hidden
meanings</u> the
poem might
contain.

<u>The poem also gives clues about the impact of death on the living.</u> By imagining how "uneasy" the narrator feels at the "contrasts" she sees, Hardy <u>gives the reader a hint of the guilt he feels</u> at moving on while she cannot. The changes described are not large, but <u>the use of an exclamation mark and the repetition of "and" in the second stanza shows how significant the poet believes they would have been to the narrator.</u> The mention of "other cups and saucers", traditionally chosen by women, hint that the dead woman's place may have been taken by another woman. This may explain the poet's guilt. However, the fact that he is so concerned with what the ghost would feel suggests, ironically, that he has not really moved on.

Give a good
<u>personal
response</u>
wherever
you can.

Mention specific
<u>language features</u>
and <u>explain why</u>
the poet used them.

<u>Sum up</u> the
<u>what</u> and <u>how</u>
in your final
paragraph.

The central message of the poem is that the living and the dead inhabit two separate worlds. Hardy explores this through his use of a ghostly first-person narrator, a gentle regular rhythm which reflects her sad drifting around the house and her eventual return to "roomy silence".

Comparing Two Poems

To do well in the exam, you'll need to be able to compare two unseen poems. Here are a few tips...

You'll have to **Compare Two** unseen poems

1) In the exam, you're going to have to compare <u>two unseen poems</u>.

2) This means that you need to write about the <u>similarities</u> and <u>differences</u> between them.

3) You'll need to discuss the <u>techniques</u> the poets use and their <u>effect on the reader</u>, so focus on the <u>structure</u>, <u>form</u> and <u>language</u> used in the two poems.

For more on how to structure an answer where you're comparing two poems, see page 60.

Four Steps to answering a comparison question

Don't start writing <u>without thinking</u> about what you're going to say — follow these <u>four steps</u> to organise your ideas:

1) Read the question

- <u>Read</u> the question carefully and <u>underline</u> the key words.

- Check whether the question asks you to write about a specific <u>theme</u>, e.g. 'conflict' or 'family'.

2) Annotate the poems

- Go through and <u>annotate</u> the poems, focusing on the <u>techniques</u> used and the <u>effect</u> they have on the reader.

- As you're annotating the second poem, look for <u>similarities</u> and <u>differences</u> with the <u>techniques</u> you picked out in the first poem.

<u>R</u>ead, <u>A</u>nnotate, <u>P</u>lan, <u>W</u>rite. To help you remember these four steps, try: <u>R</u>eally <u>A</u>ngry <u>P</u>enguins <u>W</u>obble.

3) Plan your answer

- Identify <u>three or four</u> key <u>similarities and/or differences</u> that you're going to write about.

- Write a <u>short plan</u> that outlines the <u>structure</u> of your answer.

4) Write your answer

- <u>Use</u> your plan to make sure that <u>every paragraph</u> you write discusses <u>one similarity or difference</u> between the two poems. This could be in their <u>themes</u> and <u>ideas</u>, or their <u>form</u>, <u>structure</u> and <u>language</u>.

- Use <u>linking words and phrases</u>, e.g. 'in contrast' or 'similarly', to make it really clear that you're <u>comparing</u> the two poems.

You need to write about both poems in your answer...

The examiner wants to see that you can discuss the similarities and differences between the two poems — make this easy for them by including at least one clear comparison in every paragraph.

Worked Exam-Style Question

Here's another worked example. Use it to get some ideas about how to approach a comparison question.

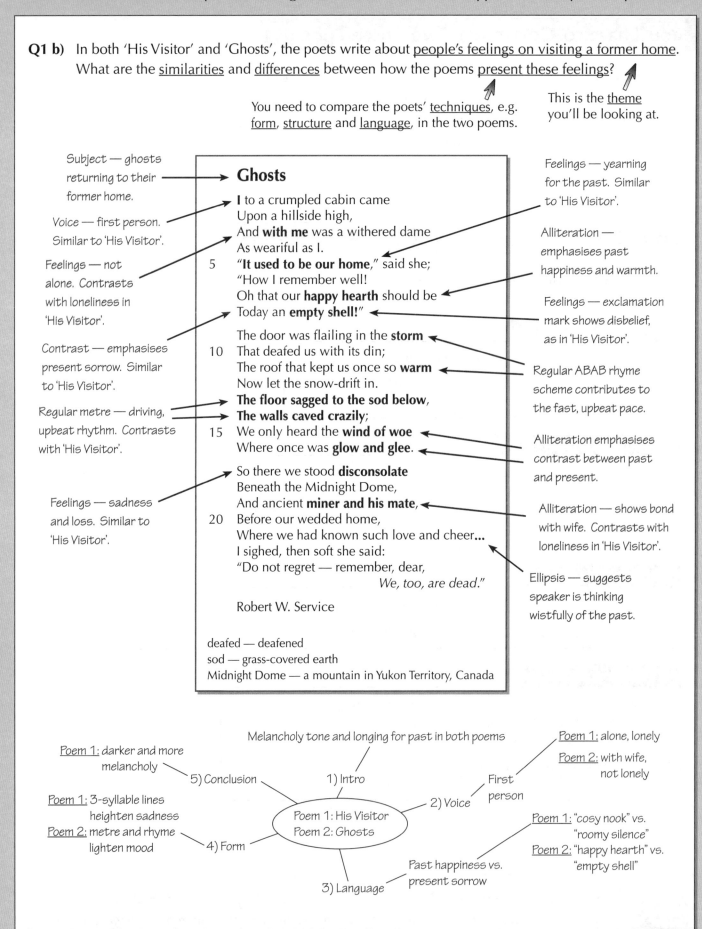

Q1 b) In both 'His Visitor' and 'Ghosts', the poets write about <u>people's feelings on visiting a former home</u>. What are the <u>similarities</u> and <u>differences</u> between how the poems <u>present these feelings</u>?

You need to compare the poets' <u>techniques</u>, e.g. <u>form</u>, <u>structure</u> and <u>language</u>, in the two poems.

This is the <u>theme</u> you'll be looking at.

Subject — ghosts returning to their former home.

Voice — first person. Similar to 'His Visitor'.

Feelings — not alone. Contrasts with loneliness in 'His Visitor'.

Contrast — emphasises present sorrow. Similar to 'His Visitor'.

Regular metre — driving, upbeat rhythm. Contrasts with 'His Visitor'.

Feelings — sadness and loss. Similar to 'His Visitor'.

Ghosts

I to a crumpled cabin came
Upon a hillside high,
And **with me** was a withered dame
As weariful as I.
5 "**It used to be our home**," said she;
"How I remember well!
Oh that our **happy hearth** should be
Today an **empty shell!**"

The door was flailing in the **storm**
10 That deafed us with its din;
The roof that kept us once so **warm**
Now let the snow-drift in.
The floor sagged to the sod below,
The walls caved crazily;
15 We only heard the **wind of woe**
Where once was **glow and glee.**

So there we stood **disconsolate**
Beneath the Midnight Dome,
And ancient **miner and his mate,**
20 Before our wedded home,
Where we had known such love and cheer**...**
I sighed, then soft she said:
"Do not regret — remember, dear,
        We, too, are dead."

Robert W. Service

deafed — deafened
sod — grass-covered earth
Midnight Dome — a mountain in Yukon Territory, Canada

Feelings — yearning for the past. Similar to 'His Visitor'.

Alliteration — emphasises past happiness and warmth.

Feelings — exclamation mark shows disbelief, as in 'His Visitor'.

Regular ABAB rhyme scheme contributes to the fast, upbeat pace.

Alliteration emphasises contrast between past and present.

Alliteration — shows bond with wife. Contrasts with loneliness in 'His Visitor'.

Ellipsis — suggests speaker is thinking wistfully of the past.

Poem 1: darker and more melancholy

Poem 1: 3-syllable lines heighten sadness
Poem 2: metre and rhyme lighten mood

5) Conclusion

4) Form

Melancholy tone and longing for past in both poems

1) Intro

Poem 1: His Visitor
Poem 2: Ghosts

2) Voice

3) Language

First person

Poem 1: alone, lonely
Poem 2: with wife, not lonely

Poem 1: "cosy nook" vs. "roomy silence"
Poem 2: "happy hearth" vs. "empty shell"

Past happiness vs. present sorrow

Worked Exam-Style Question

'His Visitor' and 'Ghosts' are both melancholy poems in which a ghostly narrator returns to their former home and is distressed to find that it has changed dramatically. Although the poems convey similar feelings about visiting a former home, the poets <u>use narrative voice, language and form in different ways to put these feelings across</u>.

Show that you've <u>understood</u> the question.

Both poems use a first-person narrator. This makes the narrators' feelings seem more real and immediate, and <u>encourages the reader to empathise with them</u>. In 'His Visitor', the narrator's isolation is conveyed by her repeated use of the first-person singular pronoun "I", which emphasises her loneliness as she revisits the once-familiar house that's now filled with "<u>strangers</u>". In 'Ghosts', however, the narrator is accompanied by his wife. The collective pronouns "we" and "us" highlight their close connection and contrast the loneliness of the narrator in 'His Visitor'.

Explain how the <u>techniques</u> in the poems affect the <u>reader</u>.

Embed <u>short quotes</u> into your writing.

<u>Both poets use language to emphasise the contrast</u> between past happiness and present sorrow. In 'His Visitor', <u>the "cosy nook" that symbolises the warmth and comfort the house once offered</u> is replaced with the afterlife's "roomy silence", and the "happy hearth" in 'Ghosts' contrasts with the now "empty shell" of the cabin. This highlights the narrators' yearning for the past, something that is emphasised by the repeated use of phrases associated with the past, <u>such as "As before" in 'His Visitor' and "used to be" in 'Ghosts'</u>, suggesting that both narrators are fixated on the way things were.

Introduce your paragraphs with a <u>comparison</u>.

Show that you understand the <u>imagery</u> in the poems.

Use <u>quotes</u> to support your <u>argument</u>.

The form of 'His Visitor' helps to convey the narrator's feelings. The three-syllable lines that end each stanza slow the poem's pace and give it an irregular rhythm, with each stanza trailing off wistfully. <u>This creates a powerful sense of sadness and melancholy.</u> In contrast, the regular metre and simple ABAB rhyme scheme of 'Ghosts' give the poem a faster pace and a driving, upbeat rhythm which lightens the mood and makes the poem seem <u>less bleak and melancholy than 'His Visitor'</u>.

Write about how <u>form</u> conveys meaning.

Remember to <u>compare</u> the two poems.

'His Visitor' and 'Ghosts' both use language to convey similar feelings of sadness, loss and longing for the past, and regret at the changes to their former homes. However, differences in the poets' use of narrative voice and form mean that, overall, the tone of 'His Visitor' is darker and more melancholy than that of 'Ghosts'.

Summarise the <u>similarities</u> and <u>differences</u> in your conclusion.

Warm-Up Questions

Before you answer the questions at the bottom of the page, read the poem all the way through and annotate anything you think is important. Once you've got an idea of what the poem's about, the techniques the poet uses and why she uses them, you'll be ready to answer the questions.

Warm-Up Questions

Spring in War-Time

Now the sprinkled blackthorn snow
Lies along the lovers' lane
Where last year we used to go—
Where we shall not go again.

5   In the hedge the buds are new,
By our wood the violets peer—
Just like last year's violets, too,
But they have no scent this year.

Every bird has heart to sing
10 Of its nest, warmed by its breast;
We had heart to sing last spring,
But we never built our nest.

Presently red roses blown
Will make all the garden gay...
15 Not yet have the daisies grown
On your clay.

Edith Nesbit

blackthorn — a bush with white flowers in spring

1) Write down what you think the poem is about, in just one sentence.

2) What do you think the narrator means by "we never built our nest" in the 3rd stanza?

3) How does the poet create a contrast between the signs of spring and the narrator's feelings in the poem?

4) What is the rhyme scheme of this poem and why do you think that the poet chose it?

5) The last line of the poem has a different rhythm. Why do you think that the poet has done this?

Exam-Style Questions

On the next two pages are questions about two poems that you probably won't have read before. They'll test your ability to analyse and compare unseen poetry, just like you'll have to do in the exam.

Q1 a) Read the poem below.

How does the poet present ideas about what it can feel like to be left alone?

At Sea

With nothing to do now he's gone,
she dusts the house,
sweeps the bleached verandah clear of sand.
The broom leaves a trail of grit on the step,
5   a sprinkling under the hook where it hangs.

A coat for a pillow,
she sleeps downstairs,
dreams the loathed ocean is coming for her,
climbing the cliffs,
10   creeping in through the door.

She wakes to the screaming gulls,
his shirts on the line
and the high tide's breakers'
chill in her arms.

Jennifer Copley

Exam-Style Questions

Q1 b) Both 'At Sea' and 'The Sands of Dee' describe the power of the sea.
What are the similarities and differences between how the poems present the sea?

The Sands of Dee

'O Mary, go and call the cattle home,
And call the cattle home,
And call the cattle home
Across the sands of Dee;'
5   The western wind was wild and dank with foam,
And all alone went she.

The western tide crept up along the sand,
And o'er and o'er the sand,
And round and round the sand,
10   As far as eye could see.
The rolling mist came down and hid the land:
And never home came she.

'Oh! is it weed, or fish, or floating hair—
A tress of golden hair,
15   A drowned maiden's hair
Above the nets at sea?
Was never salmon yet that shone so fair
Among the stakes on Dee.'

They rowed her in across the rolling foam,
20   The cruel, crawling foam,
The cruel, hungry foam,
To her grave beside the sea:
But still the boatmen hear her call the cattle home,
Across the sands of Dee.

Charles Kingsley

Sands of Dee — a sandy bay in North Wales
dank — damp and unpleasant
o'er — over
tress — a piece of hair or a plait

Here are some <u>practice papers</u> to test how well-prepared you are for your GCSE English Literature exams.

- There are <u>two</u> practice papers in this section:
  Paper 1: Shakespeare and the 19th-Century Novel   (pages 85-98)
  Paper 2: Modern Texts and Poetry   (pages 99-108)

- Before you start each exam, read through all the <u>instructions</u> and <u>information</u> on the front.

- You'll need some paper to write your answers on.

- When you've finished, have a look at the answers starting on page 119 — they'll give you some ideas
  of the kind of things you should have included in your answers.

- <u>Don't</u> try to do both of the exams in one sitting.

General Certificate of Secondary Education

GCSE
English Literature

Surname	
Other names	
Candidate signature	

Centre name					
Centre number					
Candidate number					

Paper 1:
Shakespeare and the
19th-Century Novel

Time allowed: 1 hour 45 minutes

Instructions to candidates
- You should answer **one** question from **Section A** (p.86-91)
  and **one** question from **Section B** (p.92-98).
- Write your answers in **black** ink or ball-point pen.
- Write your name and other details in the boxes above.

Information for candidates
- The marks available are given in brackets at the end of each question.
- There are 64 marks available for this exam paper.
- There are 34 marks available for Section A. This includes 30 marks for answering the question, plus
  4 marks for accuracy in spelling, punctuation and the use of vocabulary and sentence structures.
- There are 30 marks available for Section B.

Section A: Shakespeare

Answer **one** question from this section.

Macbeth

1   Read the extract below, then answer the question.

Using this extract as a starting point, write about how Shakespeare explores masculinity in *Macbeth*.
Write about:

* the ways that Shakespeare presents masculinity in this extract
* the ways that Shakespeare presents masculinity in the play as a whole.

(30 marks)
(+4 marks for spelling, punctuation and the
use of vocabulary and sentence structures)

From Act 1, Scene 7. *At this point in the play, Lady Macbeth is chastising Macbeth for his unwillingness to kill Duncan.*

Lady Macbeth:		Art thou afeard
	To be the same in thine own act and valour	
	As thou art in desire? Wouldst thou have that	
	Which thou esteem'st the ornament of life,	
5	And live a coward in thine own esteem,	
	Letting 'I dare not' wait upon 'I would,'	
	Like the poor cat i' the adage?	
Macbeth:	Prithee, peace:	
	I dare do all that may become a man;	
10	Who dares do more is none.	
Lady Macbeth:	What beast was't, then,	
	That made you break this enterprise to me?	
	When you durst do it, then you were a man;	
	And, to be more than what you were, you would	
15	Be so much more the man. Nor time nor place	
	Did then adhere, and yet you would make both:	
	They have made themselves, and that their fitness now	
	Does unmake you. I have given suck, and know	
	How tender 'tis to love the babe that milks me:	
20	I would, while it was smiling in my face,	
	Have pluck'd my nipple from his boneless gums,	
	And dash'd the brains out, had I so sworn as you	
	Have done to this.	

Romeo and Juliet

2 Read the extract below, then answer the question.

Using this extract as a starting point, write about how Shakespeare presents Romeo as a romantic lover in *Romeo and Juliet*.

Write about:

- the ways that Shakespeare presents Romeo in this speech
- the ways that Shakespeare presents Romeo in the play as a whole.

(30 marks)
*(+4 marks for spelling, punctuation and the
use of vocabulary and sentence structures)*

From Act 2, Scene 2. *At this point in the play, Romeo has gone
to see Juliet at her house and is watching her at her window.*

                 [*enter Juliet above*]

Romeo: But soft, what light through yonder window breaks?

                It is the east and Juliet is the sun!

                Arise fair sun and kill the envious moon

                Who is already sick and pale with grief

5   That thou her maid art far more fair than she.

                Be not her maid since she is envious,

                Her vestal livery is but sick and green

                And none but fools do wear it. Cast it off.

                It is my lady, O it is my love!

10   O that she knew she were!

                She speaks, yet she says nothing. What of that?

                Her eye discourses, I will answer it.

                I am too bold. 'Tis not to me she speaks.

                Two of the fairest stars in all the heaven,

15   Having some business, do entreat her eyes

                To twinkle in their spheres till they return.

                What if her eyes were there, they in her head?

                The brightness of her cheek would shame those stars

                As daylight doth a lamp. Her eyes in heaven

20   Would through the airy region stream so bright

                That birds would sing and think it were not night

                See how she leans her cheek upon her hand.

                O that I were a glove upon that hand,

                That I might touch that cheek.

The Tempest

3 Read the extract below, then answer the question.

Using this extract as a starting point, explore how far Shakespeare
presents Caliban as deserving of sympathy in *The Tempest*.
Write about:

- the ways that Shakespeare presents Caliban in this extract
- the ways that Shakespeare presents Caliban in the play as a whole.

(30 marks)
(+4 marks for spelling, punctuation and the
use of vocabulary and sentence structures)

From Act 1, Scene 2. *In this passage, Prospero and Miranda have
gone to visit Caliban, Prospero's slave.*

Caliban:	I must eat my dinner.
	This island's mine, by Sycorax my mother,
	Which thou tak'st from me. When thou cam'st first,
	Thou strok'st me and made much of me, wouldst give me
5	Water with berries in't, and teach me how
	To name the bigger light, and how the less,
	That burn by day and night, and then I loved thee,
	And showed thee all the qualities o' th' isle,
	The fresh springs, brine-pits, barren place and fertile.
10	Cursed be I that did so! All the charms
	Of Sycorax, toads, beetles, bats, light on you!
	For I am all the subjects that you have,
	Which first was mine own king, and here you sty me
	In this hard rock, whiles you do keep from me
15	The rest o' th' island.
Prospero:	Thou most lying slave,
	Whom stripes may move, not kindness! I have used thee,
	Filth as thou art, with human care, and lodged thee
	In mine own cell, till thou didst seek to violate
	The honour of my child.

The Merchant of Venice

4 Read the extract below, then answer the question.

Using this extract as a starting point, explore how Shakespeare presents ideas of justice and mercy in *The Merchant of Venice*.

Write about:

- the ways that Shakespeare presents justice and mercy in this speech
- the ways that Shakespeare presents justice and mercy in the play as a whole.

(30 marks)
(+4 marks for spelling, punctuation and the
use of vocabulary and sentence structures)

From Act 4, Scene 1. *At this point in the play, Portia, disguised as a lawyer, is presiding over Antonio's trial.*

Portia: The quality of mercy is not strained;
It droppeth as the gentle rain from heaven
Upon the place beneath. It is twice blest;
It blesseth him that gives and him that takes.
5 'Tis mightiest in the mightiest; it becomes
The thronèd monarch better than his crown.
His sceptre shows the force of temporal power,
The attribute to awe and majesty,
Wherein doth sit the dread and fear of kings;
10 But mercy is above this sceptred sway;
It is enthronèd in the hearts of kings;
It is an attribute to God himself,
And earthly power doth then show likest God's
When mercy seasons justice. Therefore, Jew,
15 Though justice be thy plea, consider this:
That, in the course of justice, none of us
Should see salvation: we do pray for mercy,
And that same prayer doth teach us all to render
The deeds of mercy. I have spoke thus much
20 To mitigate the justice of thy plea,
Which if thou follow, this strict court of Venice
Must needs give sentence 'gainst the merchant there.

Much Ado About Nothing

5 Read the extract below, then answer the question.

Using this extract as a starting point, explore how Shakespeare presents the changing relationship between Benedick and Beatrice in *Much Ado About Nothing*.

Write about:

- the ways that Shakespeare presents Benedick and Beatrice's relationship in this conversation
- the ways that Shakespeare presents Benedick and Beatrice's relationship in the play as a whole.

(30 marks)
(+4 marks for spelling, punctuation and the use of vocabulary and sentence structures)

From Act 1, Scene 1. *In this passage, Don Pedro, Benedick and Beatrice are talking.*

Don Pedro: ... Be happy, lady, for you are like an honourable father.
Benedick: If Signior Leonato be her father, she would not have his head
on her shoulders for all Messina, as like him as she is.
Beatrice: I wonder that you will still be talking, Signior Benedick: nobody marks you.
Benedick: What, my dear Lady Disdain! Are you yet living?
Beatrice: Is it possible disdain should die, while she hath such meet
food to feed it as Signior Benedick? Courtesy itself must
convert to disdain, if you come in her presence.
Benedick: Then is courtesy a turncoat. But it is certain I am loved of all ladies, only
you excepted; and I would I could find in my heart that I had not a
hard heart, for truly I love none.
Beatrice: A dear happiness to women, they would else have been troubled with a
pernicious suitor. I thank God and my cold blood, I am of your humour for
that; I had rather hear my dog bark at a crow than a man swear he loves me.
Benedick: God keep your ladyship still in that mind, so some gentleman or
other shall scape a predestinate scratched face.
Beatrice: Scratching could not make it worse, and 'twere such a face as yours were.
Benedick: Well, you are a rare parrot-teacher.
Beatrice: A bird of my tongue is better than a beast of yours.
Benedick: I would my horse had the speed of your tongue, and so good a continuer.
But keep your way, a God's name, I have done.
Beatrice: You always end with a jade's trick, I know you of old.

Julius Caesar

6 Read the extract below, then answer the question.

Using this extract as a starting point, examine the ways Shakespeare
presents Caesar as an arrogant character in *Julius Caesar*.

Write about:

- the ways that Shakespeare presents Caesar in this extract
- the ways that Shakespeare presents Caesar in the play as a whole.

(30 marks)
*(+4 marks for spelling, punctuation and the
use of vocabulary and sentence structures)*

From Act 3, Scene 1. *At this point in the play, Caesar has just been
asked to pardon Metellus Cimber's brother, Publius Cimber.*

Caesar:		I could be well moved, if I were as you;
		If I could pray to move, prayers would move me;
		But I am constant as the northern star,
		Of whose true-fix'd and resting quality
5		There is no fellow in the firmament.
		The skies are painted with unnumber'd sparks,
		They are all fire and every one doth shine,
		But there's but one in all doth hold his place:
		So in the world; 'tis furnish'd well with men,
10		And men are flesh and blood, and apprehensive;
		Yet in the number I do know but one
		That unassailable holds on his rank,
		Unshaked of motion; and that I am he,
		Let me a little show it, even in this:
15		That I was constant Cimber should be banish'd,
		And constant do remain to keep him so.
	Cinna:	O Caesar —
	Caesar:	Hence! wilt thou lift up Olympus?
	Decius:	Great Caesar —
20	**Caesar:**	Doth not Brutus bootless kneel?
	Casca:	Speak, hands for me!
		[*CASCA first, then the other Conspirators and BRUTUS stab CAESAR*]
	Caesar:	Et tu, Brute! Then fall, Caesar.
		[*Dies*]

Section B: The 19th-Century Novel

Answer **one** question from this section.

Robert Louis Stevenson: *The Strange Case of Dr Jekyll and Mr Hyde*

7   Read the extract below from 'Henry Jekyll's Full Statement of the Case', then answer the question.

Using this extract as a starting point, write about how Stevenson explores morality in the novel.

(30 marks)

In this extract, Jekyll questions whether he is to blame for the crimes that Hyde has committed.

I was the first that could thus plod in the public eye with a load of genial respectability, and in a moment, like a schoolboy, strip off these lendings and spring headlong into the sea of liberty. But for me, in my impenetrable mantle, the safety was complete. Think of it — I did not even exist! Let me but escape into my laboratory door, give me but a second or two to mix
5   and swallow the draught that I had always standing ready; and whatever he had done, Edward Hyde would pass away like the stain of breath upon a mirror; and there in his stead, quietly at home, trimming the midnight lamp in his study, a man who could afford to laugh at suspicion, would be Henry Jekyll.

The pleasures which I made haste to seek in my disguise were, as I have said, undignified;
10   I would scarce use a harder term. But in the hands of Edward Hyde, they soon began to turn towards the monstrous. When I would come back from these excursions, I was often plunged into a kind of wonder at my vicarious depravity. This familiar that I called out of my own soul, and sent forth alone to do his good pleasure, was a being inherently malign and villainous; his every act and thought centred on self; drinking pleasure with bestial avidity from any degree of
15   torture to another; relentless like a man of stone. Henry Jekyll stood at times aghast before the acts of Edward Hyde; but the situation was apart from ordinary laws, and insidiously relaxed the grasp of conscience. It was Hyde, after all, and Hyde alone, that was guilty. Jekyll was no worse; he woke again to his good qualities seemingly unimpaired; he would even make haste, where it was possible, to undo the evil done by Hyde. And thus his conscience slumbered.

Charles Dickens: *A Christmas Carol*

8 Read the extract below from Chapter 3, then answer the question.

Using this extract as a starting point, write about how poverty is presented in *A Christmas Carol*.

(30 marks)

In this extract, the Ghost of Christmas Present reveals Ignorance and Want to Scrooge.

From the foldings of its robe, it brought two children; wretched, abject, frightful, hideous, miserable. They knelt down at its feet, and clung upon the outside of its garment.
"Oh, Man! look here. Look, look, down here!" exclaimed the Ghost.
They were a boy and girl. Yellow, meagre, ragged, scowling, wolfish; but prostrate, too, in
5   their humility. Where graceful youth should have filled their features out, and touched them with its freshest tints, a stale and shrivelled hand, like that of age, had pinched, and twisted them, and pulled them into shreds. Where angels might have sat enthroned, devils lurked, and glared out menacing. No change, no degradation, no perversion of humanity, in any grade, through all the mysteries of wonderful creation, has monsters half so horrible and dread.
10   Scrooge started back, appalled. Having them shown to him in this way, he tried to say they were fine children, but the words choked themselves, rather than be parties to a lie of such enormous magnitude.
"Spirit! are they yours?" Scrooge could say no more.
"They are Man's," said the Spirit, looking down upon them. "And they cling to me, appealing
15   from their fathers. This boy is Ignorance. This girl is Want. Beware them both, and all of their degree, but most of all beware this boy, for on his brow I see that written which is Doom, unless the writing be erased. Deny it!" cried the Spirit, stretching out its hand towards the city. "Slander those who tell it ye! Admit it for your factious purposes, and make it worse. And bide the end!"
"Have they no refuge or resource?" cried Scrooge.
20   "Are there no prisons?" said the Spirit, turning on him for the last time with his own words. "Are there no workhouses?"
The bell struck twelve.

94

Charles Dickens: *Great Expectations*

9 Read the extract below from Chapter 8, then answer the question.

Using this extract as a starting point, write about how Dickens presents Miss Havisham as a frightening character.

(30 marks)

In this extract, Pip meets Miss Havisham for the first time.

She was dressed in rich materials — satins, and lace, and silks — all of white. Her shoes were white. And she had a long white veil dependent from her hair, and she had bridal flowers in her hair, but her hair was white. Some bright jewels sparkled on her neck and on her hands, and some other jewels lay sparkling on the table. Dresses, less splendid than the

5   dress she wore, and half-packed trunks, were scattered about. She had not quite finished dressing, for she had but one shoe on — the other was on the table near her hand — her veil was but half arranged, her watch and chain were not put on, and some lace for her bosom lay with those trinkets, and with her handkerchief, and gloves, and some flowers, and a prayer-book, all confusedly heaped about the looking-glass.

10   It was not in the first moments that I saw all these things, though I saw more of them in the first moments than might be supposed. But, I saw that everything within my view which ought to be white, had been white long ago, and had lost its lustre, and was faded and yellow. I saw that the bride within the bridal dress had withered like the dress, and like the flowers, and had no brightness left but the brightness of her sunken eyes. I saw that the dress had been

15   put upon the rounded figure of a young woman, and that the figure upon which it now hung loose, had shrunk to skin and bone. Once, I had been taken to see some ghastly waxwork at the Fair, representing I know not what impossible personage lying in state. Once, I had been taken to one of our old marsh churches to see a skeleton in the ashes of a rich dress, that had been dug out of a vault under the church pavement. Now, waxwork and skeleton seemed to

20   have dark eyes that moved and looked at me. I should have cried out, if I could.

Charlotte Brontë: *Jane Eyre*

10 Read the extract below from Chapter 37 (Volume 3, Chapter 11), then answer the question.

Using this extract as a starting point, write about Mr Rochester and the way he changes throughout the novel.

(30 marks)

In this extract, Jane has returned to find Rochester at Ferndean.

"Jane! you think me, I daresay, an irreligious dog: but my heart swells with gratitude to the beneficent God of this earth just now. He sees not as man sees, but far clearer: judges not as man judges, but far more wisely. I did wrong: I would have sullied my innocent flower — breathed guilt on its purity: the Omnipotent snatched it from me. I, in my stiff-necked rebellion, almost
5 cursed the dispensation: instead of bending to the decree, I defied it. Divine justice pursued its course; disasters came thick on me: I was forced to pass through the valley of the shadow of death. His chastisements are mighty; and one smote me which has humbled me for ever. You know I was proud of my strength: but what is it now, when I must give it over to foreign guidance, as a child does its weakness? Of late, Jane — only — only of late — I began to see
10 and acknowledge the hand of God in my doom. I began to experience remorse, repentance, the wish for reconcilement to my Maker. I began sometimes to pray: very brief prayers they were, but very sincere.

"Some days since: nay, I can number them — four; it was last Monday night, a singular mood came over me: one in which grief replaced frenzy — sorrow, sullenness. I had long had the
15 impression that since I could nowhere find you, you must be dead. Late that night — perhaps it might be between eleven and twelve o'clock — ere I retired to my dreary rest, I supplicated God, that, if it seemed good to Him, I might soon be taken from this life, and admitted to that world to come, where there was still hope of rejoining Jane.

"I was in my own room, and sitting by the window, which was open: it soothed me to feel
20 the balmy night-air; though I could see no stars, and only by a vague, luminous haze, knew the presence of a moon. I longed for thee, Janet! Oh, I longed for thee both with soul and flesh! I asked of God, at once in anguish and humility, if I had not been long enough desolate, afflicted, tormented; and might not soon taste bliss and peace once more. That I merited all I endured, I acknowledged — that I could scarcely endure more, I pleaded; and the alpha and omega of my
25 heart's wishes broke involuntarily from my lips in the words, 'Jane! Jane! Jane!'"

Mary Shelley: *Frankenstein*

11 Read the extract below from Chapter 24 (Volume 3, Chapter 7), then answer the question.

Using this extract as a starting point, write about how Shelley explores revenge in *Frankenstein*.

(30 marks)

In this extract, Frankenstein describes his desire for revenge on the monster.

... How I have lived I hardly know; many times have I stretched my failing limbs upon the sandy plain and prayed for death. But revenge kept me alive; I dared not die and leave my adversary in being.

5   When I quitted Geneva my first labour was to gain some clue by which I might trace the steps of my fiendish enemy. But my plan was unsettled; and I wandered many hours round the confines of the town, uncertain what path I should pursue. As night approached, I found myself at the entrance of the cemetery where William, Elizabeth, and my father reposed. I entered it and approached the tomb which marked their graves. Everything was silent, except the leaves of the trees, which were gently agitated by the wind; the night was nearly dark; and the scene would have
10 been solemn and affecting even to an uninterested observer. The spirits of the departed seemed to flit around and to cast a shadow, which was felt but not seen, around the head of the mourner.

The deep grief which this scene had at first excited quickly gave way to rage and despair. They were dead, and I lived; their murderer also lived, and to destroy him I must drag out my weary existence. I knelt on the grass and kissed the earth, and with quivering lips exclaimed, "By the
15 sacred earth on which I kneel, by the shades that wander near me, by the deep and eternal grief that I feel, I swear; and by thee, O Night, and the spirits that preside over thee, to pursue the daemon who caused this misery, until he or I shall perish in mortal conflict. For this purpose I will preserve my life: to execute this dear revenge will I again behold the sun and tread the green herbage of earth, which otherwise should vanish from my eyes for ever. And I call on you, spirits of the dead;
20 and on you, wandering ministers of vengeance, to aid and conduct me in my work. Let the cursed and hellish monster drink deep of agony; let him feel the despair that now torments me."

Jane Austen: *Pride and Prejudice*

12 Read the extract below from Chapter 1, then answer the question.

Using this extract as a starting point, explore how Austen portrays the relationship between Mr and Mrs Bennet.

(30 marks)

In this extract, Mrs Bennet is trying to persuade Mr Bennet to visit Mr Bingley, who has just moved in to nearby Netherfield Park.

"I see no occasion for that. You and the girls may go, or you may send them by themselves, which perhaps will be still better, for as you are as handsome as any of them, Mr. Bingley may like you the best of the party."

"My dear, you flatter me. I certainly have had my share of beauty, but I do not pretend to be
5   anything extraordinary now. When a woman has five grown-up daughters, she ought to give over thinking of her own beauty."

"In such cases, a woman has not often much beauty to think of."

"But, my dear, you must indeed go and see Mr. Bingley when he comes into the neighbourhood."

"It is more than I engage for, I assure you."
10   "But consider your daughters. Only think what an establishment it would be for one of them. Sir William and Lady Lucas are determined to go, merely on that account, for in general, you know, they visit no newcomers. Indeed you must go, for it will be impossible for us to visit him if you do not."

"You are over-scrupulous, surely. I dare say Mr. Bingley will be very glad to see you; and I will
15   send a few lines by you to assure him of my hearty consent to his marrying whichever he chooses of the girls; though I must throw in a good word for my little Lizzy."

"I desire you will do no such thing. Lizzy is not a bit better than the others; and I am sure she is not half so handsome as Jane, nor half so good-humoured as Lydia. But you are always giving her the preference."
20   "They have none of them much to recommend them," replied he; "they are all silly and ignorant like other girls; but Lizzy has something more of quickness than her sisters."

"Mr. Bennet, how can you abuse your own children in such a way? You take delight in vexing me. You have no compassion for my poor nerves."

"You mistake me, my dear. I have a high respect for your nerves. They are my old friends. I
25   have heard you mention them with consideration these last twenty years at least."

Sir Arthur Conan Doyle: *The Sign of Four*

13 Read the extract below from Chapter 11, then answer the question.

Using this extract as a starting point, explore how Conan Doyle presents the loving relationship between John Watson and Mary Morstan.

(30 marks)

In this extract, Watson and Mary reveal the contents of the treasure-box.

"What a pretty box!" she said, stooping over it. "This is Indian work, I suppose?"

"Yes; it is Benares metal-work."

"And so heavy!" she exclaimed, trying to raise it. "The box alone must be of some value. Where is the key?"

5 "Small threw it into the Thames," I answered. "I must borrow Mrs. Forrester's poker." There was in the front a thick and broad hasp, wrought in the image of a sitting Buddha. Under this I thrust the end of the poker and twisted it outward as a lever. The hasp sprang open with a loud snap. With trembling fingers I flung back the lid. We both stood gazing in astonishment. The box was empty!

10 No wonder that it was heavy. The iron-work was two-thirds of an inch thick all round. It was massive, well made, and solid, like a chest constructed to carry things of great price, but not one shred or crumb of metal or jewellery lay within it. It was absolutely and completely empty.

"The treasure is lost," said Miss Morstan, calmly.

As I listened to the words and realized what they meant, a great shadow seemed to pass from
15 my soul. I did not know how this Agra treasure had weighed me down, until now that it was finally removed. It was selfish, no doubt, disloyal, wrong, but I could realize nothing save that the golden barrier was gone from between us. "Thank God!" I ejaculated from my very heart.

She looked at me with a quick, questioning smile. "Why do you say that?" she asked.

"Because you are within my reach again," I said, taking her hand. She did not withdraw it.
20 "Because I love you, Mary, as truly as ever a man loved a woman. Because this treasure, these riches, sealed my lips. Now that they are gone I can tell you how I love you. That is why I said, 'Thank God.'"

"Then I say, 'Thank God,' too," she whispered, as I drew her to my side. Whoever had lost a treasure, I knew that night that I had gained one.

General Certificate of Secondary Education

GCSE English Literature

| Surname |
| Other names |
| Candidate signature |

Paper 2: Modern Texts and Poetry

| Centre name |
| Centre number | | | | | |
| Candidate number | | | | | |

Time allowed: 2 hours 15 minutes

Instructions to candidates
- You should answer **one** question from **Section A** (p.100-103), **one** question from **Section B** (p.104-106) and **both** questions in **Section C** (p.107-108).
- Write your answers in **black** ink or ball-point pen.
- Write your name and other details in the boxes above.

Information for candidates
- The marks available are given in brackets at the end of each question.
- There are 96 marks available for this exam paper.
- There are 34 marks available for Section A. This includes 30 marks for answering the question, plus 4 marks for accuracy in spelling, punctuation and the use of vocabulary and sentence structures.
- There are 30 marks available for Section B and 32 marks available for Section C.

Section A: Modern Prose or Drama

Answer **one** question from this section.

JB Priestley: *An Inspector Calls*

1   Write about how Priestley presents Arthur Birling as a selfish character in *An Inspector Calls*.
    Write about:
    • the techniques that Priestley uses to present Arthur Birling
    • how Priestley uses the character to explore ideas about selfishness.

(30 marks)
(+4 marks for spelling, punctuation and grammar)

Willy Russell: *Blood Brothers*

2   Write about the character of Mickey and the way he changes during the course of *Blood Brothers*.
    Write about:
    • how Mickey changes as the play develops
    • the techniques that Russell uses to present Mickey.

(30 marks)
(+4 marks for spelling, punctuation and grammar)

Alan Bennett: *The History Boys*

3   Write about education and the way it is presented in *The History Boys*.
    Write about:
    • ideas about education in the play
    • how these ideas are presented.

(30 marks)
(+4 marks for spelling, punctuation and grammar)

Dennis Kelly: *DNA*

4   Write about how Kelly uses the character of Leah to explore ideas about morality in *DNA*.
     Write about:
     •   how Kelly presents the character of Leah
     •   how Kelly uses the character to explore ideas about morality.

(30 marks)
(+4 marks for spelling, punctuation and grammar)

Simon Stephens: *The Curious Incident of the Dog in the Night-Time*

5   Write about honesty and dishonesty and the way they are presented in
     The Curious Incident of the Dog in the Night-Time.
     Write about:
     •   ideas about honesty and dishonesty in the play
     •   how these ideas are presented.

(30 marks)
(+4 marks for spelling, punctuation and grammar)

Shelagh Delaney: *A Taste of Honey*

6   Write about how Delaney uses the character of Jo to explore the lives of women in *A Taste of Honey*.
     Write about:
     •   how Delaney presents the character of Jo
     •   how Delaney uses the character to explore the lives of women.

(30 marks)
(+4 marks for spelling, punctuation and grammar)

William Golding: *Lord of the Flies*

7 Write about fear and the way it is presented in *Lord of the Flies*.
   Write about:
   • ideas about fear in the novel
   • how these ideas are presented.

(30 marks)
(+4 marks for spelling, punctuation and grammar)

AQA Anthology: *Telling Tales*

8 Write about death and the way it is presented in 'Chemistry' and one other story from *Telling Tales*.
   Write about:
   • ideas about death in the two stories
   • how these ideas are presented by each writer.

(30 marks)
(+4 marks for spelling, punctuation and grammar)

George Orwell: *Animal Farm*

9 Write about education and learning and the way they are presented in *Animal Farm*.
   Write about:
   • ideas about education and learning in the novel
   • how these ideas are presented.

(30 marks)
(+4 marks for spelling, punctuation and grammar)

Kazuo Ishiguro: *Never Let Me Go*

10 Write about memory and the way it is presented in *Never Let Me Go*.

Write about:

- ideas about memory in the novel
- how these ideas are presented.

(30 marks)
(+4 marks for spelling, punctuation and grammar)

Meera Syal: *Anita and Me*

11 Write about friendship and the way it is presented in *Anita and Me*.

Write about:

- ideas about friendship in the novel
- how these ideas are presented.

(30 marks)
(+4 marks for spelling, punctuation and grammar)

Stephen Kelman: *Pigeon English*

12 Write about violence and the way it is presented in *Pigeon English*.

Write about:

- ideas about violence in the novel
- how these ideas are presented.

(30 marks)
(+4 marks for spelling, punctuation and grammar)

104

Section B: Poetry

Answer **one** question from this section — **either** 'Love and Relationships' **or** 'Power and Conflict'.

Love and Relationships

> The poems in this cluster are:
>
> - *When We Two Parted* by Lord Byron
> - *Love's Philosophy* by Percy Bysshe Shelley
> - *Porphyria's Lover* by Robert Browning
> - *Sonnet 29* by Elizabeth Barrett Browning
> - *Neutral Tones* by Thomas Hardy
> - *The Farmer's Bride* by Charlotte Mew
> - *Walking Away* by C. Day Lewis
> - *Letters From Yorkshire* by Maura Dooley
> - *Eden Rock* by Charles Causley
> - *Follower* by Seamus Heaney
> - *Mother, any distance* by Simon Armitage
> - *Before You Were Mine* by Carol Ann Duffy
> - *Winter Swans* by Owen Sheers
> - *Singh Song!* by Daljit Nagra
> - *Climbing My Grandfather* by Andrew Waterhouse

13 Compare how the breakdown of a relationship is presented in Thomas Hardy's 'Neutral Tones' and one other poem you have studied.

(30 marks)

Neutral Tones

We stood by a pond that winter day,
And the sun was white, as though chidden of God,
And a few leaves lay on the starving sod;
    — They had fallen from an ash, and were grey.

5   Your eyes on me were as eyes that rove
Over tedious riddles of years ago;
And some words played between us to and fro
    On which lost the more by our love.

The smile on your mouth was the deadest thing
10   Alive enough to have strength to die;
And a grin of bitterness swept thereby
    Like an ominous bird a-wing...

Since then, keen lessons that love deceives,
And wrings with wrong, have shaped to me
15   Your face, and the God-curst sun, and a tree,
    And a pond edged with greyish leaves.

Thomas Hardy

Practice Papers — Paper 2

Power and Conflict

The poems in this cluster are:

- *Ozymandias* by Percy Bysshe Shelley
- *London* by William Blake
- *The Prelude: Stealing the Boat* by William Wordsworth
- *My Last Duchess* by Robert Browning
- *The Charge of the Light Brigade* by Alfred Tennyson
- *Exposure* by Wilfred Owen
- *Storm on the Island* by Seamus Heaney
- *Bayonet Charge* by Ted Hughes
- *Remains* by Simon Armitage
- *Poppies* by Jane Weir
- *War Photographer* by Carol Ann Duffy
- *Tissue* by Imtiaz Dharker
- *The Emigrée* by Carol Rumens
- *Kamikaze* by Beatrice Garland
- *Checking Out Me History* by John Agard

14 Compare how nature is presented in William Wordsworth's
'The Prelude: Stealing the Boat' and one other poem you have studied.

(30 marks)

The Prelude: Stealing the Boat

One summer evening (led by her) I found
A little boat tied to a willow tree
Within a rocky cave, its usual home.
Straight I unloosed her chain, and stepping in
5   Pushed from the shore. It was an act of stealth
And troubled pleasure, nor without the voice
Of mountain-echoes did my boat move on;
Leaving behind her still, on either side,
Small circles glittering idly in the moon,
10   Until they melted all into one track
Of sparkling light. But now, like one who rows,
Proud of his skill, to reach a chosen point
With an unswerving line, I fixed my view
Upon the summit of a craggy ridge,
15   The horizon's utmost boundary; far above
Was nothing but the stars and the grey sky.

Poem continues on the next page

Poem continued from the previous page

She was an elfin pinnace; lustily
I dipped my oars into the silent lake,
And, as I rose upon the stroke, my boat
20   Went heaving through the water like a swan;
When, from behind that craggy steep till then
The horizon's bound, a huge peak, black and huge,
As if with voluntary power instinct,
Upreared its head. I struck and struck again,
25   And growing still in stature the grim shape
Towered up between me and the stars, and still,
For so it seemed, with purpose of its own
And measured motion like a living thing,
Strode after me. With trembling oars I turned,
30   And through the silent water stole my way
Back to the covert of the willow tree;
There in her mooring-place I left my bark, –
And through the meadows homeward went, in grave
And serious mood; but after I had seen
35   That spectacle, for many days, my brain
Worked with a dim and undetermined sense
Of unknown modes of being; o'er my thoughts
There hung a darkness, call it solitude
Or blank desertion. No familiar shapes
40   Remained, no pleasant images of trees,
Of sea or sky, no colours of green fields;
But huge and mighty forms, that do not live
Like living men, moved slowly through the mind
By day, and were a trouble to my dreams.

William Wordsworth

Section C: Unseen Poetry

Answer **both** questions from this section.

For a Five-Year-Old

A snail is climbing up the window-sill
into your room, after a night of rain.
You call me in to see, and I explain
that it would be unkind to leave it there:
5   it might crawl to the floor; we must take care
that no one squashes it. You understand,
and carry it outside, with careful hand,
to eat a daffodil.

I see, then, that a kind of faith prevails:
10   your gentleness is moulded still by words
from me, who have trapped mice and shot wild birds,
from me, who drowned your kittens, who betrayed
your closest relatives, and who purveyed
the harshest kind of truth to many another.
15   But that is how things are: I am your mother,
and we are kind to snails.

Fleur Adcock

15a How does Adcock present the narrator's attitude to parenthood in 'For a Five-Year-Old'?

(24 marks)

The Beautiful Lie

He was about four, I think… it was so long ago.
In a garden; he'd done some damage
behind a bright screen of sweet-peas
– snapped a stalk, a stake, I don't recall,
5   but the grandmother came and saw, and asked him
"Did you do that?"

Now, if she'd said *why* did you do that,
he'd never have denied it. She showed him
he had a choice. I could see in his face
10   the new sense, the possible. That word and deed
need not match, that you could say the world
different, to suit you.

When he said "No", I swear it was as moving
as the first time a baby's fist clenches
15   on a finger, as momentous as the first
taste of fruit. I could feel his eyes looking
through a new window, at a world whose form
and colour weren't fixed

but fluid, that poured like a snake, trembled
20   around the edges like northern lights, shape-shifted
at the spell of a voice. I could sense him filling
like a glass, hear the unreal sea in his ears.
This is how to make songs, create men, paint pictures,
tell a story.

25   I think I made up the screen of sweet-peas.
Maybe they were beans, maybe there was no screen:
it just felt as if there should be, somehow.
And he was my – no, I don't need to tell that.
I know I made up the screen. And I recall very well
30   what he had done.

Sheenagh Pugh

15b In 'For a Five-Year-Old' and 'The Beautiful Lie', both poets write about relationships between adults and children. What are the similarities and differences in the way these poems present those relationships?

(8 marks)

Section Two — Prose and Drama

Pages 20-21 — Warm-Up Questions

1) a) characterisation
   b) theme
   c) mood/atmosphere

2) Answer depends on chosen text. Here are some points you could consider:
   * What did you think about the characters?
   * How did you feel at different points in the text?
   * Did you agree with the writer's message?

3) Answer depends on chosen text.

4) Answers should focus on what the character is like, how the writer presents them and how this makes you feel about them. Here are some points you could consider:
   * Actions: What does the character do in the text? How does he or she treat other people? How do their actions make you feel about them?
   * Structure: Does the character change over the course of the text? Do they learn anything?
   * Language: How is the character described? How does the character speak? Does this make them likeable or not to you?

5) Answer depends on chosen text.

6) Answers should focus on what atmosphere the writer creates, how they create it and the effect it has on the reader. Here are some points you could consider:
   * Structure: Does the writer reveal what's happening gradually or suddenly?
   * Language: What words does the writer use? How do they make you feel? Does the writer use any techniques to create or add to the atmosphere (e.g. imagery)?
   * Form: Are the sentences long or short? Do they vary in length? What effect does this have?

7) Answers should focus on what the structural feature is and the effect it creates. Here are some points you could consider:
   * What is the feature? Why do you think the writer chose to use it at this point in the story?
   * Does it add to your enjoyment of the text? If so, how?
   * How would the text be different if the writer had not used this feature or had used a different structure?

8) a) E.g. "The conch shell represents democracy — it enables the boys to impose a fair system on their meetings that allows them all a chance to put their views across."
   b) E.g. "The old chestnut tree symbolises Jane's relationship with Mr Rochester. Just as the tree is split in two by lightning, Jane and Mr Rochester are separated by the revelation that he is already married."
   c) E.g. "Driving is a symbol for freedom. The students have little control over their lives, but they believe that driving would give them some freedom and a sense of being able to escape from their lives."

9) a) Answer depends on chosen text.
   b) Answer depends on chosen text. Here are some points you could consider:
      * How does the writer describe the setting?
      * Does it seem like a generally pleasant time in which to live or not? Why or why not?
      * Do you think it's a realistic description of life during this time? Why or why not?
   c) Answer depends on chosen text. Here are some points you could consider:
      * Are men and women treated differently? Do they have different opportunities?
      * How does social class affect people's lives?
      * Are some characters treated differently on the basis of their race, beliefs or background?

10) Answer depends on chosen text. E.g. for 'A Christmas Carol', you could have picked out the following themes:
    * Social responsibility
      It is implied that Scrooge helping the Cratchits at the end of the novel saves Tiny Tim's life. This shows how important social responsibility is — it can save lives.
    * Redemption
      The contrast between Scrooge's behaviour at the beginning and at the end of the novel. This emphasises that anyone, even someone as miserly and mean as Scrooge, has the potential to be redeemed.
    * Family
      The Cratchits are "happy, grateful, pleased with one another, and contented with the time", despite their poverty. This shows that family can bring comfort and joy to life, regardless of the hardships that people have to endure.

11) Answer depends on chosen text. E.g.
    * You might write that the message of 'Macbeth' is: 'Ambition and lust for power can drive the humanity out of a person.'
    * You might write that the message of 'Pride and Prejudice' is: 'Don't judge people on first impressions or superficial qualities.'

12) Paragraph a) shows better use of quotations, because it uses short quotations that are embedded into the text.

Page 22 — Exam-Style Questions

1) For this question, you have to focus on a single scene from a Shakespeare text you're studying and then write about the rest of the play. Make sure you pick a scene that you think shows your chosen character in an interesting light, so you'll have plenty of things to write about. This answer is for the character of Beatrice in 'Much Ado About Nothing', starting with Act 2, Scene 1, but it's worth reading even if you're studying a different play. Here are some things you could mention:
   * Act 2, Scene 1 of 'Much Ado About Nothing' starts with Beatrice criticising Don John because he is "too like an image and says nothing". This shows her to be judgemental and somewhat cruel in her assessment of others.
   * Despite this, however, she appears to be well-liked. Rather than telling her off for her cruelty, Leonato just reminds her that she will never find a husband if she continues to be so "shrewd of tongue". This shows that he is more concerned about the consequences of her behaviour than how rude she is being, which implies that he cares about her future and wellbeing.
   * Beatrice's conversation with Leonato also highlights her wit. For example, she answers Leonato's hope that she will be "fitted with a husband" by arguing that "Adam's sons are my brethren, and truly I hold it a sin to match in my kindred." In this line, she plays on the biblical idea that all men are descended from Adam in order to emphasise her point. This shows her intelligence and ability to think quickly. Jokes about incest would have been considered shocking in Shakespeare's day, so this also shows the extent to which Beatrice flouts convention and ignores the rules of society.

- Beatrice shows that she is unafraid to speak directly when she asks Benedick to "Kill Claudio" in Act 4, Scene 1. Her blunt request seems shocking because it comes directly after several lines in which she and Benedick confess their love for each other. This contrast emphasises that she is willing to speak her mind and does not feel the need to be polite to Benedick. It also hints at her vulnerability: she is fearful of love, having been hurt before, and so needs proof of Benedick's commitment to her in order to trust him. This shows that her character is a mixture of toughness and vulnerability.

- Beatrice's anger towards Claudio shows that she can be very loyal. She states that Claudio has "slandered, scorned, dishonoured" Hero. The use of three strong verbs implies the strength of her feeling against him. Beatrice's loyalty to Hero — whose story she never doubts — softens her character and shows how, although she often speaks harshly, she shows loyalty to the people that she cares about.

2) For this question, you have to focus on a single passage from a prose text you're studying and then write about the rest of the book. You should focus on the ways that the author has created a feeling of tension or excitement. This answer is for tension in 'Frankenstein', starting with Chapter 23 (or Volume 3, Chapter 6), from "It was eight o'clock..." to "I rushed into the room.", but it's worth reading even if you're studying a different novel. Here are some things you could mention:

- Imagery is used to create tension in the passage, as Frankenstein awaits the monster's revenge. For example, Frankenstein's anxiety is reflected in the personification of the "restless waves" and the simile of the clouds, which move "swifter than the flight of the vulture". This constant movement creates a feeling of unease in the reader, increased by the presence of the "vulture", which is often seen as an omen of death.

- In the passage, Shelley uses the weather to reinforce this atmosphere of unease and build the sense of tension further. There is a "heavy storm of rain" and the moon's rays have been "dimmed". This creates an atmosphere of restlessness and threat, which echoes the turmoil and danger that Frankenstein faces. The wind has also risen with "great violence", which foreshadows the violence that the monster will presently unleash on Elizabeth.

- Shelley uses the structure of Frankenstein's narration in the novel to create tension. Frankenstein is writing with hindsight about things that have already happened to him, so he is able to make references to events that will occur later in the story. This includes explaining in Chapter 8 that his brother and servant were the "first hapless victims" of the monster, implying that there will be others. This makes the reader nervous about the fates of the other characters. He also says that the times during and just after his marriage to Elizabeth in Chapter 22 (Volume 3, Chapter 5) were "the last moments" of his life when he felt "happiness". This suggests that the events to come in the rest of the novel will be unhappy, creating anticipation about what will happen and increasing the sense of tension in the novel.

- The novel's settings, which include the Alps and the Arctic seas, are intimidating. In Chapter 9 (or Volume 2, Chapter 1), Frankenstein describes the "immense mountains and precipices that overhung" him in the Alps. The adjective "immense" indicates the huge size of the mountains, and the verb "overhung" suggests that they seemed threatening and powerful. The novel's extreme settings appear strange and dangerous to the reader, which makes them feel like anything could happen there. This emphasises the feeling of tension in the novel.

3) This question asks you to focus on a particular theme. Make sure you choose a theme that is relevant to the text you have studied. Focus on how the writer uses language, structure and form to present the theme. This answer is for the theme of social class in 'An Inspector Calls', but it's worth reading whatever play you're studying, because it'll give you an idea of the kind of things you should be writing about. Here are some things you could mention:

- The play emphasises the power that social class can give — Sheila uses her "power" as the daughter of the well-known, well-off Mr Birling to have Eva/Daisy fired, and it's heavily implied that as a result Eva/Daisy is forced to turn to a life of prostitution. Although this event had a huge effect on Eva/Daisy's life, Sheila says that, to her, it "didn't seem to be anything very terrible at the time". Priestley shows that a relatively unimportant decision by a middle-class woman like Sheila can prove catastrophic for a working-class woman such as Eva/Daisy.

- Eva Smith is presented as a symbol of the suffering that the working classes are forced to undergo as a result of middle-class families — there are "millions of Eva Smiths and John Smiths", which suggests that her story symbolises the difficulties of the working classes as a whole.

- The Birling family believe the working classes to be inferior, which is reflected in the way Sybil refers to Eva/Daisy dismissively as a "girl of that sort". However, Eva/Daisy is shown to be morally superior to some of the middle-class characters, turning down Eric's stolen money even though she needs it. This suggests that Priestley thought that social class didn't define a person's character or moral values.

- The Inspector, who reflects Priestley's own socialist views and acts as his 'mouthpiece', presents an alternative to the Birlings' class-obsessed perspective. He disagrees with Arthur Birling's selfish, characteristically middle-class beliefs — the Inspector says that all people "are members of one body" who shouldn't ignore each other's needs, regardless of social class.

4) This question asks you to focus on a particular theme. Make sure you choose a theme that is relevant to the text you have studied. Focus on how the writer uses language, structure and form to present the theme. This answer is about the lives of women in 'Pride and Prejudice', starting with Chapter 13, from the start of the chapter to "do something or other about it.", but it's worth reading whichever text you're studying, because it'll give you an idea of the kind of things you should be writing about. Here are some things you could mention:

- In the extract, Austen emphasises how important it is that the novel's young female characters find husbands. She describes how Mrs Bennet's eyes "sparkled" at the hope that Mr Bingley may be visiting; the verb shows how excited she is, because she hopes that he will marry Jane. Mrs Bennet's reaction is typical of her excitable and emotional character, but it also shows how important marriage was for women at the time Austen was writing — it wasn't socially acceptable for upper and middle-class women to have jobs, which meant they were unable to earn money for themselves, and so were reliant upon marrying a wealthy husband to ensure their financial security.

- Mr and Mrs Bennet's discussion in the extract of the entailment of the Bennet estate shows how the law treated women unfairly. It means that only a male heir can inherit the property, who in this case is Mr Collins. Mr Bennet explains that Mr Collins could turn the female family members out of the house "as soon as he pleases" when he is the owner. This phrase emphasises how little control the female family members will have when the entailment comes into effect. This highlights the unequal position of women in Regency England, because the law is not set up in their favour.

- Austen also explores some of the unfair expectations of women in Regency society. In Chapter 8, Miss Bingley describes how an "accomplished" woman is expected to have several abilities including "singing" and "drawing", as well as other features including a certain "tone of voice". The large number and specific nature of these requirements makes them seem unachievable, and therefore suggests that they were unfair towards women.

- Austen portrays a strong female character in Elizabeth. She is confident about breaking some social conventions. For example, in Chapter 7, she is not worried about getting "dirty stockings" when walking to see Jane, despite Mrs Bennet saying that she would "not be fit to be seen" in that state. Mrs Bennet's disapproval suggests that Elizabeth's independence and lack of social propriety are unusual, emphasising that women typically had to conform to strict expectations of appearance and behaviour to maintain their reputations.

- Austen also demonstrates how women could suffer harshly for breaking social conventions. Regency society's beliefs about social propriety for women meant that Lydia's elopement with Wickham is viewed as a very serious problem. It destroys her reputation: Mary says that Lydia's virtue is now "irretrievable", and Mr Collins claims that Lydia's death would have been a "blessing" in comparison. This highlights how breaking social conventions regarding marriage could have serious consequences for the woman involved.

Section Three — Drama

Page 35 — Warm-Up Questions

1) E.g. In 'An Inspector Calls', Priestley uses stage directions to help create an atmosphere of stately formality. For example, the furniture is described as "solid" and the room as a whole appears "substantial" but "not cosy and homelike".

2) Monologue — e.g. one person speaking alone for a long period of time. Example depends on chosen text.
Aside — e.g. a short comment that reveals a character's thoughts to the audience, but not to the other characters. Example depends on chosen text.
Soliloquy — e.g. when one character speaks their thoughts aloud for a long time, but no other character can hear them. Example depends on chosen text.

3) Answers depend on chosen text.

4) E.g. In Act 2, Scene 4 of 'Romeo and Juliet', Mercutio mocks people who swordfight for being pretentious, calling them "lisping" and "fashion-mongers". This gives the scene a light-hearted tone that reflects the events of the play at this point — Romeo is in love with Juliet and they are due to be married. The humour here suggests to the audience that all is well and things will have a happy ending. This makes the following scenes even more tragic because the audience has been misdirected into thinking the play could end happily.

5) Answers should focus on how the passage makes you feel and how Shakespeare achieves this. Here are some points you could consider:
   - How do you feel when you read the passage?
   E.g. Is it funny, sad, exciting or frightening?
   - How does Shakespeare convey the characters' feelings? Look at what they say and how they speak.
   - What has happened directly before the passage and what happens next? Does the position of the passage in the text enhance its effect or affect your reading of it?

6) a) Don Pedro's speech — blank verse
   The lines are written in iambic pentameter but they don't rhyme.
   Prince's speech — verse
   The lines are written in rhymed iambic pentameter.
   Trinculo's speech — prose
   The start of each line doesn't begin with a capital letter.
   b) The Prince's speech is written in verse form with rhymed iambic pentameter, and it has an ABAB rhyme scheme. These combine to make it sound serious and important.

Page 40 — Exam-Style Questions

1) For this question, you'll need to write about fate and free will in the extract you've been given, and then pick out specific examples from elsewhere in the play to illustrate how Shakespeare explores fate and free will. This answer is for 'Romeo and Juliet', but it's worth reading whichever of Shakespeare's plays you're studying. Here are some things you could mention:

- A conflict between fate and free will is evident in the play's prologue. Romeo and Juliet are referred to as "star-cross'd lovers", implying that their lives are controlled by fate, not by their own choices. The prologue also states that their death is the only thing that can "bury their parents' strife", or end the feud between the Montagues and the Capulets, suggesting that there is a purpose to their deaths. In this way, Shakespeare introduces the audience to the idea that Romeo and Juliet's deaths are unavoidably fated.

- The form of the prologue echoes this theme of fate: it is written in iambic pentameter, the steady rhythm of which gives the feeling of a pattern long established, which cannot be changed. The prologue is also written in rhyming verse, ending with a rhyming couplet — "attend" and "mend". This makes the declaration of Romeo and Juliet's fate seemed fixed and final, which suggests they have no free will to change their destiny.

- Having established that Romeo and Juliet are destined to die, Shakespeare gives the audience several reminders throughout the play, which strengthens the sense that their lives are controlled by fate. For example, Lady Capulet wishes that Juliet "were married to her grave" and Juliet sees Romeo "As one dead in the bottom of a tomb", foreshadowing their eventual suicides.

- However, although there is strong evidence that fate plays a significant part in the events of 'Romeo and Juliet', the importance of free will should not be underestimated. For example, it could be argued that because the characters often seem to know in advance what consequences their actions will have, they could simply act differently. This is illustrated when Romeo kills Tybalt — before he fights him he realises that killing Tybalt "begins the woe others must end." In other words, he knows that Tybalt's death will have repercussions, yet he still chooses to fight. When he kills Tybalt, he calls himself "fortune's fool", suggesting that he wants to blame fate for what he has done, and that he is simply pretending to have had no other choice.

2) For this question, you'll need to explain Shakespeare's use of comedy in your extract, and then pick out specific examples from elsewhere in the play to illustrate Shakespeare's use of comedy. This answer is for 'The Merchant of Venice', but it's worth reading whichever of Shakespeare's plays you're studying. Here are some things you could mention:

- Shakespeare's use of comedy in the extract provides light relief for the audience before a long, emotional courtroom scene. However, it also highlights themes that are important to the courtroom scene, such as the conflict between Jews and Christians that forms the backdrop of the play. This shows how Shakespeare uses the placement of comedic scenes within the structure of the play to add to its overall impact.

- In the extract, Shakespeare uses puns to create humour. For example, Jessica and Launcelot use the word "bastard" to mean both 'illegitimate' and 'pointless' when discussing the "bastard hope" that Shylock might not really be Jessica's father and therefore that she might not be Jewish herself. Since her mother is also Jewish, the word "bastard" also suggests that it is a 'pointless' hope. Shakespeare's audience would likely have been aware of the dual meaning of the word, and so may have been entertained by the cleverness of the characters. However, the pun also shows the prejudice against Jews that existed in Shakespeare's time, because it demonstrates how it was considered better to be a Christian, providing a serious undertone to the humour in the extract.

- Further comedy in the extract comes from Launcelot's complaint that Jews converting to Christianity will raise the "price of hogs" in Venice. Launcelot is making a joke about the fact that Christians eat pork and Jews do not, so more Christians will make pork more expensive as there will be greater demand for it. In this remark, Launcelot deliberately trivialises the serious issue of Jewish-Christian relations by focusing on something as unimportant as the price of pork. Although his comment may appear insensitive to modern-day audiences, an audience during Shakespeare's time would likely have been amused by Launcelot's flippant attitude and deliberate ignorance of the issues at hand.

- In Act 1, Scene 2, Shakespeare uses mockery and exaggeration to create humour. Portia and Nerissa discuss the suitors who have tried to win Portia's hand in marriage, and the use of exaggeration makes each sound ridiculous, such as Monsieur le Bon, who is so keen to show off his fencing skills that he would "fence with his own shadow". The portrayal of each man as an over-the-top cliché of a bad suitor would be amusing for the audience, as it emphasises Portia's continuing bad luck in finding an appropriate husband.

- Shakespeare's use of disguise and mistaken identity is also humorous. In Act 2, Scene 2, Launcelot's father, Old Gobbo, is blind and so cannot recognise his son. Launcelot tricks him into thinking that his son has "gone to heaven", before eventually revealing his true identity. This interaction is an example of dramatic irony, as Launcelot's identity would always be clear to the audience, which makes this interaction especially funny on stage. Launcelot's disguise also highlights one of the play's key ideas, that appearances do not always match reality. This is perhaps shown most clearly by the phrase "All that glitters is not gold", which is found inside the gold casket in Act 2, Scene 7, suggesting that something being visually impressive does not make it a good thing. Shakespeare's use of comedic disguise therefore emphasises this serious message that appearances cannot always be trusted.

3) This question requires you to think carefully about ideas about gender or growing up, so all your points need to be clearly about one of those themes. This answer is about gender in 'An Inspector Calls', but it's worth reading whatever play you're studying, because it'll give you an idea of the kind of things you should be writing about. Here are some things you could mention:

- Both Birling and Gerald have a stereotypical, often patronising, view of women, which Priestley seeks to highlight and condemn. This is most strongly seen in their treatment of Sheila. For example, Gerald tries to shut Sheila out, stating that she has "obviously had about as much as she can stand" after the questions from the Inspector. He does not make the same comment about himself or the other men, suggesting that he does not consider women capable of coping with difficult issues and that he sees them as mentally weaker than men.

- Men in the play are held to different moral standards than women. Birling appears to defend Gerald by implying that a lot of young men have affairs and telling Sheila that she "must understand" this, indicating that he thinks it is acceptable or at least should be quietly ignored. This suggests that infidelity is tolerated for men in a way that it would not be for women. Through this, Priestley reveals the unequal positions of men and women in early 20th-century Britain.

- Priestley uses the character of the Inspector to challenge the characters' prejudiced views about women. For instance, he questions whether women should really be protected from "unpleasant things". This repeats the words of Birling from earlier in the play, who wanted to protect Sheila from "unpleasant business". The repetition highlights how the Inspector is presenting a different viewpoint, one which suggests that women are capable of dealing with upsetting things as well as men. The contrast of views makes the attitudes of some of the Birlings seem overprotective and prejudiced.

- Priestley also shows female characters who challenge stereotypes about women. For instance, Sheila changes throughout the play and becomes more assertive, insisting that she has "a right to know" about Gerald's behaviour. She takes on a similar role to the Inspector, asking questions of the other characters and trying to get them to see how they have not learn their lesson — "You're just beginning to pretend all over again". By presenting Sheila as strong and independent, Priestley shows how stereotypes about women can be wrong.

4) For this question, you need to talk about your extract and then pick out specific examples of the supernatural elsewhere in the play, and explain them in detail. This answer is for 'Macbeth', but it's worth reading whatever play you're studying, because it'll give you an idea of the kind of things you should be writing about. Here are some things you could mention:

- The Witches are the first characters to appear on stage in Act 1 Scene 1, which highlights their importance. They are accompanied by "thunder and lightning", which makes them seem more threatening, increasing the audience's perception of the supernatural as something powerful and dangerous.

- The focus on the Witches in the first scene reflects how they are the most notable supernatural presence in the play. Shakespeare presents their supernatural powers of prediction as a very powerful force, which drives the play forwards and influences Macbeth to commit terrible crimes, such as murdering Duncan.

- The Witches also speak in rhyming couplets in this scene, including "done" and "won". This emphasises the fact that they are different to the other characters — they exist outside the natural order of the world, so they speak unnaturally. The rhyme and rhythm they use makes their speech sound like a chant, which gives it a magical, spell-like quality.

- Elsewhere, the three Witches are portrayed as unattractive and unnatural — they are "so withered and so wild" that they look scarcely human, and they curse a sailor to sleep "neither night nor day", which emphasises their cruelty. This hints at the negative way that society in Shakespeare's time, and especially the reigning monarch, King James I, viewed witchcraft.

- Lady Macbeth uses supernatural imagery — she calls on "spirits" to help her, which links her with the Witches and the supernatural. This helps the audience to recognise how far she will go to gain power and understand that she is a morally corrupt character.

- The supernatural elements in the play are often ambiguous — the appearance of Banquo's ghost, the dagger and the blood on Lady Macbeth's hands could all be figments of the characters' imaginations, or they could be genuine supernatural occurrences. This ambiguity adds to the complexity of the characters of Macbeth and Lady Macbeth — the reader is left wondering whether they are truly seeing supernatural visions, or if they have been driven mad by their guilty consciences. It also reinforces the fear that the supernatural causes in the play, as the visions inspire very strong feelings of horror in Macbeth and Lady Macbeth.

5) For this question, you need to write about the relationship between two characters over the course of a whole play. This means you need to pay particular attention to the changes that occur between the two characters as the play progresses. This answer is for 'Blood Brothers', but it's worth a read even if you haven't studied the play. Here are some things you could mention:

- Mickey and Edward become best friends and "blood brothers" almost as soon as they meet. This highlights their youthful innocence at that point in the play, as well as the immediate, instinctive bond between them. In contrast, at the end of the play Mickey uses the recurring motif of "Blood brothers" to express his sense of betrayal and anger. This emphasises how much the characters' relationship has changed since their first meeting as children.
- Just before Edward departs for university, Russell uses a montage to illustrate the continuing happiness of the relationship between Mickey and Edward as teenagers. The stage directions say that both characters "smile" frequently, which emphasises the joy and freedom of youth and their pleasure in each other's company. This contrasts with the characters' actions and emotions immediately after Edward returns from university: the stage directions say that Edward "laughs" and jokes, but Mickey is "unamused" and denounces their blood brother bond as "kids' stuff". This contrast highlights the turning point in their relationship — Mickey has come to view Edward as "still a kid", and resents that he himself has had to grow up too quickly. Their relationship continues to deteriorate until the end of the play.
- The balance of power in the relationship between Mickey and Edward changes as time goes on. As children, Mickey has the power in the friendship. He has knowledge that Edward wants, and behaves in a way that Edward admires. When Edward shouts at Mrs Lyons, "you're a fuckoff!", it is clear that he's already strongly influenced by what Mickey says, even when he doesn't know what it means. As adults, Edward holds the influence in Mickey's life — he gets Mickey a house and a job. Mickey resents this, feeling that he "didn't sort anythin' out" for himself, and this contributes to the final confrontation between the brothers.
- The changing relationship between the two boys as they enter adulthood, and their eventual deaths, could be interpreted as a comment on the divisions between social classes in 20th-century Britain — even a bond as strong as the one between Mickey and Edward can be destroyed. In his final speech, the narrator asks whether "class" was to blame for the deaths of the two brothers, suggesting that this is part of Russell's message in the play.

Section Four — Prose

Page 47 — Warm-Up Questions

1) Answer depends on chosen text. Here are some points you could consider:
   - The writer's choice of language — is it formal and written in Standard English, or more informal and written using slang or dialect words?
   - The sentence structures the writer uses — does the writer use long sentences to describe something in detail, or short, punchy sentences to create an exciting beginning for the reader?
   - The writer's tone — what is the overall feeling of the text in the first paragraph? Does it seem particularly cheerful, conversational or melancholy? How is this achieved?

2) Answers should focus on how the writer sets the scene and what effect the description has. Here are some points you could consider:
   - Where is the passage set? What is the place like?
   - How does the passage make you feel? Can you pick out any words or phrases that contribute to this effect?
   - Does the writer use techniques such as imagery to make the description more vivid? If so, what effect does it have on the reader?

3) For example:
   a) Elizabeth Bennet is the central character in Jane Austen's 'Pride and Prejudice'. She is important because she is involved in much of the action, and is portrayed as one of the wisest characters, so we trust her judgement. She has the strongest will of any of the Bennet sisters and she follows her own mind. Because of this, she is responsible for many of the novel's turning points.
   b) Elizabeth is a presented as sympathetic character, which helps the reader to identify with her feelings and decisions. She is presented as a caring, witty character, but her mistakes (e.g. misjudging Darcy and Wickham) make her seem like a real person.
   c) Elizabeth's opinion of Darcy and her sister's suitor, Wickham, changes as she recognises that she has misjudged them. By the end of the novel she has realised that appearances can be deceptive, and that it is wrong to judge people on first impressions.

4) E.g. In 'Anita and Me', the narrator writes in the first person, as an adult looking back on the events of her childhood. This allows the reader to follow her thought processes and empathise with her. The use of a grown-up narrator gives an adult perspective on the events and emotions of childhood, which adds humour and pathos to the narrative.

5) a) For example: "most unfortunate affair", "much talked of", "useful lesson", "loss of virtue in a female is irretrievable", "one false step involves her in endless ruin", "reputation is no less brittle than it is beautiful", "she cannot be too much guarded in her behaviour".
   b) For example: "Reputation was extremely important for women in nineteenth-century Britain. Women who damaged their reputation by behaving in an 'improper' way were regarded as having lost their "virtue", a situation that was judged "irretrievable". This shows that, once a woman's good reputation was lost, there was no way of getting it back — she would have been affected for life. Such women were used as a "useful lesson" to prevent other women from behaving in the same way."

Page 52 — Exam-Style Questions

1) For this question, don't try to pick out every point in the novel where prejudice occurs. Instead, you should pick a few key scenes and explain how the writer uses language, structure and events to portray prejudice. You should also consider other characters' reactions to it, and what effect the theme of prejudice has on the novel as a whole. This answer is for 'Anita and Me', but it should come in handy whichever novel you're studying. Here are some things you could mention:

• In 'Anita and Me', racial prejudice is often casual, such as Deirdre calling her dog "Nigger" because it's black, without realising it's offensive. This casual racism shows the ignorance of some of the residents of Tollington, who often don't realise the impact of their racism. This is reinforced later in the novel, when Sam says that he "never meant" Meena when he made racist comments.

• The novel highlights the role of education and the media in inadvertently encouraging racism — Meena says that all she learned at school about India was from "tatty textbooks" showing Indians as servants, or from "television clips" showing "machete-wielding thugs". This means that neither she nor her classmates are given a fair picture of the country on which to base their assumptions. It also makes Meena feel ashamed of her Indian heritage.

• The racist attitudes of characters in the novel reflect the views of many British people in late 1960s and early 1970s, when the novel is set. For example, Sam Lowbridge makes his racist views public by shouting "If You Want a Nigger for a Neighbour, Vote Labour!" on television — this was the slogan used by supporters of a real Conservative MP who was elected in Smethwick (a town in the West Midlands) in 1964.

• Characters in the novel react differently to racial prejudice. Mama's reaction to racism is to try to disprove racial stereotypes — for example, she purposely speaks English "without an accent". In contrast, Papa tells Meena that she shouldn't accept racist abuse: "first you say something back, and then you come and tell me." The Kumars' mild, non-violent reaction to racism paints them in a much better light than the racist characters in the novel, and emphasises how unfair and illogical racial prejudice is.

2) This question asks you to talk about your chosen text in relation to a particular theme, so make sure the examples you choose are relevant to that theme. Remember to discuss how language, form and structure are used to present the theme. This answer is about social class in 'Pride and Prejudice', but it should come in handy whichever novel you're studying. Here are some things you could mention:

• 'Pride and Prejudice' was written during the late eighteenth century, when class distinctions based on wealth and family connections were fairly rigid, and people were expected to marry within their own class. This expectation, and the struggle to overcome it, is one of the main themes of the novel.

• Most of the characters in the novel are aware of the restrictions of class. For example, Elizabeth recognises that because of her mother's family background, she and Jane are not necessarily 'good enough' to marry Darcy or Bingley, and Darcy himself describes Elizabeth's family as "decidedly beneath" his own.

• Although Elizabeth is aware of the barrier that class creates between herself and upper-class characters like Darcy and Lady Catherine, she is never intimidated by them. For example, whilst Mr Collins is "employed in agreeing to every thing her Ladyship said", Elizabeth is not afraid to speak her mind and criticise Lady Catherine's behaviour, for example telling Lady Catherine that she has "no right" to interfere in her business. Austen uses Elizabeth to criticise the restrictions of the class system, suggesting that they don't need to be as strictly adhered to as some in Regency society might think.

• Austen satirises attitudes to social class using the character of Lady Catherine. Lady Catherine is so convinced that her upper-class status makes her superior that it does not occur to her that the other characters might not agree with her views. For example, she is "shocked and astonished" that Elizabeth won't promise not to marry Darcy.

• Lady Catherine is determined that Darcy will marry her daughter because they are "descended… from the same noble line", despite the fact that Anne is "pale and sickly" and "spoke very little", making it clear that she would not be a good wife for Darcy. This contains an implicit judgement of those who see social class as the most important factor in a happy marriage.

3) This question asks you about the writer's methods, so you need to pay close attention to things like structure and language in your answer. Remember to pick out key events and quotations to illustrate your points, and make sure you relate your points to the historical context of the novel. This answer is for 'Animal Farm', but it's worth reading whatever your set text is, because it gives you an idea of the kind of things a good answer should mention. Here are some points you could include:

• The feeling that all is not well on Manor Farm is present from the beginning of the novel. In the first sentence we are told that Mr Jones is "too drunk" to do his job, showing that he does not have control over the farm. This impression is furthered by the fact that the meeting takes place at night and in secret, and involves Major's "strange dream", which makes it seem almost supernatural.

• Major talks about the "hideous cruelty" of slaughter, uses emotive language such as "slavery" and repeatedly refers to humans as the "enemy". This builds the sense that something is about to happen, so the reader feels the same suspense as the animals, because they know that they are plotting a rebellion that could lead to failure and death. The feeling of fear increases once we realise what Napoleon is capable of. The clearest example of this is when he violently expels Snowball from the farm, and it becomes clear that he has been planning this takeover for some time. We find out that Napoleon took the puppies that he uses to terrorise the other animals from their mother and "reared them privately", implying that he has been planning to seize power since the beginning.

• Following Snowball's expulsion, the mood of fear and uncertainty grows. The scene in which Napoleon slaughters animals he believes are "in touch" with Snowball is terrifying because it shows his power over the other animals. This reminds the reader of Stalin's secret police in the Soviet Union, who tortured and executed politicians who were not loyal to Stalin.

• Perhaps the most horrifying image in the novel occurs right at the end, when the animals realise that they cannot distinguish between man and pig. The line "The creatures outside looked from pig to man, and from man to pig… but already it was impossible to say which was which" creates a real sense of fear, because it is a macabre and disturbing image which reminds the reader of fairytales where men are turned into the beasts that they resemble. The reader realises that the utopian society described by Major can never be achieved, and that the animals will never be free of tyranny and oppression. Again, this echoes events in the Soviet Union, where Stalin's expulsion and subsequent assassination of Trotsky effectively wiped out the possibility of a utopian communist society and resulted instead in fear and oppression.

4) For this question, you need to work out what the author's ideas about the nature of evil are, then explain how these ideas are presented. This answer is for 'Lord of the Flies', but it's worth reading if you're studying a different set text. These points give you some ideas of the kind of things you could include:

- The main message of 'Lord of the Flies' is that evil is present in everyone, that it is only the constraints of society that prevent people from committing evil acts, and that evil can be easily brought to the surface by fear. Golding served in the navy during World War II, and was shocked by the fact that civilians were bombed and by the way that prisoners in concentration camps were treated. It was this experience that made him believe that humans are essentially savage, and that outside of the boundaries of civilisation people are capable of great evil.

- In the novel, the boys don't realise that the evil is inside them, so they make it into a real being — "the beast" — which gives them something to "hunt and kill". This allows them to think of themselves as good, backing up Jack's statement that they are inherently capable: "We're English; and the English are best at everything", and building their belief that by hunting they are ridding themselves of evil. However, the more savagely they act and the more they hunt the beast, the stronger the evil inside of them grows and the more real the beast seems. The beast continually changes shape, from a "snake-thing", to something that "comes out of the sea" to "something like a great ape". In this way, Golding shows the reader that the beast is not real, and also demonstrates how evil continually changes shape depending on what the boys are most scared of.

- When Simon says of the beast that "maybe it's only us", the others laugh at him — they are unable to accept the idea that there could be evil in each of them. Simon's death therefore symbolises the end of reason and goodness. In the scene in which Simon is killed, the boys are nameless and act as a "single organism" which kills with "teeth and claws". This animal imagery shows how savage the boys have become, and how they are losing the final traces of civilisation. Even Ralph feels "a kind of feverish excitement" when he talks about Simon's murder, which shows how strong evil is and how it is present even in the characters that are usually considered 'good' and 'civilised'.

- The novel is set against the backdrop of a nuclear war: Piggy talks about the "atom bomb" and says "They're all dead." This, together with the appearance of the naval officer at the end, reminds the reader that the boys' evil is minor on the wider scale of human evil, and reinforces Golding's message that savage behaviour is man's natural state.

5) For this question, you can write about any prose text that you've studied, so make sure you pick one that you can think of plenty to write about. You need to write about the ways in which the main character has changed, and the ways in which they've stayed the same through the course of the novel. This answer is for 'Great Expectations', but it'll give you an idea of the sort of points you need to make whatever text you're studying. Here are some things you could mention:

- The novel is a Bildungsroman, which means that it follows the progress of one character, in this case Pip, as he grows up. At the start of the novel, Pip is a young, naive boy. His main aspiration is to be Joe's apprentice, and he has no ambition to better himself. This changes when he first sees Satis House and meets Estella, and begins to feel that his own home is "coarse and common". In much the same way, his home becomes a metaphor for his character and he starts trying to improve himself. It is this struggle for education, social class and wealth that causes the first big change in Pip's character.

- This change is demonstrated by the way that Pip acts towards Joe. At the start of the novel, Pip says that he "was looking up to Joe in my heart." However, following his move to London, and once he feels that he has become a gentleman, Pip treats Joe coldly because Estella "would be contemptuous" of Joe. This shows how Pip is blinded by wealth and status, and how his 'rise' in society has made him a harder, more selfish person, who judges people by their social standing and is prepared to hurt his oldest friend in order to impress Estella.

- Pip eventually starts to understand that wealth and status do not bring happiness. This realisation is foreshadowed by Dickens' description of London, a place that in the 19th century was associated with wealth and status, as having "the most dismal trees in it, and the most dismal sparrows, and the most dismal cats, and the most dismal houses". Repetition of the word "dismal" shows how disappointed Pip is with London, and later with his own social advancement.

- A second great change in Pip's character occurs when he meets Magwitch for the second time. Pip's realisation that his wealth, education and social standing are the result of a convict's generosity, rather than a favour from Miss Havisham, challenges his views about the social hierarchy he believes in, and makes him recognise his own "worthless conduct" towards Joe. This is a major turning point in Pip's character, as it makes him realise that social class and status are very different from generosity and goodness of heart, and that the latter qualities are more important in a person.

- Dickens uses the character of Pip to represent the failings of a society that believed happiness could be attained through social climbing and wealth. By having Pip recognise the error of his ways, Dickens showed that he believed people were capable of altering their views and placing greater importance on decency, loyalty and hard work than on money and status.

Section Five — Poetry

Page 61 — Warm-Up Questions

1) a) A word that sounds like the noise it's describing, e.g. splash, creak.
   b) A pause or break in a line, often marked by punctuation.
   c) A sentence that runs over from one line to the next.

2) "the fizzy, movie tomorrows / the right walk home could bring."
   E.g. "The onomatopoeic word "fizzy" sounds lively and bubbly, emphasising the feeling of excitement about the future."

   "They accuse me of absence, they circle me."
   E.g. "Sibilance creates a hissing sound, which highlights the menacing tone."

   "Slowly our ghosts drag home"
   E.g. "The assonance of the long 'o' sounds makes the journey sound difficult and lengthy.

   "a blockade of yellow bias binding around your blazer."
   E.g. "The alliteration causes hard 'b' sounds to dominate the line, creating a harsh tone which suggests the narrator is distressed."

3) Your answer should consider how dawn is personified in the extract and what this tells the reader about the speaker's feelings (e.g. lonely, scared, depressed). Here are some things you could mention:

- Dawn is personified as an "army". This reminds the reader of soldiers preparing to attack, and suggests that the speaker dreads the coming day.

- Dawn is normally a positive symbol, associated with light and new beginnings. The speaker views it negatively, suggesting that he has lost hope.

- Dawn is described as "melancholy" — this reflects the feelings of the soldiers in the trenches. They are weary and depressed rather than energised and ready to fight.
- The words "once more" show that the attack continues with no respite, and creates a sense that there will be no end to the war or to the soldiers' suffering.

4) a) E.g. "The strict rhyme scheme uses rhyming couplets (AABB etc.) to emphasise the Duke's obsessive need for order and control."
    b) E.g. "The direct address brings the narrator to life, making his presence a dominant feature of the narrative."
    c) E.g. "The Duke's speech often runs on from one line to the next, which creates the impression that he doesn't give his visitor a chance to speak, and shows his desire to dominate the conversation."

Section Six — Poetry Anthology

Page 69 — Warm-Up Questions

1) E.g. 'War Photographer' by Carol Ann Duffy has a regular rhyme scheme — it is "set out in ordered rows" like the photographer's spools. This helps to emphasise the care that the photographer takes over his work.

2) E.g. In 'The Charge of the Light Brigade', the narrator uses the third person to describe a battle between British cavalry and Russian forces during the Crimean War. This makes it more difficult to empathise with the soldiers because there is no insight into their individual thoughts or feelings, which creates distance between them and the reader. In contrast, in 'Poppies', Jane Weir uses the first person to explore the experience of a mother whose son has gone off to war. The first-person perspective allows for an intensely personal description of her emotions and reaction to her son leaving, which makes it easier for the reader to empathise with the speaker.

3) a) E.g. "'Forward, the Light Brigade!' / Was there a man dismay'd?"
        (Charge of the Light Brigade, Alfred Tennyson)
        Effect: End-stopping imposes order on the poem, reflecting the way that the soldiers' actions are controlled by the officers.
    b) E.g. "My father spins / A stone along the water. Leisurely"
        (Eden Rock, Charles Causley)
        Effect: This caesura slows the pace of the poem, which emphasises the feeling of peace.
    c) E.g. Porphyria's Lover, Robert Browning
        Effect: It emphasises the sense of the narrator's control over Porphyria, because his is the only perspective the reader hears.
    d) E.g. "spits like a tame cat / Turned savage."
        (Storm on the Island, Seamus Heaney)
        Effect: Enjambment places emphasis on the word "Turned", which highlights how suddenly the storm arrives.

4) E.g. Tennyson uses form to convey a sense of order in 'Charge of the Light Brigade'. For example, end-stopping in the lines "'Forward, the Light Brigade!' / Was there a man dismay'd?" creates a controlled rhythm that reflects the way that the soldiers' actions are controlled by the officers. In contrast, in 'Storm on the Island' Heaney uses enjambment to describe the storm: for example, he says that it "spits like a tame cat / Turned savage." Here, enjambment is used to emphasise the word "Turned", which highlights how suddenly the storm arrives, and how little power the islanders have against nature.

5) a) E.g. "I struck and struck again"
        (The Prelude: Stealing the Boat, William Wordsworth)
        Effect: The repetition of "struck" emphasises the narrator's fear and desperation to get away.
    b) E.g. "the waterlogged earth / gulping for breath"
        (Winter Swans, Owen Sheers)
        Effect: The word "gulping" helps the reader to imagine the sound made by the walkers as they walk across the muddy ground.
    c) E.g. "With sidelong flowing flakes that flock"
        (Exposure, Wilfred Owen)
        Effect: Alliteration emphasises the relentlessness of the snow.
    d) E.g. "a green-blue translucent sea"
        (Kamikaze, Beatrice Garland)
        Effect: The smooth, long 'u' sound makes the sea seem appealing.

6) E.g. 'Kamikaze' uses assonance to emphasise the beauty of nature. For example, the repeated long 'u' sound in the phrase "green-blue translucent sea" creates a smooth sound that emphasises the beauty of the sea. This highlights the pilot's appreciation of the natural world and hints that it influenced his decision to return home. In contrast, 'Exposure' uses alliteration to emphasise the terrible conditions the soldiers are experiencing: the snow is described as "flowing flakes that flock", which makes it sound relentless and overwhelming. This contributes to the cumulative sense of threat in the stanza, which reflects Owen's negative depiction of war overall in the poem.

7) E.g. In 'Follower', Seamus Heaney uses nautical imagery to emphasise the father's strength and skill. One effective image in the poem is the description of the father's shoulders as "globed like a full sail strung". This simile likens the father to a ship, which creates an image of strength and power for the reader.

Page 74 — Exam-Style Questions

1) For this question, you have to think about the way that the poets use form, structure and language to describe feelings towards another person, so make sure you choose a second poem that has plenty to write about on the subject. Comparing them means writing about the similarities and differences, so make some links between the poems in your answer. This answer is for 'Sonnet 29' by Elizabeth Barrett Browning and 'Love's Philosophy' by Percy Bysshe Shelley, but it gives you an idea of the kind of things you need to write whichever poems you're analysing. Here are some points you could make:
- Both poets use form to help convey a sense of longing for another person. In 'Love's Philosophy', the final line of each stanza is shorter than the other lines, which makes it stand out. This adds weight to the rhetorical question in each stanza, which emphasises the narrator's desire to be with his lover. The short lines also slow the pace of the poem — this creates a sense of wistfulness, which emphasises the narrator's yearning for his lover. In contrast, 'Sonnet 29' uses the sonnet form to link the narrator's feelings to a tradition of love poetry. However, whereas in a standard sonnet the solution often arrives in line 9, in 'Sonnet 29' it arrives early: "Rather, instantly / Renew thy presence" appears in line 7, hinting that the narrator cannot wait for her lover's arrival. The enjambment of these lines emphasises the words "instantly" and "Renew", which further underscores the narrator's eagerness to see her lover.

- 'Love's Philosophy' has a regular ABAB rhyme scheme, reflecting the constancy of the narrator's feelings towards his lover. However, half-rhymes such as "river" / "ever" create a note of discord, emphasising the narrator's sorrow at the fact that he and his lover are not together. This half-rhyme also emphasises the words "for ever", which underscores the narrator's desire for an eternal connection with his loved one. 'Sonnet 29' also has a strong rhyme scheme, with half the lines ending with the same sound, for example "tree" / "see". This helps to drive the poem forward, reflecting the narrator's impatience to be reunited with her lover. The end-rhyme "thee" is repeated four times, which emphasises the narrator's obsession with her lover and longing for him to return.
- 'Love's Philosophy' and 'Sonnet 29' both use natural imagery to emphasise feelings of longing for another person. In 'Love's Philosophy', Shelley personifies nature, for example "the mountains kiss high heaven", to suggest that all of nature craves intimacy. This adds weight to the narrator's argument that he and his lover should be together. Similarly, Barrett Browning's narrator compares her thoughts to "wild vines" to show that her longing for her lover is uncontrollable. The natural metaphor extends to her lover, who she likens to a "strong tree" about which she grows. This suggests that she yearns for his support.

2) For this question, you have to think about the way that the poets use form, structure and language to present time, so make sure you choose poems that have plenty to write about on the subject. Remember, you're comparing the two poems, so you need to think about similarities and differences between them. This answer is for 'The Emigrée' by Carol Rumens and 'War Photographer' by Carol Ann Duffy, but it gives you an idea of the kind of things you need to write whichever poems you're analysing. Here are some points you could make:

- Both 'The Emigrée' and 'War Photographer' use form to emphasise the changes in the main characters' circumstances that have occurred over time. 'War Photographer' is made up of four equal-length stanzas, and it has a regular rhyme scheme, which reflects the safety and security of the photographer's present situation. This contrasts with phrases such as "running children in a nightmare heat", which describe the chaos the photographer has witnessed in the past. This contrast between the poem's form and language emphasises how the photographer's past is very different from the life he currently leads. 'The Emigrée' also uses form to emphasise the differences between the narrator's past and present. The first two stanzas use lots of enjambment, but the final stanza includes more end-stopped lines. This underscores the contrast between the freedom of the narrator's past and the confined "city of walls" that characterises her present life.
- In 'The Emigrée', time is presented as a destructive force using a war metaphor: "time rolls its tanks / and the frontiers rise between us". By comparing time to an army, and suggesting that it has created the "frontiers" between herself and the past, the narrator suggests that time is responsible for the fact that she is unable to return. Similarly, in 'War Photographer' the influence of the past is presented as something that is personally destructive to the photographer. This is shown by the "tremble" of his hands as he develops the photographs, which is linked to the events of the past by the references to both "then" and "now" in the stanza.

- The main characters in both poems are symbolically taken back through time at the end of their narratives. In 'The Emigrée' this is presented positively: although the narrator says that there's "no way" for her to physically return to the old city, a personified version of her old home appears to her and takes her "dancing". This hints that her memories of the past are strong enough to overcome her present unhappiness. 'War Photographer' ends with the suggestion that the photographer is flying to another war zone, showing that the past is repeating itself. The final rhyming couplet makes his return seem unavoidable; because of his job, the photographer has no choice except to return to another version of the past that haunts him.

3) For this question, you have to think about the way that the poets use form, structure and language to present ideas about war, so make sure you choose a second poem that has plenty to write about on the subject. Comparing them means writing about the similarities and differences, so make some links between the poems in your answer. This answer is for 'Remains' by Simon Armitage and 'Exposure' by Wilfred Owen, but it gives you an idea of the kind of things you need to write whichever poems you're analysing. Here are some points you could make:

- 'Remains' has no regular rhyme scheme; this contributes to the conversational tone of the poem, which highlights the involvement of ordinary individuals in war and helps the reader to relate to the narrator of the poem. In contrast, in 'Exposure', Owen uses a regular rhyme scheme (ABBAC), which reflects the monotonous nature of the men's experience of war, but the rhymes are often half-rhymes (for example "snow" and "renew"). The rhyme scheme offers no comfort or satisfaction — the jagged rhymes reflect the confusion and fading energy of the soldiers.
- Both poets use the experience of soldiers in war to convey a message about how violent, but often monotonous, conflict can be. This is partly conveyed in both poems through the use of structure. 'Remains' has a repetitive structure: the events recounted in the first half of the poem are repeatedly mentioned in the second half. This highlights the traumatic impact of war on those who fight in it, as it shows that the narrator has flashbacks to the death of the looter even when he is "on leave". 'Exposure', on the other hand, has a repetitive structure that emphasises the static, hopeless nature of war. All of the stanzas end with half-lines, and in four of them the phrase "But nothing happens" is used. This simple half-line highlights the lack of change or hope for the men in the trenches, and makes clear that for them the war seems endless and inescapable.
- Both poets use alliterative techniques to emphasise the danger that soldiers are exposed to as part of war. In 'Remains', Armitage uses sibilance to create a sense of the difficult conditions the soldiers must live in. The phrase "sun-stunned, sand-smothered land" emphasises how hot and dusty the desert is, and places emphasis on the violent verbs "stunned" and "smothered", which indicate the violent nature of the conflict. In line 4 of 'Exposure', meanwhile, sibilance is used to mimic the sound of the sentries' "whisper", which creates a sense of ominous quiet that helps the reader to understand the tense atmosphere. Then, in the fourth stanza, alliteration is used to create a sense of chaos and danger in the phrases "sudden successive flights of bullets" and "flowing flakes that flock". This emphasises the danger that the soldiers face, not just from "bullets" but from the "deathly" winter weather.

- Both poets explore war in relation to the soldiers' lives at home. In 'Remains', the writer focuses on how the trauma of war disrupts the narrator's home life. All the narrator has to do is "blink" for the memories to return to haunt him; this emphasises the long-term psychological impact that the realities of war can cause for a person. In 'Exposure', on the other hand, Owen makes the soldiers' homes seem pleasant and appealing, using personification to describe the "kind fires" of home and the "smile" of the sun. This contrasts with the poor conditions, such as the "merciless" winds, that the soldiers experience whilst at war, and helps to emphasise the harshness of conflict.

4) For this question, you have to think about the way that the poets use form, structure and language to describe a particular place. You could choose to analyse poems that use different language to describe a similar place, or poems that describe very different places — just make sure you can think of plenty to say about the similarities and differences between the poems. This answer is for 'London' by William Blake and 'The Prelude: Stealing the Boat' by William Wordsworth, but it gives you an idea of the kind of things you need to write whichever poems you're analysing. Here are some points you could make:

- Both poems use form to help create a sense of place. 'London' uses an unbroken ABAB rhyme scheme, which echoes the relentless misery of the city, and contributes to the sense that London is a place full of pain and sorrow. In contrast, the extract from 'The Prelude' uses blank verse. The regular, unrhymed iambic pentameter of the poem makes it sound serious and important, which emphasises the power of the looming mountains.

- The places described in both poems are presented as confining and inescapable. In 'London', Blake repeats the word "chartered", meaning 'legally defined' or 'mapped out', even using it to describe the River Thames. This makes it seem like natural features are controlled by human rules, which emphasises the power that authorities such as the monarch and the ruling classes have over the physical place and make the city seem oppressive. In contrast, Wordsworth uses repetition to make nature seem powerful and uncontrollable: in the phrase "a huge peak, black and huge", the word "huge" is repeated, which emphasises the sheer size of the mountain. This highlights that it dominates the narrator's view and makes it seem like he can't escape from it.

- Blake uses sensory imagery to present London as a place that is full of sadness and pain. For example, the emotive image of the "chimney-sweeper's cry" appeals to the reader's sense of hearing, which helps them to imagine the chimney sweeper's misery at the dangerous work he has to do. Wordsworth also uses sensory imagery to appeal to the reader's sense of hearing: he twice uses the word "silent" to describe the waters of the lake, which helps the reader to imagine the sense of quiet in the narrator's surroundings.

5) For this question, you have to think about the way that the poets use form, structure and language to present the power of humans in the poems you choose. Remember, you're comparing the two poems, so you need to think about similarities and differences between them. This answer is for 'Ozymandias' by Percy Bysshe Shelley and 'Checking Out Me History' by John Agard, but it gives you an idea of the kind of things you need to write whichever poems you're analysing. Here are some points you could make:

- Both poems examine the power of an individual. In 'Ozymandias', the individual (Ozymandias) was extremely powerful during his lifetime — he was a "king of kings" — but now he is reduced to the "colossal wreck" of a statue in the middle of a desert, showing that he is completely powerless. Conversely, in 'Checking Out Me History', the narrator had little power in the past: he repeats the phrase "Dem tell me" to highlight how little control he had over his own education and therefore his "identity". However, by the end of the poem he has taken power from the authorities: he says that he is "carving out" his own identity. 'Ozymandias' hints that striving for power is ultimately pointless because power doesn't last; in contrast, 'Checking Out Me History' suggests that it is vital in order to overcome injustice.

- The poets both use form to emphasise their message about striving for power. Agard uses a mixture of stanza forms, non-standard English, and no regular rhyme scheme. This indicates a rebellion against the formal structures of poetry and spelling that he would have been taught in school and shows that he is in control of his own education now. On the other hand, 'Ozymandias' is written in sonnet form, but it doesn't follow a regular sonnet rhyme scheme. This reflects the way that human power and structures can be destroyed by time and nature.

- Both poets use strong, aggressive language to show that those in power can be brutal. For example, in 'Ozymandias' the statue's "wrinkled lip" and "sneer" hint at his cruelty and lack of care for his subjects. There is no mention of Ozymandias's subjects rebelling against him, but by emphasising the ruler's brutality, Shelley may be hinting that such an attempt to gain power may be justified. In 'Checking Out Me History', violent verbs such as "Blind me" show the damage the narrator feels the authorities have done to him, emphasising their lack of concern for his wellbeing. In both poems, the use of strong, violent language may hint that striving for power over oppressive regimes is justified.

Section Seven — Unseen Poetry

Page 82 — Warm-Up Questions

1) E.g. It's about the narrator's sense of loss after someone she loves dies.

2) E.g. The narrator means that she and her lover never got the chance to live together and make a home, because he died.

3) E.g. The descriptions of spring are vivid and life-like, which contrasts with the narrator's dead lover. Phrases like "the violets peer" and "Every bird has heart to sing" describe the beauty and joy of spring and rebirth. At the same time, the final line of each stanza describes the narrator's feelings — she is unable to appreciate the beauty around her, and feels only loss and regret, rather than joy.

4) E.g. The rhyme scheme is ABAB. This gives the poem a simple rhythm, which emphasises the sadness of what the narrator is saying.

5) The final line is missing four syllables compared to the other lines. This emphasises the last line and makes it feel like it finishes too soon, which reflects the relationship between the narrator and her lover — it ended too soon, and now something is missing.

Pages 83-84 — Exam-Style Questions

1a) For this question, you have to think about what the poet is saying about loneliness and solitude, and how she says it. Make sure you comment on how form, structure and language are used to present feelings and ideas in the poem. Here are some points you could make:

* The poem has a nightmarish quality — the woman is alone, waiting nervously for her husband's safe return. The atmosphere is tense, as if something bad may be about to happen. The second stanza deals with the woman's actual nightmare, and the alliterative words "coming", "climbing" and "creeping" make the sea feel very menacing and hostile. It's like someone creeping in and stealing her lover. She wakes up, but with the "screaming gulls" and the sea "chill in her arms" it still feels as if she's in a nightmare.
* The main feeling of the first stanza is boredom — she has "nothing to do now he's gone". She needs to keep busy, so she cleans the house. But the cleaning is futile; the broom "leaves a trail of grit". This could show that the act of cleaning can't cleanse her mind of her fear and anxiety.
* The second stanza describes the woman going to bed. She "sleeps downstairs", perhaps because she can't bear to be alone in their shared bed. This shows how even small things can be a painful reminder of the person you're missing. She also uses a "coat for a pillow" — the coat could well be her partner's, and by sleeping with it she may feel closer to him.
* In the third stanza, the onomatopoeic "screaming gulls" creates a vivid image that contrasts with the silence of the rest of the poem, where the only sounds are the sweeping of the broom and the sibilance of the sea creeping closer. The screaming gulls might also be reminiscent of the screams of drowning sailors, highlighting the woman's fear that her partner will die at sea.
* His shirts are hanging on the washing line, which is a reminder that he's coming back, and feels homely and hopeful for a moment. But the final two lines, "and the high tide's breakers' / chill in her arms", immediately recall the sea and the woman's constant fear that her partner will never return. The "chill" of the waves in the woman's arms seems like a forewarning of death — as if she's holding her partner's cold, drowned body in her arms.
* The structure of the poem, broken into three stanzas, mimics the structure of the woman's life whilst her partner is away — it's divided into day, night, day. There's no rhyme, which reflects her slightly panicky state of mind. The final stanza is heavily enjambed, which creates a feeling of time moving faster, of disorder and confusion. The final stanza is also a line shorter, possibly reflecting her partner's early death.

1b) For this question, you have to think about how the power of the sea is presented in the two poems. Make sure you comment on how form, structure and language are used to present feelings and ideas in the poem. You're comparing the two poems, so you need to think about similarities and differences between them. Here are some points you could make:

* Both poems present the sea as something dangerous and powerful. The subject of 'At Sea' fears that her partner will die at sea, while 'The Sands of Dee' describes the death of a girl who is drowned by 'The western tide'.
* Both poets use language to convey the sounds of the sea. In 'The Sands of Dee', the use of repetition (e.g. "o'er and o'er", "round and round") mirrors the sound of the waves and creates a sense of the relentless, unstoppable power of the sea. Similarly, in 'At Sea', the sibilance in the first stanza (e.g. "she dusts the house, / sweeps") echoes the sound of the sea and suggests its inescapable presence.
* The poets both create a tense, frightening atmosphere through the imagery they use. For example, the onomatopoeic image of "screaming gulls" in 'At Sea' creates tension and anxiety by suddenly breaking the silence of the poem with a sound that suggests fear and suffering. In 'The Sands of Dee', the imagery of the "rolling mist" and the alliterative description of the "wild" "western wind" creates a sense of danger and of the power of nature.
* The two poets personify the sea in similar ways. Kingsley describes it as "cruel, crawling" and "hungry", while Copley depicts it "coming", "climbing" and "creeping". In both cases, the imagery the poets use and the harsh alliterative 'c' sounds make the sea sound menacing and unstoppable.
* The form of the two poems is very different, and is used to create different effects. 'At Sea' is written in free verse, with variable line lengths and no rhyme, which makes it seem unstructured and chaotic. This reflects the way the sea affects the woman, mirroring the lack of structure in her life when her partner is away at sea. In contrast, the form of 'The Sands of Dee' reflects the movement of the sea. Unlike 'At Sea', Kingsley's poem has a regular rhyme scheme, AAABAB, which creates a strong rhythm, mirroring the relentless movement of the waves.

Practice Papers

Pages 86-91 — Paper 1: Section A (Shakespeare)

1) For this question, you have to write about masculinity, so you need to pick out important bits of the play where Shakespeare addresses this theme, and explain how each bit you write about relates to the question. Don't forget to write about the extract in detail as well as the rest of the play. Here are some points you could make:

* In Act 1, Scene 7, Lady Macbeth links the idea of masculinity to bravery and violence. She bullies her husband into killing Duncan by questioning his masculinity: "When you durst do it, then you were a man". From Lady Macbeth's perspective, the ability to commit violent acts is a key element of masculinity.
* Macbeth's view of masculinity in the extract contrasts with that of Lady Macbeth. He explains that to kill his king would not "become" a man, and that if he commits the murder he is "none": not a man at all. Macbeth incorporates concepts of honour and loyalty into his ideas about masculinity, which shows that he is morally more principled than Lady Macbeth.

- However, as the scene progresses, Lady Macbeth persuades Macbeth to change his mind, and he decides once again that he will kill the king. It is clear that Lady Macbeth's attacks on his masculinity have influenced him, as he tells Lady Macbeth that due to her "undaunted mettle" (bravery) she deserves to "Bring forth men-children only". This shows that, like Lady Macbeth, he has come to associate masculinity with the desire to commit violent acts, regardless of whether or not it is the moral thing for someone to do.
- Shakespeare challenges this view of masculinity by presenting Macbeth and Lady Macbeth's actions as cowardly. They kill Duncan in his sleep, and they pin his murder on his innocent servants. Audiences at the time would have considered Macbeth's actions to be unmanly and dishonourable. His lack of honour and unmasculine behaviour sets the scene for his eventual downfall.
- As the play progresses, Macbeth becomes less willing to commit 'masculine' acts of violence; instead he acts like Lady Macbeth, manipulating other people to achieve his own ends. This suggests that he is moving away from the "brave" warrior of Act 1, which was the masculine ideal of the Middle Ages, when the play is set.

2) For this question, you have to write about Romeo as a romantic lover, so you need to pick out important bits of the play where Shakespeare addresses this idea, and explain how each bit you write about relates to the question. Don't forget to write about the extract in detail as well as the rest of the play. Here are some points you could make:

- In Act 2, Scene 2, there is a strong sense of Romeo's physical attraction for Juliet, as he enjoys looking at her and imagining being with her: "See how she leans her cheek upon her hand. / O that I were a glove upon that hand". Shakespeare shows that Romeo physically desires Juliet, but also hints that his romantic feelings for her at this stage in the play are relatively shallow and rooted in lust rather than true affection.
- However, we also see how strongly Romeo admires Juliet. For example, he compares her to the sun: "what light through yonder window breaks?". This makes it seem as though he feels that the world is lit up by Juliet's presence. He goes on to say that the moon is jealous of her, "pale with grief / That thou... art far more fair than she." This metaphor suggests the power of Romeo's romantic feelings and his sense of awe at her beauty. The comparison is particularly dramatic given that the two have just met; this emphasises Romeo's ability to fall in love very quickly, but also suggests the depth of his new love for Juliet.
- At the start of the play, Romeo's romantic feelings for Rosaline appear juvenile. Mercutio mocks him for crying "Ay me!", and Friar Lawrence criticises him for "doting" on her rather than "loving" her. This shows that the other characters think Romeo is being silly about his romantic feelings for Rosaline. By portraying Romeo's romantic feelings for Rosaline as childish and unrealistic, Shakespeare makes the audience doubt whether his love for Juliet is any more authentic.
- Romeo's devastation at Juliet's apparent death suggests that his love for her is deeper than it was for Rosaline. He uses aggressive language, including grotesque verbs such as "Gorged", to portray death as greedy, showing that he is disgusted by the way Juliet has been taken and considers it unfair. This extreme emotional reaction implies that he had a true affection for Juliet. This is further emphasised by his subsequent suicide in order to be with her, which suggests to the audience that his feelings of love were so strong that he felt he could not live without her. By the end of the play, the audience is therefore encouraged to view Romeo as a character who is capable of feeling romantic love to an extreme extent.

3) For this question, you have to write about Caliban as deserving of sympathy, so you need to pick out important bits of the play where Shakespeare addresses this idea, and explain how each bit you write about relates to the question. Don't forget to write about the extract in detail as well as the rest of the play. Here are some points you could make:

- In the extract, Caliban claims to have been betrayed by Prospero. Commenting on how he initially trusted him, he cries "Cursed be I that did so!". The strong exclamation shows that Caliban feels very upset, and his distress invites the audience to feel sympathy for him. Furthermore, his belief that he should be "Cursed" implies that he feels trusting Prospero was a mistake that he regrets. This hints that Prospero has betrayed his trust. The idea that Caliban has been betrayed incites further sympathy for him from the audience.
- Caliban believes the island was stolen from him, claiming that Prospero "tak'st" it from him. His knowledge of the area is shown in his description of its "fresh springs, brine-pits, barren place and fertile". The detailed list suggests that he has a deep understanding of the island, giving support to his claim that it belongs to him. This encourages the audience to agree with his claim that Prospero is a thief who has stolen his land. Caliban's treatment may represent how, during the time that Shakespeare was writing, European colonists were taking over lands in other parts of the world, often oppressing the people living there, in the same way that Caliban's lands are taken from him before he is enslaved. The moral issues around colonisation and how people were being mistreated were often debated at the time; Shakespeare may be encouraging the audience to similarly consider whether Caliban has been mistreated and may therefore deserve sympathy.
- However, Caliban's immoral behaviour makes him less deserving of sympathy. In Act 1, Scene 2, Prospero claims that Caliban "didst seek to violate / The honour of my child", suggesting that he tried to rape Miranda. Later in the play, in Act 3, Scene 2, Caliban encourages Stephano to use Miranda to have a "brood" of children. This callous attitude towards Miranda, seeing her only as a possession to be taken or as a means for having children, portrays Caliban as crude and violent, especially towards women. This makes the audience doubt whether the earlier sympathy they felt for Caliban was rightly placed, and question whether Caliban or Prospero's version of events about what happened when Prospero came to the island is closer to the truth.
- Moreover, in Act 3, Scene 2, Caliban initiates the plot to take revenge on Prospero. This shows he is inclined to vengeance and violence. He suggests to Stephano various ways to kill Prospero, including that he should "Batter" him with a log, "paunch" him with a stake or "cut" his wind-pipe. The detail of the description and the violence of the verbs Caliban uses suggests that he relishes the idea of killing Prospero. Caliban's enjoyment of violence implies that he is an immoral character, and therefore someone who Shakespeare intends the audience to have only limited amounts of sympathy for.

4) For this question, you have to write about justice and mercy, so you need to pick out important bits of the play where Shakespeare addresses these themes, and explain how each bit you write about relates to the question. Don't forget to write about the extract in detail as well as the rest of the play. Here are some points you could make:

- Portia's speech in the extract explores in detail the two related themes of mercy and justice. The speech is written in blank verse, which makes it seem more important than if it were written in prose. This emphasises that these are key themes in the play.

- The speech presents the concepts of mercy and justice as two very different things. Portia links justice with the laws of Venice: if Shylock follows his "plea" for "justice", then the "strict court" of Venice will be forced to sentence Antonio. Mercy, on the other hand, is presented as a human quality that can be used to "mitigate" the law; in this speech, Portia asks Shylock to consider abandoning his case against Antonio in the name of "mercy", even though "justice" would convict him.
- Portia's speech hints at a negative portrayal of justice that is reinforced throughout the play. Many of the characters associate justice with the character of Shylock, who is obsessed with "justice and his bond." His cruel quest for revenge on Antonio relies on the justice of the court, which shows that Venetian justice is unreliable and can lead to unfair consequences.
- In contrast, the portrayal of mercy in Portia's speech is strongly positive. She calls mercy an "attribute to God" that comes from "heaven", and says that if justice alone were followed then nobody would "see salvation". This suggests that mercy is a divine attribute, which is required in order to reach heaven. This would have resonated strongly with the predominantly Christian audiences of the Elizabethan era, who would have understood mercy as an important quality that a good Christian person should have.
- The idea that showing mercy is the right thing to do under any circumstances is reinforced throughout the play. Despite Portia's speech, and Bassanio's offer of money, Shylock refuses to show mercy to Antonio, insisting that "no power in the tongue of man" can persuade him to change his mind. His insistence on justice and refusal to be merciful condemns him: Portia twists the rules of the court so that justice no longer works in his favour, and he can no longer harm Antonio; furthermore, Shylock's own life and fortune are forfeit.
- Antonio's final request as part of Shylock's punishment is to insist that he "become a Christian". Audiences in Shakespeare's time would have associated Christianity with mercy, so it is appropriate that Shylock's final punishment is to be forced to embrace the ideals of mercy and forgiveness that he previously rejected.

5) For this question, you have to write about the changing relationship between Benedick and Beatrice, so you need to pick out important bits of the play where this is shown, and explain how each bit you write about relates to the question. Don't forget to write about the extract in detail as well as the rest of the play. Here are some points you could make:
- At the start of the play, Benedick and Beatrice have a combative but playful relationship. Both characters use wordplay, which emphasises their wit and suggests that they enjoy arguing with each other. Between them, they cleverly develop the same extended metaphor using animal imagery: Benedick calls Beatrice a "parrot-teacher", and in return, Beatrice replies, "A bird of my tongue is better than a beast of yours." She also suggests that she is cleverer than Benedick by linking his intelligence to that of a "beast" that cannot speak. This interplay is likely to persuade the audience that, although their relationship appears antagonistic, they are perfectly matched in character and intelligence and may well fall in love by the end of the play. This is reinforced by the audience's prior expectations of the play: based on Shakespeare's other comedies, they'll be expecting a happy ending.

- However, on an underlying level, Beatrice seems to have a poor opinion of Benedick at this point in the play. For example, she uses a metaphor to describe how "disdain" cannot die as long as Benedick is there to "feed" it, implying that she will always feel disdain for him. She also comments that he "always" ends with "a jade's trick", hinting that he has treated her badly in the past. Shakespeare makes it clear that she has some negative feelings towards Benedick, and that their relationship is not wholly positive at this stage.
- Later in the play, Benedick and Beatrice's relationship changes as they fall in love. They confess how they feel about each other in Act 4, Scene 1, when Benedick says "I do love nothing in the world so well as you", and Beatrice says "I love you with so much of my heart that none is left to protest". The use of exaggeration shows their strong feelings for each other, and the openness and honesty of these declarations contrasts with their usual witty language, highlighting how their relationship has changed to the point where they now openly express love for each other.
- Towards the end of the play, in Act 5, Scene 2, Benedick and Beatrice continue to argue playfully. For instance, Benedick asks Beatrice which of his "bad parts" she first fell in love with; Beatrice replies by claiming that he has no space for "any good part" to fit. These teasing insults show that their witty and playful relationship will continue even though they are now in love, suggesting that this aspect of their relationship has not changed.
- Furthermore, the pair acknowledge that their playful conversation may have always been a way of expressing their affection for each other. Benedick claims that they are "too wise to woo peaceably". This suggests that their playful banter is an important part of their courtship. It also implies that they may have had feelings for each other even in the first scene, when they used similar language. This makes it clear that, while their relationship has changed in the sense that they now know and accept how they feel about each other, their affection for each other may well have been present all along.

6) For this question, you have to write about Caesar as an arrogant character, so you need to pick out important bits of the play where Shakespeare addresses this idea, and explain how each bit you write about relates to the question. Don't forget to write about the extract in detail as well as the rest of the play. Here are some points you could make:
- In the extract, Caesar describes himself as superior to other people. He uses a simile to compare himself to the "northern star", to show how his mind cannot be changed, because the northern star does not appear to move in the sky. His statement that the northern star has "no fellow" in the sky to match it also implies that he believes he is superior to all other people, because of his refusal to change his mind. Since he is the leader of Rome, this is partly true, however the extreme extent to which he stresses his uniqueness and superiority makes him appear vain and arrogant.
- Caesar's arrogance proves to be flawed when, immediately after this speech, he is murdered by the assassins. Dramatic irony is used in this scene, for the audience is aware of the assassins' plan. This is partly because the structure of the play means it has been discussed in previous scenes, and partly because an audience of the time would likely have known about Caesar's murder from their knowledge of Roman history. This dramatic irony means that Caesar appears especially foolish to the audience. Shakespeare suggests that Caesar's high view of himself is misplaced, and that his position is not as "unassailable" as he believes it to be.

- Throughout the play, Caesar shows arrogance in ignoring omens about him. For example, in Act 1, Scene 2, a soothsayer tells him to "beware the ides of March", but Caesar calls him "a dreamer". He also ignores other warnings, such as the advice of priests in Act 2, Scene 2, and Calphurnia's dream in the same scene of people washing their hands in his blood. The repeated motif of Caesar's failure to heed the advice he is given shows that he only values his own opinion, which emphasises his arrogance. His refusal to listen ultimately leads to his death, which suggests that Shakespeare intended the audience to view arrogance as a fatal flaw in Caesar's personality.
- Brutus's motivations for killing Caesar include a fear of his arrogance. He describes his fear that Caesar, as a future ruler, will look only "in the clouds, scorning the base degrees" — those who helped him gain power. The metaphor of clouds suggests that Brutus believes Caesar wants to be higher up than others, while believing that his supporters are "base", indicating that they are still on Earth and therefore inferior. One of Brutus's stated motivations for killing Caesar is the desire to "prevent" this from happening, which implies that Caesar's arrogance, or Brutus's fear of it, contributed in part to his death.

Pages 92-98 — Paper 1:
Section B (The 19th-Century Novel)

7) For this question, you have to write about morality, so you need to pick out important bits of the novel where the writer addresses this theme, and explain how each bit you write about relates to the question. Don't forget to write about the extract in detail as well as the rest of the novel. Here are some points you could make:

- The novel emphasises the internal conflict that can be caused by immoral desires. This can be seen in the extract, as Jekyll says that he has "called" Hyde from his "own soul". This highlights the link between them, and reinforces the idea that Hyde's "depravity" represents the dark side of Jekyll's personality. Elsewhere in the novel, Stevenson uses the language of battle to show how Jekyll struggles to suppress this dark side: there is a "war" within Jekyll, and the "two natures that contended in the field" of his mind sound like two forces meeting on a battlefield. Jekyll claims that this struggle applies to all of mankind: he says that "man is not truly one, but truly two". This reflects Stevenson's message that all humans have an immoral side.
- Jekyll's language in the extract hints at his ambiguous morality: he describes Hyde's behaviour using some positive language, suggesting that he cannot bring himself to entirely condemn Hyde's actions. Whilst he claims to be "aghast" at Hyde's behaviour, he also describes the "sea of liberty" that Hyde brings him, and he reacts to Hyde's "depravity" with "a kind of wonder". This hints at the conflict between how Victorian ideas of morality dictate that Jekyll should feel and how he actually feels: whilst he feels forced to condemn Hyde's actions in writing, there is a sense that underneath he envies and almost admires him.
- Stevenson also uses other characters in the novel to illustrate the flaws in Victorian views of morality. Victorian society had a rigid set of moral values, so to maintain a good reputation, people had to repress many of their true feelings and desires in public. For the characters in the novel, preserving a good reputation appears to be more important than actually acting morally. For example, Utterson is more concerned about preserving Jekyll's reputation than bringing Hyde to trial: after Carew's murder, he says to Jekyll, "If it came to a trial, your name might appear." This shows his concern for Jekyll's reputation, and emphasises that he prioritises it over the pursuit of justice.

- The novel suggests that evil is ultimately more powerful than moral behaviour. Hyde grows stronger as the novel progresses, and eventually he overpowers Jekyll, and causes his death. This highlights Stevenson's message that trying to hide immoral desires beneath a civilised, moral exterior is very dangerous.

8) For this question, you have to write about poverty, so you need to pick out important bits of the novel where the writer addresses this theme, and explain how each bit you write about relates to the question. Don't forget to write about the extract in detail as well as the rest of the novel. Here are some points you could make:

- Scrooge's encounter with Ignorance and Want in this extract represents a turning point for his character, as he has a strong reaction to the way they look and begins to understand the effects of his attitude towards the poor. Ignorance and Want look like starving children: they are "ragged" and "wretched", which causes Scrooge to feel "appalled". By presenting Ignorance and Want as children, Dickens reinforces the message that the poor are not to blame for their situation, and that they should be helped rather than punished.
- Scrooge's emotional reaction to Ignorance and Want in the extract contrasts with the portrayal of him as unfeeling at the beginning of the novel, where he asks "Are there no prisons?" for the poor to go to. This suggests that he regards poverty as a crime, which is in keeping with the attitudes of many people in Victorian society: people in debt could be thrown into 'debtor's jail', and they were not released until they had repaid their debts.
- Dickens also uses the characters of Ignorance and Want to convey a wider message to his audience. The Ghost of Christmas Present explains that the children are a result of "Man's" neglect, which reflects Dickens's belief that Victorian society was to blame for the lack of education (Ignorance) and basic amenities such as food (Want) among poor children. The spirit explains that ignoring the problems of poverty will lead to "Doom", which suggests that Dickens thought upper- and middle-class attitudes to poverty would have negative repercussions for the whole of society.
- Dickens uses Scrooge's character to attack the mentality that Victorian society had towards the poor. Scrooge initially represents selfish members of the middle and upper classes in Victorian society. He refuses to give to charity, and he calls poor people "surplus population", saying it would be better if they died. The description of Scrooge as a "sinner" shows that his attitude to the poor is ungodly and morally wrong.
- As the book continues, Scrooge learns to reject his selfish views: in the final chapter, he buys the Cratchits a "prize Turkey", and he makes a large donation to a charity that helps the poor. Helping those less fortunate makes him happy: he greets everyone with a "delighted smile" and repeatedly acts with a "chuckle". Scrooge's happiness at the end of the novel shows that it can be satisfying and enjoyable to help the poor. His actions also have a dramatic effect on the Cratchit family, as Tiny Tim survives thanks to Scrooge's financial help. Dickens highlights the ability of the middle and upper classes to have a huge effect on the lives of those in poverty.

9) This question requires you to think carefully about the importance of a single character, so all your points need to be clearly about that character. Don't forget to write about the extract in detail as well as the rest of the novel. Here are some points you could make:

- In the extract, Dickens's use of Pip as a first-person narrator emphasises how intimidating Miss Havisham appears. He compares her to a "ghastly waxwork" and a "skeleton"; these frightening images suggest that Miss Havisham is almost inhuman in her appearance, and reflect Pip's sense of fear. The comparison to a waxwork emphasises that Miss Havisham appears to be frozen in time on the day she was left at the altar, and describing her as a "skeleton" as well implies that perhaps she is frozen in a state similar to death. This increases the eerie atmosphere around her.

- Dickens uses bold, almost grotesque imagery to show how obsessed Miss Havisham is with her own despair: for example, she keeps her mouldy wedding cake, despite the fact that it is covered with insects and "black fungus". This indicates that she hasn't been able to move on from the past, and the unpleasant image suggests that her obsession is dangerous and unhealthy. The use of such dark imagery incites fear in the reader. By using this imagery during Miss Havisham's introduction as a character, Dickens invites the reader to associate this feeling of fear with her as a character.

- Miss Havisham is manipulative throughout the novel: she has raised Estella to "wreak revenge on all the male sex", which the reader sees when she deliberately directs Pip's attention to Estella's beauty in order to manipulate him into falling in love with her. This love hurts Pip emotionally: he says that he is "as unhappy" as Miss Havisham could "ever have meant" him to be. This makes her seem cruel and intimidating, as she had purposely intended Pip to be hurt by Estella.

- However, Miss Havisham's past allows the reader to begin to understand her cruel actions. Herbert describes her treatment at the hands of Arthur as "cruel mortification", which helps the reader to understand why she behaves in such a peculiar manner. Later, when Magwitch is revealing more about Miss Havisham's story, he only refers to her in passing as "a rich lady". This hints at the callous way in which Compeyson treated Miss Havisham as disposable, and presents her as a victim of a crime, which makes the reader feel more sympathetic and less fearful towards her.

10) This question requires you to think carefully about the importance of a single central character and how they change throughout the novel, so all your points need to be clearly about that character. Don't forget to write about the extract in detail as well as the rest of the novel. Here are some points you could make:

- Mr Rochester undergoes a series of dramatic changes over the course of the novel. In the extract, he describes his younger self as "stiff-necked" and "proud", a judgement that is supported by Jane's early encounters with him. The extract takes place after Jane has been absent from his life for some time; when she returns, he is presented as a changed man. The hardships he has gone through have made him understand and overcome the flaws in his character, and he has learned "humility".

- The most obvious change in his character that the extract reveals is his newfound respect for and worship of God: he admits that he initially "almost cursed" the fate that had taken Jane away, but believes that the hardships he went through were "chastisements" from God, which re-establish his faith in a "beneficent" God who "sees... far clearer" and "judges... far more wisely" than man. For the novel's 19th-century audience, Rochester's newfound piety would have been a sign of his virtue and goodness. Later, he regains his sight in one eye, which Jane describes as a sign of God's "mercy". This indicates that Rochester has earned forgiveness for his past sins, and has become a virtuous man.

- This newfound virtue manifests itself in Rochester's actions. Earlier in the novel, Rochester calls his younger self a "trite, commonplace sinner" for his relationship with Céline Varens. His treatment of his wife, Bertha Mason, could also be seen as sinful: he locks her in an attic and denies her existence. However, by attempting to rescue her from the Thornfield fire, Rochester demonstrates that he has already begun to change for the better. This hints that Jane's departure is a necessary step that allows him to re-evaluate his past behaviour and atone for his mistakes.

- Rochester is "humbled" by his experiences, and this is also reflected in his attitude towards wealth and material possessions: when he and Jane first become engaged, he is excited to "pour" jewels into her lap and dress her in "satin and lace". However, when Jane finds Rochester at Ferndean he is no longer interested in "fine clothes and jewels"; instead Jane is described as "the most precious thing he had". This progression of character shows that he has come to understand what is truly valuable in life, and to reject the shallow obsession with wealth and status that characterises the upper classes in the novel.

- By the end of the novel, Rochester has overcome his flaws, and the reader sees that he is now worthy of marrying Jane. This makes the novel's resolution satisfying for the reader, who sees that the characters have received the outcome they deserve.

11) For this question, you have to write about revenge, so you need to pick out important bits of the novel where the writer addresses this theme, and explain how each bit you write about relates to the question. Don't forget to write about the extract in detail as well as the rest of the novel. Here are some points you could make:

- Frankenstein's language in the extract presents revenge as a powerful and violent force: he uses emotive, visceral phrases such as "drink deep of agony" to show the strength of his anger and indicate his desire to do real harm to the monster. Similarly, the monster often speaks violently of his revenge: for example, he promises to bring about Frankenstein's "destruction" when his creator initially refuses to create a female companion.

- The idea that revenge is something unhealthy and harmful is established early on in the novel. After William's death, Alphonse begs Frankenstein to avoid "brooding thoughts of vengeance", as they will end up "festering, the wounds" of his mind. The use of the word "festering" suggests that revenge is like a disease, foreshadowing the harm it will cause.

- The monster and Frankenstein are linked by their desire for revenge, and this becomes a damaging cycle that destroys both of their lives. Revenge isolates Frankenstein permanently from society, and drives him to the Arctic, eventually leading to his death; meanwhile, the monster is made miserable, describing his quest for revenge as "deadly torture".

- The monster's idea of revenge is more complicated than Frankenstein's. Frankenstein has one goal: to kill the monster in order to avenge the deaths of his family. In contrast, the monster's revenge is more calculated: he kills Frankenstein's loved ones first, in order to inflict on Frankenstein the kind of loneliness he has suffered. This shows that his thirst for revenge has made him cruel and scheming.
- Shelley makes it clear that Frankenstein's quest for revenge has affected his sanity. In the extract, he talks about the "spirits of the departed" as if they are really there, and his exaggerated language as he describes his "deep and eternal grief" and swears an oath to "the spirits" emphasises that his behaviour is irrational. This shows the reader that he has been emotionally destroyed by the suffering he has faced, and helps them to understand his motivation in setting out on a fatal quest for revenge on the monster.
- Shelley makes it clear that revenge is an ultimately unsatisfying endeavour. Even though the monster achieves the destruction he wants, he is still "miserable" because he has been "polluted" by his crimes, so he decides that the only option is to kill himself. This suggests that he has been irrevocably tainted by the murders he has committed, and shows that even though he has been able to fulfil his revenge, it is not satisfying enough to overcome his sense of guilt and shame.

12) For this question, you have to write about Mr and Mrs Bennet's relationship, so you need to pick out important bits of the novel where the writer addresses this, and explain how each bit you write about relates to the question. Don't forget to write about the extract in detail as well as the rest of the novel. Here are some points you could make:

- The extract shows how Mr and Mrs Bennet have an unequal and often difficult relationship. When they discuss Mr Bingley's arrival at Netherfield, Mr Bennet mocks Mrs Bennet's vanity by suggesting that "Mr Bingley may like you the best of the party." This shows that Mr Bennet is more intelligent and witty than Mrs Bennet, and does not regard her as an equal, but rather makes fun of her, realising that she won't understand the joke. His behaviour is quite cruel, which also reveals his lack of affection for her. The fact that she does not appear to be offended by his teasing and lack of respect for her may be due in part to the fact that society in the early nineteenth century would not have allowed a woman like Mrs Bennet to earn a living, so she would have been entirely dependent on Mr Bennet, and could not afford to drive him away.
- Mrs Bennet switches between berating her husband for not doing as she asks, and treating him affectionately when he does what she wants. For example, in the extract she is angry and resentful when he refuses to visit Bingley, and says "You take delight in vexing me", but when she later learns that he has visited Bingley, she is delighted and immediately forgives him: "What an excellent father you have, girls". The speed with which her attitude to Mr Bennet changes shows how shallow her feelings towards him are. This highlights that their marriage isn't based on deep feelings of love, respect or equality, which reinforces the idea that they are not particularly happy together in their relationship.

- Mr and Mrs Bennet are both largely comic characters, Mr Bennet because of his quick, dry wit, and Mrs Bennet because of her ignorance and lack of decorum. However, their relationship has more serious undertones; it is clear that the marriage was a mistake and they are fundamentally unsuited to one another. For example, Mr Bennet is described as "a mixture of quick parts", whereas Mrs Bennet is "a woman of mean understanding", which illustrates the difference in their intellect. We are told that Mr Bennet was initially "captivated by youth and beauty", showing that his feelings were superficial, and all "Respect, esteem, and confidence" for his wife were quickly lost. This illustrates one of Austen's messages: that it is important to select a partner on the basis of intellect, compatibility and love, rather than on the basis of wealth or sexual attraction.
- The Bennet's unhappy marriage is echoed in other marriages in the novel that are motivated by financial or superficial reasons, namely Charlotte and Mr Collins, and Lydia and Mr Wickham. In this way, Austen uses Mr and Mrs Bennet as a way of foreshadowing what will become of these couples, and as a way of emphasising that the cycle of unhappy marriages will never be broken until people realise that the only good reason to marry is for love.

13) For this question, you have to write about Watson and Mary's relationship, so you need to pick out important bits of the novel where the writer addresses this, and explain how each bit you write about relates to the question. Don't forget to write about the extract in detail as well as the rest of the novel. Here are some points you could make:

- In the extract, Watson and Mary are finally able to admit their feelings for each other after they find out the treasure is lost. Watson says "Thank God!" when he discovers that the box is empty. This short statement, which is also punctuated with an exclamation mark, emphasises Watson's immediate joy and elation. Such a quick and emotional reaction suggests that his desire for a loving relationship with Mary is strong and genuine.
- Watson describes Mary as being within his "reach" again now that the "golden barrier" of the treasure between them has gone: describing it as a "barrier" emphasises how the treasure has kept them apart for most of the novel. This highlights the significance of the treasure in their relationship; although it is the mystery surrounding it that brings them together, their relationship is impeded by its impact.
- Mary expresses ambivalence towards the treasure. For example, she reacts "calmly" when the treasure is revealed to be lost, and says "'Thank God,' too" when Watson declares his love for her. Mary is more happy about gaining Watson than sad about losing her potential fortune, which shows that she values Watson and their loving relationship over money.
- The first meeting of Watson and Mary illustrates his immediate attraction towards her. He describes her in a positive way: she is "dainty" and "dressed in the most perfect taste". Even after she has gone, he cannot stop thinking about her "smiles" and the "deep rich tones of her voice". Such specific and detailed description highlights his attraction to her. However, while Watson describes Mary in a positive way, his observations are realistic: he notices that her face lacks both "regularity of feature" and "beauty of complexion", which suggests that the love he has for her is not just idealistic or superficial.

- Watson's position as a narrator gives the reader insight into their relationship, as he is able to narrate the events of the novel with the benefit of hindsight. For example, when Watson fails to console Mary during the cab journey, he reveals that Mary later told him he appeared "cold and distant". The phrase "She has told me since" implies that the pair stay in touch after the events of the text. As this is revealed before they admit their feelings for each other, it allows the reader to view their relationship as more likely to develop into love, despite Mary's negative impression of Watson at this point in the text.
- Part of the reason Watson is distant is his concern that he will be perceived as a "vulgar fortune-seeker" because Mary is "rich". In Victorian society, it was traditional for wives to be dependent on their husbands, and the Agra treasure threatens to reverse this. This shows that, despite their love for one another, Watson and Mary's relationship is dependent on the rules of society. It is only when the treasure is gone and their relationship conforms to these rules that they can be together.

Pages 100-103 — Paper 2:
Section A (Modern Texts)

1) This question requires you to think about a single central character, so all your points need to be about that character. You need to write about how Priestley presents Arthur Birling as a selfish character, so make sure you mention the techniques that he uses. These points give you some ideas of the kind of things you could include:
- Birling's selfish nature first becomes apparent in Act One, when he uses a congratulatory speech for Sheila and Gerald as an opportunity to talk about himself. He explains how their marriage means "a tremendous lot" to him, because it will bring together his company and a rival company, suggesting that his feelings about the marriage are focused on how it will benefit him in business. This portrays him as a self-interested character, who thinks about his own interests over the needs and interests of his family.
- Birling's attitude towards his workers suggests that he does not care about other people. He refused their request for a wage increase in order to "keep labour costs down", showing that he cared more about his business costs than the welfare of his employees. This indicates that his main concern in life is his own profit rather than other people. Birling's behaviour towards Eva triggers the events that lead to her death, showing that selfishness can have harmful consequences.
- Birling lacks social conscience: he doesn't feel any responsibility to society as a whole. For example, he tells Eric and Gerald that a man has to "look after himself and his own". Priestley uses dramatic irony to emphasise that this selfish opinion is misguided. During the same conversation, Birling makes false predictions about other things, saying that there "isn't a chance" of war with Germany and that the Titanic is "unsinkable". These references to famous events that hadn't occurred in early 1912, when the play is set, would have been proven wrong by 1945, when the play was first performed. This makes Birling seem foolish and implies that he could be wrong about his attitude to society too. This helps to strengthen Priestley's message in the play that the middle and upper classes should act more selflessly and do more to help those around them.

- Birling is at first shaken by the Inspector's visit, moving "hesitatingly" after he leaves. However, when Gerald reveals that the Inspector was a "hoax", he decides that the family's problems are "All over now". This shows that he wasn't upset because he and his family had acted in a way that was morally wrong, but because of the "scandal" that the information could have caused and the damage it would have done to his reputation. This shows that the Inspector's visit hasn't made him reconsider his selfishness and lack of social conscience, suggesting that he is incapable of change.

2) This question requires you to think about a central character and how they change throughout the play, so all your points need to be about that character. You're asked to write about how Mickey is presented, so make sure you write about the techniques Russell uses. These points give you some ideas of the kind of things you could include:
- As a child, Mickey is friendly, and he easily bonds with Edward: he suggests that they become "blood brothers" and promise to "always defend" each other only a short time after they first meet. As the play goes on, he starts to push away the people he loves: he denounces his bond with Edward as "kids' stuff" and refuses to listen to Linda's concerns about his medication, repeatedly telling her to "leave me alone". His desire to break these bonds reflects the fact that he feels isolated by his circumstances, and emphasises that he has been let down by society.
- Mickey loses his innocence and sense of hope for the future over the course of the play. As a child, he longs to be older because he can "go to bed dead late" and "play with matches", but later in the play he bitterly tells Eddie that he "grew up" because he had to, and he can't be a child any more, however much he might now "wish" he was. This shows that he has come to believe that adulthood doesn't bring freedom, but rather pain and loss.
- As a child, Mickey is childishly excited by naughty behaviour: he admires Sammy when he "wees straight through the letter box". This contrasts with his attitude towards the robbery he participates in later in the play: Sammy has to persuade him to take part, and he eventually only agrees to do so because of his desperate need for the "fifty notes" that Sammy promises him. This shows that as an adult, Mickey has no appetite for crime or breaking rules; it is only desperation that forces him to take part in criminal activity.
- Mickey's changes in personality are caused by the lack of opportunities that his low social class affords him: he has a menial, insecure job from which he is fired, and this leads to his criminal behaviour, imprisonment, depression and eventual death. Even though he tries hard to find another job after he is fired — he says he's been "walking around all day, every day, lookin' for a job" — he is unable to. This emphasises that he has few options, linking him to the millions of unemployed working-class men in the UK in the 1980s and reinforcing Russell's message about the unfairness of the class divide.

3) In this question, you're asked to write about education, so all your points need to be about this idea. You need to write about how Bennett presents ideas about education, so make sure you mention the techniques that he uses. These points give you some ideas of the kind of things you could include:
- The character of Hector represents the belief that education should be well-rounded and not constrained by examinations, which he describes as "the enemy of education". He also thinks that all learning is "precious" even if it doesn't have "the slightest human use", which reflects his belief that education and knowledge is valuable in its own right, rather than being merely a means to an end.

- The Headteacher's views on education contrast with Hector's. Like Hector, he thinks that wider education is important, but for different reasons: he tells Mrs Lintott that "something more" than good grades is required, but only in order for the boys to get places at a good university. His motivations are shallow: he is interested in how the boys' achievements will affect "league tables", which shows that he is primarily motivated by his desire to improve the reputation of the school. This makes his perspective on education seem short-sighted, in contrast to Hector, who is trying to prepare the boys for "Grief. Happiness." and even "dying": he wants their education to equip them for life outside of formal education.

- After Hector's death at the end of the play, the Headteacher speaks positively about Hector's teaching: he uses a metaphor to describe the "bank of literature" in which Hector's pupils have become "shareholders". This suggests that the events of the play have caused him to re-evaluate his stance on Hector's value as a teacher. However, his choice of words indicates that he still doesn't understand Hector's perspective: the language he chooses is linked to money and profit, which shows that he still sees education as a tool that should be used to achieve wealth and success.

- Irwin's teaching style involves disregarding the truth in order to achieve an academic objective. He explains to the boys that an interesting opinion is more important than the facts: he says that truth in an exam is as unimportant as "thirst at a wine-tasting or fashion at a striptease". These activities are frivolous and unimportant, which highlights Irwin's dismissive attitude towards the truth. At some points during the play, there are hints that Bennett disagrees with Irwin's views. For example, when Dakin suggests that Nazi "death camps" have to be "seen in context", Irwin's view is that this is "inexpedient", as opposed to Hector's more humane, compassionate view that they were an "unprecedented horror". This gives the audience more perspective on Irwin's claims, making them lose sympathy for his particular views, and thereby strengthening their support for Hector's approach.

4) This question requires you to write about one central character, so all your points need to be about that character. You need to show how Kelly uses Leah to explore ideas about morality, so make sure you discuss how she is connected to this theme. These points give you some ideas of the kind of things you could include:

- Leah's monologues are used by Kelly to introduce key moral questions to the play, such as whether humans are more like chimps (killing outsiders) or bonobos (welcoming them). Leah's speech uses varied sentence lengths, such as the very short "Empathy." These emphasise her main points — in this case, that humanity's nearest animal relatives are known for caring about the needs of others. The monologue comes relatively early on in the play, which encourages the audience to think about how questions of morality, and especially the importance of kindness and empathy, relate to the events of the play as they are watching.

- Leah expresses moral beliefs, in contrast with much of the group. When Phil asks "What's more important: one person or everyone?", she replies "It's Adam, Phil, Adam!" The repetition of Adam's name emphasises his humanity and individuality, suggesting that Leah disagrees with Phil's view that the welfare of the group should come first. She therefore presents an alternative view to Phil's that shows greater empathy for Adam. As the play was written in response to media concerns about 'feral' teenagers acting immorally, Kelly may be using Leah to suggest that not all teenagers are wholly immoral or unable to feel empathy.

- Leah is very dependent on Phil's opinion. This is indicated by the many times where she asks him his view, such as "Phil, what would you do?", and continues talking to him even when he doesn't answer her. She continues this pattern of speech even after Phil demonstrates how Adam could be killed in Act Three, implying that she still accepts his authority. This suggests that, at this point in the play, her morality is still limited by her obsession with Phil.

- Towards the end of the play, Kelly indicates that Leah overcomes some of her dependency on Phil. A stage direction indicates that she "Storms off." from him, suggesting that she no longer supports his behaviour. However she does not seem to inform anyone about what the group has done, which is hinted at by Mark when he explains that she has gone "without saying a thing". This makes her morality as a character ambiguous — while she protests against the group's behaviour and eventually leaves them, she does not appear to report on the group's actions or make any obvious effort to try and get help for Adam.

5) In this question, you're asked to write about honesty and dishonesty, so all your points need to be about these ideas. You need to write about how Stephens presents ideas about honesty and dishonesty, so make sure you mention the techniques that he uses. These points give you some ideas of the kind of things you could include:

- Stephens uses the play to explore the reasons why people might not be honest. For example, Ed explains that he lied about Judy dying because he was "in such a mess" and "didn't know how to explain" what had happened. This suggests that people can be dishonest because they are upset or confused, rather than to deliberately hurt someone else. Stephens therefore shows how families do sometimes lie to each other, but that this is not always done with malicious intent.

- Stephens explores the effects of lying and dishonesty on families by showing how it can undermine trust. Christopher finding out about his father's lies is the main turning point of the play, pushing him away and forcing him to make the journey to London: after discovering his father is Wellington's killer, Christopher refuses to touch his hand, which he would usually do as a sign of affection, and he subsequently runs away in fear. This example of the negative repercussions of dishonesty in the play suggests that it is important for families to be truthful with each other, underlining the play's message that "if you don't tell the truth now, then later on it hurts even more".

- Judy, in contrast to Ed, is very honest in her letters, including about her own failings, such as confessing that she "was not a very good mother". Although this openness is painful for Christopher, causing him to throw up, Judy's perspective on the experiences she had when looking after Christopher gains the audience's respect, and Christopher's decision to stay with her in London shows that she has his trust even though the truth has upset him. Judy's honesty therefore reflects positively on her character, reinforcing the view that being honest is the better approach for people to take.

- Christopher views some forms of speech as dishonesty. For example, he believes that a metaphor "should be called a lie". His objection to the phrase "a real pig of a day" on the grounds that "a pig is not like a day" makes it seem absurd by applying logic to it. This perspective highlights how complicated language can be, because it can seem untruthful even though the person speaking means to be honest. Christopher's strong dislike of this sort of speech shows that honesty and dishonesty are not always as straightforward as they seem, particularly from Christopher's point of view.

6) For this question, you're asked to write about women's lives, so all your points need to be about that theme. You need to discuss how Delaney uses Jo to explore this theme, so make sure you write about this character. These points give you some ideas of the kind of things you could include:

- Delaney portrays Jo as an independent character. She repeats "mine" when expressing her pleasure at having her own flat — "But it's mine. All mine", which shows her strong desire to be self-reliant. The idea of an independent woman having her own flat contrasts the typical picture of women as dependent wives, which was common in the 1950s when the play was written. In this way, Delaney uses Jo to give a alternative view of women, showing how they often do want self-reliance and independence.

- Jo also rejects traditional ideas about motherhood, for example saying "I hate babies". The powerful verb "hate" emphasises the strength of her feelings. Her attitude is very different to the one expected of women at the time the play was written, when it was commonly believed that a woman's most important role was to care for her children. This view is shown in the play through Geof's remark that motherhood was expected to be "natural" for women, which highlights Jo's lack of a maternal instinct as something unusual in the context of the play. In this way, Delaney uses Jo to show that not all women fit into 1950s social expectations of motherhood.

- Jo faces criticism because she becomes pregnant without being married. For example, she is insulted using offensive terms such as "whore", and "slut". This reflects how having sex outside of marriage, especially for women, was disapproved of in the 1950s, so those who did often faced prejudice. This shows how difficult some women's lives could be if they failed to follow society's expectations of their behaviour.

- The theatrical context of the play emphasises the idea that Delaney wanted to highlight and explore the lives of women. The play was unusual for its time, when men were usually the main characters, in having working-class women like Jo as protagonists, and for having the mother-daughter relationship between Jo and Helen as a central theme. This centrality is reflected in the play's structure, as the first and last characters on stage are Jo and Helen. This means that they are the first and last characters the audience encounter, which makes them more memorable and emphasises their experiences and relationship above those of other characters.

7) For this question, you're asked to write about the author's ideas about fear, so all your points need to be about that theme. You need to write about how Golding presents fear, so make sure you mention the techniques that he uses. These points give you some ideas of the kind of things you could include:

- There are many different types of fear in 'Lord of the Flies'. Over the course of the novel, the boys' fears shift from fear of remaining stranded on the island to fear of the unknown, and finally to fear of each other. Fear is also crucial to Golding's message, which is that evil exists inside everyone; through the events of the novel he shows how evil can be brought to the surface by fear.

- The events of the novel take place against a backdrop of fear in the form of nuclear war. Piggy suggests in the first chapter that they will never be rescued because of "the atom bomb" which means their potential rescuers are "all dead". We are reminded again about this war at the end of the novel when the naval officer arrives and behind him "another rating held a sub-machine gun." This backdrop of fear serves to remind us that fear and evil are not confined to life on the island, but exist all over the world.

- Fear of the unknown is first shown by the littluns' nightmares. They "suffered untold terrors in the dark" and Jack and Ralph agree that building shelters is important so that the littluns feel they have some sort of 'home'. At this point in the novel, the boys are trying to fight their fear of the unknown by recreating something familiar — the comforts of civilised society. The boys' feeling that creating a society can fend off fear continues throughout the novel.

- The fear of the unknown gradually shifts and becomes fear of the beast. The beast changes form during the novel — it starts off as a "snake-thing" and then the dead airman is mistaken for "something like a great ape". These changes in form indicate to the reader that the beast only exists in the boys' imaginations, although they become increasingly afraid of it.

- Only Ralph and Simon understand that the "beast" is the evil inside them, such as when the Lord of the Flies says to Simon, "You knew, didn't you? I'm part of you?" They realise that believing in the beast gives the boys a way of focusing their fear of the unknown and of each other. Ralph recognises the evil inside himself and is terrified of becoming savage, but he has little choice when he is hunted like an animal. This makes his terror when he is being hunted all the more harrowing for the reader, and Golding emphasises this by saying he "became fear," showing that he has been completely overwhelmed by fear and is no longer really human.

8) For this question, you're being asked to write about ideas about death in 'Chemistry' and another story from *Telling Tales*, so make sure you choose a second story that has plenty to write about on the subject. This answer is for 'Chemistry' and 'Odour of Chrysanthemums', but it gives you an idea of the kind of points you could make whichever stories you're analysing:

- In 'Odour of Chrysanthemums', Lawrence shows how Elizabeth's reaction to death is affected by the circumstances of her life. Her first reaction to her husband's possible death is to consider how her family will survive financially and how she will care for an injured husband. These thoughts are presented in a long paragraph made up of broken sentences split up with long dashes. These increase the pace of the text, reflecting how many practical concerns she has to instantly consider, and emphasising that the responsibility she has towards her husband and family outweighs any emotional reaction she has. Her worries about money may reflect the hard situation of many widows in an era when many working-class women were financially dependent on their husbands. By presenting the practical as well as emotional impacts of death, Lawrence gives a realistic picture of death in this era.

- In Lawrence's story, chrysanthemums are clearly associated with Walter and Elizabeth's marriage: Elizabeth describes how she was given chrysanthemums at their wedding. However, Walter also had "brown chrysanthemums" in his button-hole the first time he was brought home drunk. The colour of these chrysanthemums suggests they are dead, symbolising the lack of love between Elizabeth and Walter by implying that, just as he left the flowers to die, Walter did not tend to his relationship with Elizabeth properly. The traditional meaning of chrysanthemums, which are often placed at graves and are therefore associated with death, further reinforces the idea that chrysanthemums are used to symbolise the 'death' of Walter and Elizabeth's relationship.

- In 'Chemistry', death is shown to bring characters together. The narrator's father's death "reconciled" his mother and grandfather and created a "delicate equilibrium" between the three. The use of the word "equilibrium" shows that they found a balance together; because the word can be used in a scientific sense to describe a chemical reaction that is balanced, it emphasises how their relationship has become more settled. This shows how death can alter people's relationships, as well as simply causing grief and sadness. In this way, Swift shows the complexities of the impact that death can have.

- Swift also uses 'Chemistry' to show how death can provide an opportunity for new perspectives, such as the narrator's conclusion that "though things change they aren't destroyed". This idea is reinforced by the story's cyclical structure: the boat that appears at the start of the story reappears at the end, but this time it is "unstoppable" and "unsinkable". The two similar words are placed in the middle of the sentence, giving them a greater impact to emphasise that the boat's course cannot be changed. This image acts as a symbol of how the relationship between the narrator and his grandfather cannot be destroyed, even if it exists only in memory. This implies that death can offer new outlooks that are not always wholly negative.

9) In this question, you're asked to write about education and learning, so all your points need to be about these ideas. You need to write about how Orwell presents ideas about education and learning, so make sure you mention the techniques that he uses. These points give you some ideas of the kind of things you could include:

- Education is related to power in the novel: for example, the pigs are "the cleverest of the animals", so they "naturally" take over the running of the farm. The ability to read, write and reason allows the pigs to persuade the other animals that the pigs are superior to them. The less-learned animals lack the intelligence they would need to challenge the pigs' authority, leaving them powerless.

- The pigs' intelligence and education allows them to use language to repress the working classes. The way the Seven Commandments are changed to suit Napoleon's aims is an example of the pigs using language to control the less educated animals. The pigs have power because they have learned to "read and write perfectly", and therefore change the commandments to suit their own purposes. For example, the sixth commandment is changed so that it reads, "No animal shall kill any other animal *without cause*" to defend Napoleon's "execution of traitors". This reflects the way Stalin used propaganda to control the people of Russia and relates to the Great Purge, the killing of people thought to be traitors to instil fear in others. Because the other animals have not learned to read, they don't immediately notice when the commandments are changed, and when they do notice, they can't prove it.

- Snowball attempts to teach the other animals to read, though his attempts are frustrated because the other animals lack the intelligence or motivation to learn – most of the animals on the farm are unable to "get further than the letter A." In contrast, Napoleon chooses to concentrate his teaching on a select few, such as the puppies, who he trains to attack anyone who objects to him. He only teaches the puppies what they need to know to be useful to him, which contrasts with Snowball's attitude to education. Napoleon also teaches the sheep to loudly repeat the phrase "Four legs good, two legs bad" whenever they are agitated, which effectively "put an end to any chance of discussion." The little learning that they receive makes them a powerful tool for Napoleon, showing how he educates selectively in order to continue the oppression. They use the words without understanding what they mean, which shows how the less-educated animals simply accept the terms of the revolution and their own repression.

10) For this question, you're asked to write about the author's ideas about memory, so all your points need to be about that theme. You need to write about how Ishiguro presents memory, so make sure you mention the techniques that he uses. These points give you some ideas of the kind of things you could include:

- Kathy approaches memory in an analytical way. She explains that she wants to "order" her memories, and particularly go over her childhood memories "carefully"; the adverb "carefully" emphasises that she wants to take a thought-out approach. Throughout the story she makes choices about which memories to discuss and when, including jumping "three years later" at one point. This structure implies that she uses the process of remembering to help her make sense of her life and her identity. The novel therefore shows some of the psychological and emotional benefits of remembering the past.

- Kathy sees things that remind her of Hailsham throughout the novel. For example, she recalls driving around and 'seeing' Hailsham in a "misty field" or some "poplar trees". The list shows how often she is reminded of the school and how well she remembers it, including small details like the type of trees. This emphasises how strongly she values these memories. The significance she places them may reflect how limited her life is as a clone, meaning her happy memories of the past are more significant to her.

- Characters often use memory as a way of avoiding their fears about the present or future. Kathy's patient in the first chapter tries to create false memories of Hailsham to cope with the trauma of his situation. He asks her for more detail about the school so that the memories will "really sink in", reflecting his desire to remember it as if it had been his own school. This suggests that memories, including those of other people, can be a form of escapism in response to a frightening present or future. This may reflect a desire to return to a simpler, happier past; readers may relate to this due to fears at the time the novel was published about cloning and stem cell research.

- However, Ishiguro also suggests that memories can be unreliable. Kathy believes that her most valued memories will not "ever" fade. Yet she also acknowledges that her early memories could "blur into each other", and that different people can remember an event differently, such as her and Ruth's differing memories of how long the "'secret guard' business" lasted. This makes it clear to the reader that Kathy is an unreliable narrator, and Ishiguro suggests that memories can be untrustworthy, even if, as in Kathy's narrative, care is taken over how they are recalled and arranged.

11) For this question, you're asked to write about the author's ideas about friendship, so all your points need to be about that theme. You need to write about how Syal presents friendship, so make sure you mention the techniques that she uses. These points give you some ideas of the kind of things you could include:

- Syal portrays two types of friends in the novel: false friends, like Anita, and true friends, such as Robert. Meena's realisation that Anita isn't a true friend is a key part of her character development throughout the novel.

- Initially, Meena values and is heavily influenced by Anita's friendship. She feels "privileged" to be her friend, thinks of her as a "kindred spirit", and tries to emulate Anita's behaviour, using coarse language such as "shag the arse off it". Because she values Anita's friendship, she is a good friend to her: for example, she tries to stop Anita finding out about the relationship between Deirdre and Dave, because she knows that Anita would feel hurt if she found out.

- In contrast, it is clear to the reader that Anita doesn't value Meena's friendship. Meena explains that "Anita talked and I listened", and Anita abuses her trust by trying to steal her belongings. This suggests that, instead of trying to engage with Meena's life and form a meaningful relationship with her, Anita simply wants to exploit Meena for her own personal gain. This emphasises the unhealthy, unbalanced nature of their friendship.
- Eventually, Meena comes to feel "pity" rather than "love" for Anita, and to understand that Anita has been using her, so she decides to "erase" her from her mind. This is an important turning point for Meena, as she starts to appreciate her own value and potential instead of trying to become someone she's not. Her realisation that her friendship with Anita wasn't healthy or fair is linked to the development of her own identity and personality.
- Syal presents examples of healthy friendships in the novel in order to highlight the inequality of Anita's relationships. For example, the Kumar family have close friendships with other people who have left India for England. Their friends are presented as a valuable source of love and support: Uncle Amman helps Shyam to find a job, and the Kumars rush to hospital to support Uncle Amman after he has a heart attack. This contrasts directly with Anita, who doesn't visit Meena at all when she's in hospital.

12) For this question, you're asked to write about the author's ideas about violence, so all your points need to be about that theme. You need to write about how Kelman presents violence, so make sure you mention the techniques that he uses. These points give you some ideas of the kind of things you could include:
- Images of violence appear regularly in the novel, creating an atmosphere of threat that builds up as the novel progresses. The first line focuses on the dead boy's blood, and Harri recalls this image at other points in the novel, such as remembering how he "saw the blood. His blood." The repetition of "blood", in these lines and throughout the novel, suggests that Harri cannot stop thinking about the boy's death. This emphasises that violence has affected him deeply on an emotional level.
- Kelman uses the structure of the novel to emphasise that Harri's violent death is not an isolated incident. For example, connections are made between Harri and the dead boy, such as when he takes on the part of the dead boy in a role-play, saying "I was the dead boy." It is not immediately clear from this sentence that Harri is acting, making the link between him and the dead boy clear and hinting that he is vulnerable to the same violence that caused the dead boy to be killed. Furthermore, the first line of the novel, starting "You could see the blood", is repeated in the final paragraph. The cyclical structure stresses the similarity between Harri and the dead boy, emphasising that he, like Harri, was an innocent victim of violence. This underlines Kelman's message that many young people have died needlessly as a result of youth violence (such as Damilola Taylor, whose death informed Kelman's novel), and that Harri's story represents just one of the lives lost due to violent acts.
- The novel's depiction of harm towards animals highlights how violence can be cruel and unnecessary. Harri describes the killing of ducklings, stating that "The babies just got crushed." The brutal verb "crushed" makes the action appear especially barbaric. The violence shown here seems particularly cruel, as the baby animals are helpless and pose no threat, which encourages the reader to sympathise with them. The ducklings act as a symbol of children such as Harri, who are also innocent, which helps the reader to understand how unjust it is that they are hurt or killed.

- Kelman uses the third-person perspective of the pigeon to reflect on the wider causes of human violence. The pigeon uses the rhetorical question "Wasn't that a sickly sweet epiphany?" to describe an infant killing an ant. The adjective "sweet" suggests that the child experiences pleasure in killing the ant. However, the adjective "sickly" suggests that there is a negative aspect to the child's joy, because it can be nauseating, implying that violence is also bad for us. Kelman's use of a child in this image implies that it is instinctive to humans to enjoy violence; however, the language he uses portrays this instinct as harmful to those who indulge in it as well as those who are victims of it.

Pages 104-106 — Paper 2: Section B (Poetry)

13) For this question, you have to think about the way that the poets use form, structure and language to present the breakdown of a relationship, so make sure you choose a second poem that has plenty to write about on the subject. Comparing them means writing about the similarities and differences, so make some links between the poems in your answer. This answer compares 'Neutral Tones' by Thomas Hardy with 'When We Two Parted' by Lord Byron, but it gives you an idea of the kind of things you need to write whichever poems you're analysing. Here are some points you could make:
- The two poems have a similar subject matter — the end of a romantic relationship — and they use similar narrative voices to present this. Both poems are written in the first person, which gives the reader an insight into the thoughts and feelings of the narrators. Both narrators also use second-person pronouns, such as "thee" and "your", throughout the poems, which indicates that they are addressed directly to their former lovers and emphasises the fixation that both narrators have on the women they address.
- However, the two narrators express different emotions towards the breakdown of their relationships. In 'Neutral Tones', there is a time jump at the end of the third stanza, which is introduced by an ellipsis. This creates a sense of distance between the events of the past and the narrator's present-day life: although he is still haunted by the loss of his lover, he seems calm about it. The emotions that the narrator expresses in 'When We Two Parted', on the other hand, seem stronger and less controlled. For example, in line 20 he uses a rhetorical question, asking "Why wert thou so dear?" This emphasises his sense of desperation and shows how upset he is at the loss of his lover.
- Both poems have a cyclical structure that reinforces the narrator's sense of regret and loss. The final line of 'When We Two Parted' refers back to the poem's opening stanza by repeating the phrase "silence and tears". This emphasises that the breakdown of the relationship has been a traumatic experience for the narrator, as well as suggesting that he is unable to move on from it. In 'Neutral Tones', the final two lines of the poem repeat the images of the "sun", "tree" and "pond" that were introduced in the first stanza. This reflects the narrator's inability to forget the pain that his former lover inflicted on him. The return of the 'A' rhyme in the ABBA rhyme scheme reinforces this sentiment, reflecting how the narrator's memory of the break-up returns to affect him.

14) For this question, you have to think about the way that the poets use form, structure and language to describe nature, so make sure you choose a second poem that has plenty to write about on the subject. Comparing them means writing about the similarities and differences, so make some links between the poems in your answer. This answer compares 'The Prelude: Stealing the Boat' by William Wordsworth with 'Storm on the Island' by Seamus Heaney, but it gives you an idea of the kind of things you need to write whichever poems you're analysing. Here are some points you could make:

- 'The Prelude: Stealing the Boat' and 'Storm on the Island' both present nature as a powerful force, which can have a profound effect on humans. In Wordsworth's poem, the narrator experiences nature's "power" when he sees a "huge" mountain while rowing on a lake, which causes a "darkness" to hang over his thoughts for "many days" afterwards. Meanwhile, in Heaney's poem an island community experiences the violent power of nature in the form of a storm that "pummels" them. Both poems present nature as having power over humans — in Heaney's poem the impact of this power is physical, whereas in Wordsworth's poem it is psychological.

- Wordsworth and Heaney both use personification to present nature as a conscious force that can threaten humans. Wordsworth's narrator uses personification to describe how the mountain "Strode after" him with "measured motion". The word "measured" and the use of alliteration in this phrase suggest that the mountain is chasing the narrator, enabling the reader to share in his fear. Heaney also personifies nature, using language usually associated with war, such as "strafes" and "bombarded", to compare the actions of the wind to those of a fighter pilot. The use of such violent imagery emphasises the power of the storm, and suggests that the wind is deliberately attacking the island. This highlights how destructive the storm could be, which helps to clarify the islanders' fear.

- Both poems have a distinct turning point, which heightens the presentation of nature as changeable and dramatic. In 'The Prelude: Stealing the Boat', the volta in line 21 represents the moment when the narrator first encounters the "huge peak", and at this point the mood of the poem shifts from confidence to fear. Similarly, in 'Storm on the Island', the volta in line 14 represents the sudden arrival of the storm. The poem's tone is subsequently transformed by the storm's arrival — the confident opening statement, "We are prepared", now sounds empty, as the island community is powerless in the face of the storm. As in Wordsworth's poem, this change of tone reflects how changeable nature can be, and emphasises how unsettling this changeability can be for humans.

Pages 107-108 — Paper 2: Section C (Unseen Poetry)

15a) For this question, you have to think about what the poet is saying about the speaker's attitude to parenthood and how she presents this attitude. Make sure you comment on how form, structure and language are used to present feelings and ideas in the poem. Here are some points you could make:

- 'For a Five-Year-Old' is about the relationship between a mother and a child, and the responsibility that the mother feels for her child's upbringing. This responsibility is emphasised using the form of the poem: it is mostly written in iambic pentameter, which creates a steady rhythm that reflects the narrator's dedication and commitment to her child.

- The poem's narrator addresses the narrative directly to the child, repeating the pronouns "you" and "your" throughout. This reflects the narrator's constant awareness of how her actions affect her child's development, and emphasises the idea that parenthood affects every aspect of a parent's life.

- The poem is structured using two distinct stanzas. In the first stanza, the narrator describes a specific interaction with the child, and then in the second stanza she describes some of the unkind things she has done at other times in her life. The child's "careful hand" in the first stanza contrasts with violent verbs such as "trapped", "shot", "drowned" and "betrayed" in the second stanza. This makes it clear that the narrator behaves differently around the child in order to set a good example, and emphasises her belief that it is important to teach children the correct lessons in life, regardless of one's personal experience.

- The snail could be seen to symbolise the child; the care and delicacy with which the narrator teaches her child to handle the snail reflects her belief that the responsibilities of parenthood must be carried out with similar care and delicacy. In the first stanza, the snail is presented as fragile using the alliterative phrase "carry it outside, with careful hand". This makes the word "careful" stand out to the reader, which shows the care and attention that the child pays to the snail, and hints at the snail's fragility. In the second stanza, the narrator refers to the child's "gentleness" and her own ability to 'mould' the child. This suggests that, like the snail, the child is fragile, and highlights the responsibility that the narrator feels to make sure that the child is treated with the same kindness and care that they show to the snail.

15b) For this question, you have to think about how the relationship between an adult and a child is presented in the two poems. Make sure you comment on how form, structure and language are used to present feelings and ideas in the poems. You're comparing the two poems, so you need to think about similarities and differences between them. Here are some points you could make:

- Adcock and Pugh both write about the process of a child learning about the world around them. Both poems are written in the first person, which allows the reader an insight into the narrators' thoughts and feelings and makes their descriptions of their relationship and experience feel more personal.

- Both poems contain characters who feel responsible for a child's moral education. In 'For a Five-Year-Old', the narrator understands that her child's "gentleness" is "moulded" by her own words; the verb "moulded" emphasises the patience and care that goes into such teaching. In 'The Beautiful Lie', the child's grandmother asks the boy, "Did you do that?", in order to teach him that his actions are wrong. The hard 'd' and 't' sounds in this phrase make the grandmother sound harsh and angry. This increases the reader's pleasure in the unexpected side-effect of her words: they "showed him" he had the "choice" of lying.

- Although both poems are about the joy of watching a child learn, the poets present different messages about what it is important for a child to learn. Adcock focuses on the innocence of the child, and the mother's pleasure in preserving this innocence. In contrast, Pugh's narrator takes pleasure in seeing a small loss of innocence, as the child learns how to lie.

- The poets reinforce their messages using their rhyme schemes. The middle six lines of each stanza of 'For a Five-Year-Old' use rhyming couplets; this careful use of form highlights the care and attention with which the narrator tries to preserve the child's "gentleness". In contrast, 'The Beautiful Lie' has no rhyme scheme and an irregular rhythm. This reflects the freedom that the narrator believes the boy gains by learning how to "*tell a story*": the realisation that he is able to lie opens up a world of imagination. The poem presents this as a "moving" and "momentous" occasion for the narrator, showing how an adult can experience the world afresh through a child, and hinting at how, for an adult, the achievements of a child they love can be more important than their own accomplishments.

Glossary

allegory	When the characters, settings and events of a story are used to represent something else, e.g. 'Animal Farm' is an allegory for the Russian Revolution.
alliteration	When words that are close together start with the same sound. E.g. "the beat of the band".
aside	When a character in a play makes a short comment that reveals their thoughts to the audience, and no other character can hear it.
assonance	When words share the same vowel sound but their consonants are different, e.g. "in this deep joy to see and hear thee".
audience	The person or group of people that read or listen to a text.
autobiographical	Describing something that happened in the writer's life.
blank verse	Lines from a play or poem that are written in iambic pentameter and don't rhyme.
caesura (plural caesurae)	A pause in a line of poetry. E.g. the full stop in "Over the drifted stream. My father spins" in 'Eden Rock' by Charles Causley.
chronological	When events are arranged in the order in which they happened.
cliffhanger	A break or ending to a text that leaves the reader in suspense about what will happen next.
colloquial language	Informal language that sounds like ordinary speech, e.g. "with your pals".
comedy (Shakespeare)	A type of Shakespeare play that tries to make the audience laugh, often by using exaggerated events and characters.
consonance	Repetition of a consonant sound in nearby words, e.g. "And fit the bright steel-pointed sock".
context	The background to something, or the situation surrounding it, which affects the way it's understood. E.g. the context of a text from 1915 would include the First World War.
couplet	A pair of lines in a poem, which usually have the same metre and often rhyme.
cyclical structure	Where key elements at the start of the text repeat themselves at the end.
dialect	A variation of a language spoken by people from a particular place or background. Dialects might include different words or sentence constructions, e.g. "what happen to de Caribs".
dialogue	When two or more characters talk to each other in a text.
direct address	When a narrator or writer speaks directly to another character or to the reader, e.g. "you might recall..."
doppelgänger	A character who is presented as if they are a version (or double) of another character.
double negative	A sentence construction that incorrectly expresses a negative idea by using two negative words or phrases, e.g. "I don't want no trouble."
dramatic irony	When the reader or audience knows something that a character does not know.
dramatic monologue	A form of poetry that uses the assumed voice of a single speaker who is not the poet to address an implied audience.

Glossary

embedded narrative	Where several different stories are told within the main story, e.g. in 'Dr Jekyll and Mr Hyde'.
emotive	Something that makes you feel a particular emotion.
empathy	The ability to imagine and understand someone else's feelings or experiences.
end-stopping	Finishing a line of poetry with the end of a phrase or sentence, usually marked by punctuation.
enjambment	When a sentence or phrase runs over from one line or stanza to the next.
first person	A narrative viewpoint where the narrator is one of the characters, written using words like 'I', 'me', 'we' and 'our'.
flashback	A writing technique where the scene shifts from the present to an event in the past.
foreshadowing	A literary device where a writer hints or gives clues about a future event.
form	The type of text (e.g. a novel, a novella) or poem (e.g. a sonnet or a ballad).
frame narrative	A narrative in which one story is presented within another.
free verse	Poetry that doesn't rhyme and has no regular rhythm or line length.
Gothic	A genre of text that was popular in the 19th century, which usually involved mysterious locations, supernatural elements, troubling secrets and elements of madness. E.g. 'The Strange Case of Dr Jekyll and Mr Hyde'.
half-rhymes	Words that have a similar, but not identical, end sound. E.g. "plough" and "follow".
history (Shakespeare)	A type of Shakespeare play based on real historical events.
iambic pentameter	Verse with a metre of ten syllables — five of them stressed, and five unstressed. The stress falls on every second syllable, e.g. "Two households both alike in dignity".
imagery	Language that creates a picture in your mind, e.g. metaphors, similes and personification.
imperative	An order or direction, e.g. "run away" or "stop that".
inference	A conclusion reached about something, based on evidence. E.g. If you read the phrase "They tiptoed from room to room", you could infer that the characters don't want to be heard.
internal rhyme	When two or more words in the same line rhyme, e.g. "The soft young down of her; the brown".
irony	When words are used to imply the opposite of what they normally mean. It can also mean when there is a difference between what people expect and what actually happens.
limited narrator	A narrator who only has partial knowledge about the events or characters in a story.
metaphor	A way of describing something by saying that it is something else, e.g. "his feet were blocks of ice".
metre	The arrangement of stressed and unstressed syllables to create rhythm in a line of poetry.
monologue	One person speaking alone for a long period of time.

Glossary

monosyllabic	When a word only has <u>one syllable</u>, e.g. "had", "thought", "play".
montage	A <u>series</u> of <u>short scenes</u> that are put together, often to show how something <u>changes</u> over <u>time</u>.
mood	The <u>feel</u> or <u>atmosphere</u> of a text, e.g. humorous, peaceful, fearful.
narrative	Writing that tells a <u>story</u> or describes an <u>experience</u>.
narrative viewpoint	The <u>perspective</u> that a text is written from, e.g. <u>first-person</u> point of view.
narrator	The <u>voice</u> or <u>character</u> speaking the words of the narrative.
novella	A <u>prose text</u> that is longer than a short story, but <u>shorter</u> than a <u>novel</u>, e.g. 'A Christmas Carol'.
omniscient narrator	A narrator who <u>knows</u> the thoughts and feelings of all the characters in a narrative.
onomatopoeia	A word that <u>imitates</u> the sound it describes as you say it, e.g. 'whisper'.
pace	The <u>speed</u> at which the writer takes the reader through the events in a text or poem.
paradox	A statement that <u>contradicts itself</u> or <u>cancels itself out</u>.
paraphrase	Describing or rephrasing something in a text <u>without</u> including a direct quote.
personification	Describing a non-living thing as if it's a <u>person</u>. E.g. "The sea growled hungrily."
phonetic spellings	When words are spelt as they <u>sound</u> rather than with their usual spelling, e.g. "yow" instead of "you". It's often used to show that someone is speaking with a certain <u>accent</u> or <u>dialect</u>.
prose	Any kind of writing that <u>isn't poetry</u>, and doesn't have a set <u>metre</u> or <u>rhyme scheme</u>.
pun	A word or phrase that's deliberately used because it has <u>more than one meaning</u>, often for <u>humorous</u> effect.
quatrain	A type of stanza which has <u>four lines</u>.
rhetoric	Using <u>language</u> techniques (e.g. repetition or hyperbole) to achieve a persuasive <u>effect</u>.
rhetorical question	A question that <u>doesn't need an answer</u> but is asked to <u>make</u> or <u>emphasise</u> a point, e.g. "Do you think the planet is worth saving?"
rhyme scheme	A <u>pattern</u> of rhyming words in a poem, e.g. if a poem has an <u>ABAB</u> rhyme scheme, this means that the <u>first</u> and <u>third</u> lines in each stanza rhyme, and so do the <u>second</u> and <u>fourth</u> lines.
rhyming couplet	A <u>pair of rhyming lines</u> that are next to each other.
rhyming triplet	<u>Three rhyming lines</u> that are next to each other.
rhythm	A <u>pattern of sounds</u> created by the arrangement of <u>stressed</u> and <u>unstressed</u> syllables.
romance (Shakespeare)	A type of <u>Shakespeare play</u> that is similar to a <u>comedy</u> but with <u>darker elements</u>.
Romantic	A <u>genre</u> of text that was popular in the late 18th and early 19th centuries, which tried to capture <u>intense emotions</u> and <u>experiences</u>, and presented <u>nature</u> as a <u>powerful force</u>, e.g. Wordsworth's 'The Prelude'.

Glossary

sarcasm	Language that has a scornful or mocking tone, often using <u>irony</u>.
sensory language	Language that appeals to the <u>five senses</u>.
sibilance	Repetition of '<u>s</u>' and '<u>sh</u>' sounds, e.g. "a <u>sh</u>rill whi<u>s</u>tle <u>sh</u>attered the <u>s</u>tifling <u>s</u>ilen<u>ce</u>".
simile	A way of describing something by <u>comparing</u> it to something else, usually by using the words 'like' or 'as'. E.g. "The apple was as red as a rose".
slang	Words or phrases that are <u>informal</u>, and often specific to one <u>age</u> group or <u>social</u> group.
soliloquy	When a <u>single character</u> in a play speaks their thoughts <u>out loud</u>, but no other characters can hear them.
sonnet	A form of poem with <u>fourteen lines</u>, that usually follows a <u>clear rhyme scheme</u>.
stage directions	<u>Written instructions</u> in a play that describe how the play should be <u>staged</u> or <u>performed</u>.
staging	How a play appears on the <u>stage</u>, including the <u>set</u>, <u>costumes</u> and where the <u>actors</u> stand.
Standard English	English that is considered to be <u>correct</u> because it uses formal, standardised features of <u>spelling</u> and <u>grammar</u>.
stanza	A <u>group of lines</u> in a poem.
structure	The <u>order</u> and <u>arrangement</u> of ideas in a text. E.g. how it begins, develops and ends.
syllable	A single <u>unit of sound</u> within a word. E.g. "all" has one syllable, "always" has two.
symbolism	When an object <u>stands for something else</u>. E.g. a cross symbolises Christianity.
syntax	The <u>arrangement</u> of words in a sentence or phrase so that they make sense.
tense	Writing about the <u>past</u>, <u>present</u> or <u>future</u>. E.g. "I walked" is the past tense, "I walk" is the present tense and "I will walk" is the future tense.
tercet	A type of stanza which has <u>three lines</u>.
third person	A <u>narrative viewpoint</u> where the narrator remains <u>outside</u> the events of the story, written using words like 'he' and 'she'.
tone	The <u>feeling</u> of a piece of writing, e.g. happy, sad, serious, light-hearted.
tragedy (Shakespeare)	A type of <u>Shakespeare play</u> that has a <u>serious tone</u>. It is usually about the <u>downfall</u> of the main character and often has a <u>moral message</u>.
unreliable narrator	A narrator who isn't necessarily <u>trustworthy</u>, and who might present things from <u>their own point of view</u>, e.g. Kathy from 'Never Let Me Go'.
viewpoint	The <u>attitude</u> and <u>beliefs</u> that a writer is trying to convey.
voice	The <u>characteristics</u> of the <u>person</u> narrating a poem or text.
volta	A <u>turning point</u> in a poem, when the argument or tone <u>changes dramatically</u>.

Index

Index

ELAS41